The
MASTERS
of
PRIVATE
EQUITY
and
VENTURE
CAPITAL

Management Lessons from the Pioneers of Private Investing

ROBERT A. FINKEL
with DAVID GREISING

New York • Chicago • San Francisco • Lisbon • London
Madrid • Mexico City • Milan • New Delhi • San Juan
Seoul • Singapore • Sydney • Toronto

The *McGraw·Hill* Companies

67890   QFR/QFR   1654321

ISBN   978-0-07-162460-2
MHID   0-07-162460-0

This publication is designed to provide accurate and authoritative information in regard to the subject matter covered. It is sold with the understanding that neither the author nor the publisher is engaged in rendering legal, accounting, or other professional service. If legal advice or other expert assistance is required, the services of a competent professional person should be sought.

—From a Declaration of Principles Jointly Adopted by a Committee of the
American Bar Association and a Committee of Publishers.

McGraw-Hill books are available at special quantity discounts to use as premiums and sales promotions, or for use in corporate training programs. To contact a representative, please e-mail us at bulksales@mcgraw-hill.com.

This book is printed on acid-free paper.

For Matt and Allison, may you never stop learning.
R.A.F.

For Wes, Greta, and Claire, who make it all worth while.
D.G.

CONTENTS

APPENDICES: TOOLS OF THE TRADE

ACKNOWLEDGMENTS

I need to acknowledge a group of people who made it possible for me to put this project together:

First, thank you to the wonderful people whose life work is herein profiled; each interview was a master class for me. I wish to thank the Illinois Venture Capital Association for the opportunity to create mentoring panels that were the inspiration for the book. Also, my professional mentor, Art DelVesco, and the good partners at Wind Point Partners, for teaching me the ropes with a loose tie.

Joan Shapiro, a guiding hand in my very fortunate life, introduced me to David Greising. Leslie Pratch thoughtfully aided in our quest to reach the masters. Emily Thornton of *BusinessWeek* was kind enough to introduce me to McGraw-Hill. And to our editor at McGraw-Hill, Leah Spiro, thank you for your steadfast commitment to doing this right and on time. I am grateful to each of you.

To my loyal Partners at Prism, thank you for your patience as I traveled to conduct interviews. To my top-notch assistant, Lauren Belcher, for transcribing so long and so well and to the passionately focused Renata Johns, for your skillful research, well-crafted editing, and attention to detail, I thank you.

Through this process I have gained a friend in David Greising. Thank you, David, for being a terrific collaborator, writer, and interviewer. David artfully and faithfully incorporated the voice of the professional masters who very generously agreed to participate. When looking for a writer for the project, a friend of a friend, Terri Savage, advised me what I knew in my heart but was good to hear again: "If you gave John Canning a referral for a plumber, you would make damn sure it was a good one, right?" For me and this book, David Greising is the Harry Tuttle of writers (in the movie *Brazil*, Robert DeNiro plays the heroic and good-natured craftsman who always appears when you need him).

To my lovely and supportive wife Linda, for being my life's partner, and to my parents, who taught me that persistence is everything, thank you.

—Robert Finkel

It is one thing to come up with a good idea and quite another to exert the energy, resources, persistence, and creativity to bring the idea to life. I would like to thank Robert Finkel, first, for conceiving the notion that in these times of challenge and trial there ought to be a book about the core values of the private-equity and venture capital industries. The good humor, patience, and trust Robert embodied as we worked to bring his idea to fruition helped make this a mission, not just a piece of work.

When Robert set out to find a writer to share the work with him, Joan Shapiro steered him to my friend and former colleague R.C. Longworth, who directed him to me. For that, I thank both Joan and, especially, Dick, whose wisdom and grace have meant so much to me over the years.

I wish to thank my editors at the *Chicago Tribune*, editor-in-chief Gerould Kern and managing editor Jane Hirt, for their support of this work and their recognition that newspaper reporters grow professionally through projects outside the newsroom. My friend Jim Kirk, business editor at the time, gave an early green light, and his successor Mike Lev was generous in his encouragement and flexibility. Tim Jones and Jim Miller provided what is sorely needed during a project such as this: friendship and fresh-ground coffee.

This book renewed a working relationship and friendship with Leah Spiro, our editor and a former colleague from *Business Week*. Leah's advice, judgment, and trust in us proved invaluable. I wish to thank Joel Weisman for offering astute counsel during negotiations and unflagging encouragement in all respects. Rafe Sagalyn represented us well in talks with McGraw-Hill.

Renata Johns provided invaluable research assistance and tracked countless details, and Lauren Belcher's transcriptions and other work were timely, accurate, and good humored. Numerous *aides-de-camp* to our pioneers provided important assistance on short notice and contributed mightily to our work.

Finally, of course, comes family. My wife, Cindy, kept us happy and healthy and up to date on obligations, while handling the demands and transitions at her own job, and still had time to help me work through the latest challenges with the book. Wes, Greta, and Claire provided welcome relief from the pressures of work and book, and our dog, Nopi, was always ready for a walk when Cindy and I needed one most.

—David Greising

INTRODUCTION

Robert A. Finkel
Prism Capital

During dinner when I was young, the conversation frequently turned to business, a topic that often prompted my father both to entertain and teach with an almost vaudevillian impersonation of a Harvard Graduate School of Business professor named Georges Doriot. In a voice that combined Peter Sellers' Inspector Clouseau with Colonel Klink from the "Hogan's Heroes" television show, Dad doled out Doriot's truisms like so many Danish cookies from a blue tin on the countertop nearby.

I didn't know it then, but Professor Doriot widely was considered the founding father of venture capital and private-equity investing—even in the days before venture capital built Silicon Valley and private equity reinvigorated thousands of companies. When he formed American Research and Development in 1946, Doriot did more than raise a pool of money that would go on to fund Digital Equipment and other start-ups. He created a way of thinking and operating in business: pooling investors' money and deepening its impact by putting discipline, accountability, and a sense of purpose to work on its behalf. By harnessing the capital and commitments needed to support innovation, Doriot was introducing a new chapter to the history of capitalism.

Doriot as sketched during class by the author's father, Stanley Finkel, MBA '39.

The Doriot *bon mots* that my dad tossed across the dinner table no longer survive.

But, as I reviewed Doriot's writings recently, I found a passage that captures the essence of his thinking and shows why his voice rang so powerfully, not just among Harvard Business School graduates but also among a new industry of private investors:

> The study of a company is not the study of a dead body. It is not similar to an autopsy. It is the study of things and relationships. They are very much alive and constantly changing. It is the study of something very much alive which falls or breaks up unless constantly pushed ahead or improved. It is the study of men and men's work, of their hopes and aspirations. The study of the tools and methods they selected and built. It is the study of conceptions and creations—imagination—hopes and disillusions.

What Prof. Doriot described, in his misleadingly simple phrase as "the study of a company," is really the essence of what private investment is all about. Companies are hardly cadavers. Rather, they are complex, living networks of people, capital, products, and markets. Likewise, private investment is not a simple transaction of buyer meets seller. It is the beginning of a relationship—one that requires nurturing, discipline, sharing, and accountability. If the relationship works, the rewards are rich. If it does not, the company suffers and, eventually, so does the private-investment firm, because it shares responsibility for the failure, especially in the eyes of the investors who support the fund and expect success.

If Doriot's surviving teachings are quotations from a founding father of private investment, then the lessons contained in this book are the embodiment of his ideas by the modern masters of what is now a full-fledged trade. Just as Doriot was a mentor to hundreds of would-be businesspeople in the mid-20th century, so these present-day practitioners can be mentors to people today who strive for achievement as managers, investors, or students of business.

A Growth in Scale

The people who share their experiences in this book are leaders of an industry that has built a track record that merits attention. Even in the face of economic uncertainty and rising public scrutiny, private-equity

and venture capital investment has continued to grow in scale and impact. As recently as 2000, large private-equity deals, those valued at over $1 billion, totaled only $28 billion worldwide. In 2006, that number reached $502 billion, and in 2007 private-equity firms put together some $501 billion of such large deals—in just the first half of the year alone. Between 2000 and 2007, a record 2,173 venture capital funds raised approximately $272 billion. In 2008, the pace of private-equity investment slowed, as the availability of credit dried up and many firms started realizing they had significantly overpaid in many of the large deals of the prior two years. As with other industries, private equity and venture capital go through times of expansion and contraction, at which point the winners survive and the losers find other work.

There is general agreement, among private investors, economists, and others, that the period from 2006 to 2007 was one of excess in which some in the private-equity industry lost their way. That, too, is another purpose of this book. The professionals profiled here, both the private-equity and the venture capital investors, had built records of success long before many of their peers paid too much money in too many deals during the latter years of this decade. They earned their money and built their records of success through patient and intelligent investing and a surprising knack for strategy and management that has contributed greatly to their success. While even these high-caliber investors were not immune from mistakes during the difficult phase beginning in 2006, we are inclined to consider those errors against the backdrop of the successful careers that preceded them, as well as the adjustments these masters have made since credit dried up, making transactions more difficult to close.

As the size of private-equity and venture capital funds has grown, so has their impact on the economy, particularly on the companies where the funds invest their money. As private investment has matured and become a style of investment and management in its own right, it has had a growing impact on how companies are run, who leads them, what strategies they pursue, and how their assets are maximized. Along with the investment capital they contribute, private-equity and venture capital investors also bring resources of experience and insight to the table.

The private-investment professionals who have contributed a great deal, both in capital and in strategic expertise, clearly have much to share with people who want to understand how businesses succeed or fail. Choosing to absorb what these successes or failures teach is akin to adopting mentors for our own careers. In all aspects of life, including in our careers, we are best off if we seek advice from the best brain trust we can find. The selection of a mentor is one of the most important decisions a person can make. It literally can be the first step in directing our own destiny. Our parents influence us profoundly, but not by our choice. Our mentors, on the other hand, we choose. Their ideas, their habits, their ethics, their successes, their failures—we embrace the best of these winning qualities because we want to emulate the people who embody them.

The voices that populate this book are the very best mentors of an important part of our capitalist system: private investment. (We will use the term to represent both private equity and venture capital.) Individually and as a group, these pioneers of the trade have built tremendous track records and helped to turn the private-equity and venture capital businesses into major forces in our economy. Admittedly, some private-investment professionals have paid too much for companies they acquired, and others fairly can be accused of using too much leverage and managing for short-term profit. But the vast majority of private-equity investors have breathed new life into countless companies that otherwise might have floundered in an increasingly competitive global economy, starved for capital, or closed down altogether. The venture capitalists, meanwhile, have helped make Silicon Valley a mecca of capitalism and helped entrepreneurs everywhere realize their dreams and build new industries.

Fundamental Principals

Why do the lessons of private-equity professionals and venture capitalists belong together? Because the guidance they share applies to all of those participating in private enterprise, and their insights are useful to anyone interested in learning more about the art of management. Although they invest in different parts of the life cycle of business, their role in the economy is much the same. Venture capitalists support start-up and early-stage companies. Private-equity investors finance or purchase more mature companies, middle-aged even, and give them new leases on life. What they share is what they do: inject capital, provide counsel and governance, devise and implement stock and compensation systems, help with strategy and tactics, and, in most cases, prepare their companies for private or public sale.

Both venture capitalists and private-equity professionals invest primarily with money they raise in the form of investment partnerships. With those funds in hand, they use the same disciplines: assessing hundreds of business plans or buyout opportunities, weighing the arguments for and against investing in companies, and peering into the hearts and minds of the entrepreneurs or business people who need their backing. When the risks are large, they often invest in syndicates, spreading the risk—and the potential reward—among several firms. They charge fees for managing their limited partners' capital and participate in their investors' profits when they successfully exit their investments.

When venture capital and private-equity funds go to raise money, they typically turn to pension funds, endowments, and wealthy families. There they compete against other so-called "alternative assets": hedge funds, real estate, and a host of commodities. These are distinctions with a huge difference. Even hedge funds, which seem similar to private investment to many outsiders, bear little resemblance to private-equity or venture investments.

The typical hedge fund manager spends much of the day paying rapt attention to multiple plasma screens, closely monitoring the ups and downs of the equity and derivatives markets. They trade actively, often relying on rocket-scientist types, "quants," who run exotic financial models. For at least a decade, the hedge fund model succeeded exceedingly well. A muscular bull market in stocks and easy credit helped fuel the growth of hedge funds, making them a nearly $2 trillion business.

While the alternative asset pie grew as a whole, the hedge fund industry took an outsized share of that growth, and in some senses it posed a competitive threat to private investment. Hedge funds competed for deals, recruited the same junior talent, and sought backing from the same limited partners. The financial troubles that began in 2007 introduced new troubles that many hedge funds were ill-equipped to handle. The reverses in performance that resulted have caused havoc in the hedge fund community. In January of 2008, well before the financial markets broke down in late 2008, three-quarters of all hedge funds reported losses, in large part due to the tightening of the easy credit that funded much of their trading. The losses intensified after the collapse of the Lehman Bros. investment firm in September of 2008, further exposing the vulnerability of hedge funds to the collapse of credit and extreme market volatility.

Patient Capital

The conditions that have assailed hedge funds—tight credit, tough stock markets, and economic uncertainty—have created challenges for private-equity and venture funds, too. Yet, the approach of these funds has proven out over a much longer period of time, through numerous investment cycles. Except for a small number of high-profile mishaps, private-investment funds have relied on their experience and savvy—and their more patient investment mindset—to succeed in the face of a credit crunch and unprecedented economic stress. A key component of their resilience is due in large part to the fact that their successes have been built on their ability to promote sound management practices in their portfolio companies, not just the latest investment fad or the momentum of fast moving markets.

Hedge fund managers rely on their ability to time markets and gauge changes in stock prices and the related derivatives markets to create competitive advantage. Private-investment professionals use similar analytical skills, but to different effect. They use them to confirm hypotheses and assessments about how a company might perform over a long time frame. In fact, many of the major sources of competitive advantage for the private-investment asset class are qualitative in nature: picking the right companies, mentoring their managements, measuring their performance, and driving them toward success. Structuring deals requires the conceptual skills of a master negotiator, the sleuthing skills of a private detective, and the steely stomach of a risk manager. Moving from deal to a successful long-term investment requires patience, a human touch, strategic insight, and, ultimately, a keen assessment of a company's market value and potential.

There are many styles of both venture capital and private-equity investment. Some such investors try to get in at the earliest possible stage, when risks and potential rewards are both extreme. Others prefer more mature companies. Some move in and out, buying the distressed shells of outmoded companies, stripping out what is valuable, and then eventually turning over the streamlined company to new ownership. Some focus on specific sectors. Some buy and hold, almost as if they are investing on behalf of their grandchildren.

There is plenty to learn from each of these investment methods, but this book is focused on the mainstream of success, the professionals who on behalf of others in primarily private companies stay in their investments for roughly five years. It is this group that represents the core of the business and its most profound contribution to the capitalist economy. This is the group that has the greatest impact on how companies are managed. They stay with their investments long enough to have a lasting effect, but also exit them speedily enough to move on and spread their capital elsewhere, in effect pollinating the economy with new energy and new ideas.

Hallmarks of Success

Regardless of technique or investment preference, all private investors must be expert at selecting, nurturing, and assessing their CEOs and other company management. It is company management that makes the key decisions of setting strategy and budget, allocating capital, managing inventory, and recruiting, hiring, and firing employees. Whether providing helpful guidance or actively coaching, the private investor still remains on the sidelines. The better the company performance, the more passive the investor can afford to be.

The best private investors are walking sources of wisdom based on broader experiences than most of the managers with whom they work. They frequently do not have the industry knowledge or possess the operating talent needed to run their portfolio companies, but they do have what few corporate CEOs can hope to have: knowledge about patterns of success based on data points acquired from up-close experience in dozens of companies and several industries. The veteran venture or private-equity investor likely has sat on as many as 30 boards—both successes and failures—and learned to navigate through the many potential minefields that a manager must traverse to create value in a private company. They also often draw on informal networks of advisors, people who can add additional operating and global perspective.

Ultimately, all of the attributes must add up to bottom-line returns. Those who do succeed tend to share certain traits. They are those who, while motivated by a desire for wealth, also value other aspects of the trade. They enjoy coaching the entrepreneurs they choose to work with, supporting innovation, encouraging enthusiasm, establishing good governance practices, and promoting an adherence to bottom-line discipline. This requires extensive investment, not just of money but also of time and attention. Not only are the successful practitioners rewarded handsomely for their efforts, but the marketplace also corrects for those who do not behave this way. Private-investment managers who do not deliver results will not attract or retain investment capital. This is a very difficult business and, despite the casual caricatures of some business press, it is no place for quick-hit artists.

In other words, the successful private investors are people who value the sort of holistic approach to business that Doriot preached. They figure out how to ask the right questions in the right order. They value intellectual honesty and let the facts speak for themselves. They do not let emotions cloud their decisions. Their ability to be self-critical, reflective, and adaptive is the lifeblood of their livelihoods. They see companies not as mere numbers on a balance sheet but as living entities that need support and encouragement to survive. Sometimes, the decisions are difficult. Other times, they are inspired. Not all companies can make it, and sometimes it falls to the private-investment professional to decide whether the company can survive: are the challenges temporary or final?

Both Failures and Success

Most people do not dwell on their mistakes. They prefer to think and talk mainly about their greatest triumphs. However, the most successful few in any profession constantly examine and improve on their past performances, both winners and losers. They know what worked, what did not, and how to improve the next time around. Such is the case with the best private-equity and venture capital investors. The super successful, the masters of the business, succeed in large part because of their ability to learn from both their triumphs and disasters. They remain students of their own histories and humble about what the future could bring—remarkable success or devastating failure.

There are two ways to benchmark: from success and from failure. This book will use both. Uncommon success is rarer than failure. It is remarkably difficult to achieve. That's why it is important to learn from the successes profiled here, especially if we can distill from them what made the difference and what made their decisions right. We fail to learn from our many mistakes at our peril, so the missed opportunities shared by these pioneers of the profession are important lessons, too. Taken together, these lessons offer powerful insights into the science and art of managing toward success.

Like any industry where it takes many years of listening and learning to come up to speed, private investment has evolved as a classic master–apprentice business. It takes a long time to learn enough that one can responsibly invest someone else's money. It helps to experience the life cycles of many different companies in a variety of economic environments. Living through a failure and its consequences on people's lives is sobering. If we had all the time in the world, we could afford repeated mistakes, but we do not have that luxury. The clock that measures return on investment never stops ticking, not just for investors but also for managers, their employees, and anyone who is trying to achieve. Those who can evolve and adapt most quickly win.

What is it like to work in the business? The investment process requires a certain bifocal view: the need to work on long-term projects that require great patience yet acting, when necessary, with great impatience and urgency. Private investors have to enjoy both the process of investing and the hard work of adding value. As the job description entails very little instant gratification, I sometimes refer to the long-term horizon of our business as similar to listening to a Yiddish joke: Because the verb does not arrive until the end, you do not know until then whether it was worth waiting for.

The patience required to create a track record of success should weed out the sort of person who likes to measure accomplishment from day to day or week to week. Whenever advising people who are contemplating entering the business, I try my best to apprise them of how long it takes to come up to speed and be meaningfully successful. When it does not go well, one is fighting a multiple-front war with lenders, other stakeholders and co-investors, management, and vendors. When it does go well, the satisfaction of being part of building something is real and lasting.

Gems from the Pros

The inspiration for this book arose out of a series of panels I helped arrange as a co-founder of the Illinois Venture Capital Association. Dubbed "VC Confidential," the series was designed to pass the secrets of our trade from elder statesmen to junior professionals in the business. The discussions were as fascinating to the senior people in our audiences as to the novices. Listening to the pioneers of our profession was like reading an inspiring book for the first time, but because we made no record of the remarks those words were lost to history.

With this book, gems from a carefully selected group of veterans have now been written down. In assembling this book, I have turned to some of the most important pioneers of private investment. Some names will be recognizable to any regular reader of the business press. Others are virtual unknowns to the general public—though quietly legendary among investors who have placed billions of dollars at their disposal. What our masters have in common is that they all are founding partners and professionals who, while having an eye for a bargain, also know how to help create wealth where they put their money.

Few have ever memorialized their credos, missions, lessons, or tenets to share with their own partners, much less anyone else. Now that the private-investor business has become an industry and a major source of jobs in this country, it is time to place this wealth of wisdom in the public domain. This way, everyone can learn at the pens of some of the most successful investors and advisors of our time. We have taken an added step, in an appendix to the chapters, to elicit actual tools of the trade from the masters: valuation spreadsheets, risk analyses, personnel evaluations, portfolio appraisals, and other mechanisms by which these experts practice their craft.

These are private people—not just by trade, but typically by personality, too. They are more comfortable advising behind the scenes. Although they may view themselves mainly as investors, experience has taught them a great deal about management theory, too. They got into the business to learn and to profit, not to teach, but they wound up doing all three. For most, the exercise of memorializing these ideas was a rare opportunity for them to proactively organize their thinking about their methods and to share wisdom they had gathered in a career's worth of experience.

When John Canning shares with us that managing a partnership means having to be fair, it really means that in order to manage a high-performing partnership one has to share the firm's economic pie, in a sense overpaying the up and comers in order to retain and groom them. When Joe Rice informs us that his firm views companies from an operating perspective, it is interesting to note that his firm is one of the very few that splits the firm's share of investment returns evenly between deal makers and operating partners. From Jeff Walker, we learn that measuring metrics—whether tracking revenue per employee for an operating company or tracking the number of mosquito nets deployed per week for an African charity—are the grist of managing from the board level. Carl Thoma emphasizes the importance of impatience, and Warren Hellman shows how a private-equity investor can bring new strategic vision that can improve the fortunes of companies, particularly in our post-industrial economy.

The venture capitalists in these pages educate us, as Pitch Johnson and Bill Draper do, with intriguing stories about the origins of the industry that tell us a great deal about the vision and risk-tolerance required to be a successful long-term investor. Patricia Cloherty shares how she maintains discipline and achieves success in the hurly-burly of Russia's fast-changing economy. Dick Kramlich explains how a megafund still manages to focus on the details of performance in the many companies in its portfolio, and Steve Lazarus explores the nuances of taking breakthrough technologies out of university laboratories and bringing them to market.

Management Metrics

These are the lessons as the masters have learned them. I have asked each of these teachers to focus on a different aspect of the trade, but with a strong emphasis on how their efforts help to improve management in the companies in their portfolios. The private-equity pioneers have particular expertise in improving the performance of existing companies—from corporate orphans to carve-outs to merged entities. The venture capitalists, meanwhile, are expert at identifying and nurturing entrepreneurial genius. This involves selecting novel ideas that will succeed in creating new businesses in a fast-changing, highly competitive world. It also requires an ability to help visionary entrepreneurs become successful managers, identify the right advisors to help build successful strategies, and decide when a business is mature enough to seek new infusions of capital.

Cross-pollination of ideas among the masters of private equity and venture capital can shed new understanding on the requirements for success in the field of private investment. It also is an effective way to transmit some of the most piercing insights about management theory and technique to a broad audience of readers. Yet, somehow, even after exploring these ideas with the masters, I still felt the need for a framework in which to view and digest their information. Powerful as the lessons are, they require context, a sense of connection to the history of private investment and the broader world of business.

To explore the unique qualities of private investment from an independent perspective, we turn to academia, to two key leaders in the growing field of entrepreneurial studies. Steve Kaplan of the University of Chicago Booth School of Business explains the role that private equity plays in the economy and the impact it can have on enterprises that seek to expand or refinance. Garth Saloner, the dean of Stanford University's Graduate School of Business, discusses the role that venture capital has played in supporting invention and growing start-up enterprises, while also sharing his insights on the inevitable tensions between entrepreneurs and the venture investors who help them pursue their dreams.

On the surface, my career would seem to have a fairly simple objective: to make money for my firm's investors, my partners, and myself. Yet, the richest personal rewards—and the ones that make the more commercial objectives achievable—are those I gain from activities such as encouraging innovation, finding economic ways for companies to operate, and mentoring business leaders to pursue their own destinies. As a mid-career professional, one striving to take my own firm to a higher level, I feel a renewed passion to learn best practices and document the experience and insights of the leading colleagues in the realm of private investment. The first step toward greatness is striving to achieve it, and one can take that step by listening to and learning from the greats. With this book, I am seeking to expand my own interest in their accomplishments and channel it, in written form, into a kind of virtual classroom, one open to public viewing.

The Social Impact of Private Capital

For the purposes of society, private investment plays a simple but essential role in the process of capital allocation. Private investors have to make tough decisions about what companies and ideas to endorse. Imagine if the task were not done well. Millions of dollars would be misallocated, with potentially dire results. It happened in the late 1990s, at the height of the dot-com bubble, when many in the private-investment business literally flushed billions down the drain, a very unproductive use of resources. It has happened again to some who paid too much for companies in the private-equity buyout frenzy of 2006 and 2007. The extremely low average returns for funds of these periods reflected the impact of the many fund managers who fell prey to the irrational exuberance of the times. After such periods of excess, it can take years for private-investment managers to rebuild their credibility.

Although those in the private-equity industry are at times vilified and at others lionized, after a period in which some lost their way—in very high-profile ways—I feel it may be helpful to put forward this book as a means of reconnecting with the foundational philosophies and techniques that can help make private investment a positive force in our economy and our society. The originals in this industry, the true masters, were attracted to it before there was a hint of the unthinkable success that was to come their way. We can both model ourselves after their achievements and use their ideas to blaze new paths. Harkening back to our industry roots grounds us, and can be good therapy. For the general business reader, seeking new foundations after the economic breakdown that started in late 2008, the management and investment insights from these masters can help lead the way first to survival and ultimately to success.

It would be naïve, and inaccurate, to characterize even the most successful private-investment partnerships as purely altruistic or community oriented. What can be said is that, in the pursuit of profit, they create opportunities and allocate capital in ways that benefit society. They identify good managers, support them, and help elevate their performance. They add real value. The strengths of the many who responsibly and successfully practice this form of investment overshadow the shortcomings of a few. The most successful leaders among them, the pioneers who first showed the way, have learned to make a mistake only once, and to repeat their successes, again and again, ever more quickly and on an ever-grander scale.

When an industry springs to prominence as suddenly as private investment has, it helps to take a measure of the early results. Why do they behave as they do? Who benefits? What are their core values? Perhaps the newest generation of private-investment professionals is attracted to the trade by headlines boasting about instant wealth. Their elders, though, had no such inducement. When they were starting out, big funds were measured in the tens of millions, not in the billions, as happens today. For them, a career in private investment promised mainly hard work, learning the tempo of business cycles, finessing the intricate world of business relationships, and introducing their niche to institutional investors.

In other words, they operated as Doriot had, according to a credo that saw companies as living entities, one that prized innovation, instinctively nurtured effective managers, and valued ethical standards. As private investors, they acted within the context of partnerships that also lived and breathed with a culture and a soul. They recognized, as Doriot did, that they and their portfolio companies were "something very much alive which falls or breaks up unless constantly pushed ahead or improved."

The pioneers of private investment took it upon themselves to push ahead, and to help companies improve. Society is the better for it. These masters, who share their experiences in this book, embody some of the best tenets of the profession of private investment. It is not just their financial success we admire and respect; it is also their wealth of knowledge, the ways in which they have acquired it, and how that knowledge can help others.

PART I

PRIVATE EQUITY

1

METHOD OVER MAGIC: THE DRIVERS BEHIND PRIVATE-EQUITY PERFORMANCE

Steven N. Kaplan

Neubauer Family Professor of Entrepreneurship and Finance
University of Chicago Booth School of Business

More than two decades of research and writing have established Steve Kaplan as a thought leader on the role of private equity in the economy and society. Tracking the industry through economic cycles, Kaplan identifies methods and tools that private-equity investors use to consistently improve performance. Kaplan also debunks the notion that private-equity investment leads to outsized layoffs at portfolio companies, and finds no evidence to support contentions that private-equity firms benefit from access to privileged information when making investment decisions.

The strong track record of private-equity firms, Kaplan finds, results from a combination of techniques. They use equity compensation and leverage to align management with efforts to increase efficiencies. They make changes in firm governance that lead to better oversight and decisions. Finally, private-equity firms increasingly bring industry and operating experience to help improve their companies.

⌗⌗⌗

The investment firms that we once called "leveraged-buyout firms" today are called "private-equity firms," but the rebranding has not changed the basics of what these firms do. They use modest doses of their own investment capital, backed by outside debt, to buy companies and attempt to improve their performance. Proponents of leveraged buyouts argue that private-equity firms improve the operations of the companies they buy and create economic value by applying financial, governance, and operational engineering to their portfolio companies. Others argue quite the opposite. Private-equity firms, these people say, take advantage of tax breaks and superior information but do not create any operational value. Moreover, critics sometimes argue that private-equity activity relies on market timing—and market mispricing—between debt and equity markets.

I largely agree with the private-equity proponents. Overall, private-equity firms create economic value by improving management incentives, providing better governance oversight, and, increasingly, providing advice on cost cuts or strategic improvements. This sort of operational engineering—the use of management techniques and tactics to enhance firm performance—is a thematic focus of this book. The empirical evidence from academic research leads to the clear conclusion that these changes lead to operating improvements and add value, on average. That said, it also appears to be the case that market timing matters and in some instances leads to negative results. From time to time, in the late 1980s and most recently from 2005 to 2007, plentiful availability of very aggressive debt financing allows private-equity investors to finance large public-to-private buyouts. And the record on those transactions, particularly post-1980s, is mixed.

The stereotype of the private-equity investor as a mercurial taskmaster prone to squeezing out costs, firing management, and flipping companies is at least in part a legacy of the frenzied leveraged-buyout boom of the 1980s. Leveraged-buyout activity mushroomed in that decade and culminated with the $25 billion buyout of RJR Nabisco in early 1989. Shortly thereafter, the junk bond market crashed. A number of high-profile leveraged buyouts resulted in default and bankruptcy, and leveraged buyouts of public companies—taking them private—virtually disappeared by the early 1990s.

While leveraged buyouts of public companies were relatively scarce in the 1990s and early 2000s, private-equity firms continued to buy private companies and divisions. In the mid-2000s, public-to-private deals reappeared when the United States led the world's rediscovery of a second private-equity boom. Then, in 2006 and 2007, pension funds, university endowments, and other institutional investors were among those who committed a record amount of capital to private equity, both in nominal terms and as a fraction of the overall stock market. Private-equity commitments and transactions rivaled, and in some respects overtook, the activity of the first wave in the late 1980s; however, in 2008, with the turmoil in the debt markets, private-equity transactions declined markedly again as they had in the late 1980s.

The Rising Tide of Private Equity

We can track the ebb and flow in the popularity of private equity by measuring the amount of capital committed to private-equity funds over the years. Nominal dollars committed each year to U.S. private-equity funds have increased exponentially since private equity achieved its first big wave of growth during the 1980s. In a quarter century, the scale of commitments to private equity grew from $0.2 billion in 1980 to over $200 billion in 2007, meaning commitments that year were a thousand times greater than the total in 1980.

Given the large increase in the market value of firms over this period, it is appropriate to measure committed capital as a percentage of the total value of the U.S. stock market. The data suggest that private-equity commitments are cyclical, tracking in part the ups and downs in the way the investment sectors performed. Commitments increased in the 1980s, peaked in 1988, declined in the early 1990s, and increased through the late 1990s. They peaked in 1998, declined again in the early 2000s, and then began climbing in 2003. By 2006 and 2007, private-equity commitments appeared extremely high by historical standards, exceeding 1% of the value of the U.S. stock market. Perhaps not merely by coincidence, many large private-equity buyouts occurred during those two years, and an inordinate number of those deals seemed to run into financial trouble in fairly short order.

One caveat to this observation is that many of the large U.S. private-equity firms have only recently become global in scope. Foreign investments by U.S. private-equity firms were much smaller 20 years ago, so the comparisons are not exactly apples to apples. Even so, the trends are clear, and, if the past record is any indication, the recent poor results of private-equity funds that began to be reported in 2008 seem likely to affect investor commitments to private-equity funds, which likely will find it difficult to raise new capital, at least until investment returns begin to improve.

The Levers of Performance

While commitments to private-equity firms have ebbed and flowed over the years, the improvement in operating results of companies bought by private-equity firms has been consistent across time and geographies. Private-equity firms improve firm performance, and maximize their investment returns, by engineering changes to the financial, governance, and operational aspects of the companies they buy. Private-equity investors also appear to take advantage of market timing—and market mispricing—between debt and equity markets, particularly when they take publicly owned companies private.

Equity participation by management is a key tool affecting performance. Private-equity firms typically give the management teams of portfolio companies a large equity upside through stock and options—a practice that was unusual among public firms in the early 1980s. Private-equity firms typically also require management to make a meaningful investment in the company. This is designed to align management with the private-equity investors to give management not only a significant upside but a significant downside as well. Moreover, because the companies are private, management's equity is illiquid— that is, management cannot sell its equity or exercise its options until the value is proved by an exit transaction. This illiquidity reduces management's incentive to manipulate short-term performance.

To illustrate the continued importance of equity stakes, my colleague Per Stromberg and I collected information on 43 leveraged buyouts in the United States from 1996 to 2004 with a median transaction value of over $300 million. In a little more than half of these deals, the private-equity firm was taking a public company private. After the deals closed, management ownership was substantial. The chief executive officer received 5.4% of the equity upside—both in stock and options—while the management team as a whole got 16%. These magnitudes have not changed much since I first studied them in the 1980s. Even though stock- and option-based compensation has become more widely used in public firms since the 1980s, management's ownership percentages—and management's upside—remain greater in leveraged buyouts than in public companies.

The second key ingredient is leverage, the borrowing that is done in connection with the transaction. Leverage creates pressure on managers not to waste money, because they must make interest and principal payments. In the United States, and in many other countries, leverage also potentially increases firm value through the tax deductibility of interest. On the flip side, if leverage is too high, the inflexibility of the required payments increases the chance of costly financial distress. This contrasts with the flexibility of payments on equity: Dividends and the like can be reduced or eliminated as market conditions change. Because the very inflexibility of leverage is itself a motivating factor, private-equity firms in a sense impose discipline on their firms' managers by virtue of the fact that they impose higher levels of debt on the companies they acquire.

A third technique, what I call *governance engineering*, refers to the greater involvement of private-equity investors in the governance of their portfolio companies compared to the directors of public companies. Private-equity portfolio company boards are smaller than comparable public company boards and meet more frequently, around 12 formal meetings per year and many more informal contacts. We can infer, too, that the pressure on management increases because private-equity firms have established a willingness to replace poorly performing managers. Viral Acharya and Conor Kehoe report that one-third of chief executive officers of these firms are replaced in the first 100 days, while two-thirds are replaced at some point over a four-year period. Financial and governance engineering were common by the late 1980s and have remained as common features of private-equity portfolio companies ever since.

Today, most large private-equity firms have added another type of activity that we call *operational engineering*. This refers to industry and operating expertise that they apply to add value to their investments, and this book seeks to redress the relative lack of attention that this particular aspect of private-equity investment has received. Indeed, most top private-equity firms are now organized around industries. In addition to hiring dealmakers with financial engineering skills, private-equity firms now often hire professionals with operating backgrounds and an industry focus. For example, Lou Gerstner, the former chief executive officer of RJR Nabisco and IBM, was affiliated with The Carlyle Group, while Jack Welch, the former chief executive officer of General Electric, is affiliated with Clayton, Dubilier & Rice. Most top private-equity firms also make use of internal or external consulting groups.

Private-equity firms use their industry and operating knowledge to identify attractive investments, to develop value creation plans for those investments, and to implement the value creation plans. A plan might include elements of cost-cutting opportunities and productivity improvements, strategic changes or repositioning, and acquisition opportunities, as well as management changes and upgrades. The operating partners of these firms can enhance the implementation of such plans by sharing their real-world experience with portfolio company management, offering unique perspectives that aid in the execution of plans and help to enhance results.

Impact on Cash Flow

As far back as the 1980s, when I first studied the impact of private equity on the operating performance of companies, I found that the operating performance of companies improved after they were purchased through leveraged buyouts. For U.S. public-to-private deals in the 1980s, the ratio of operating income to sales increased by 10 to 20%, both in absolute terms and relative to industry peers. The ratio of cash flow (operating income less capital expenditures) to sales increased by roughly 40% among public companies acquired and taken private by private-equity firms. The ratio of capital expenditures to sales declined. These changes coincide with large increases in firm value, again both in absolute terms and relative to industry peers.

Most post-1980s empirical work on private equity and leverage buyouts has focused on buyouts in Europe, largely because of data availability. Consistent with U.S. results during the 1980s, this work finds that leveraged buyouts are associated with significant operating and productivity improvements in the United Kingdom, in France, and in Sweden. In a 2007 paper, the economists Douglas Cumming, Don Siegel, and Mike Wright summarized the research in the United States and Europe and concluded that there "is a general consensus across different methodologies, measures, and time periods regarding a key stylized fact: LBOs, and especially management buyouts, enhance performance and have a salient effect on work practices."

There has been one exception to the largely uniform positive operating results: more recent public-to-private deals. In a study looking at U.S. public-to-private transactions completed from 1990 to 2006, Edie Hotchkiss and colleagues found modest increases in operating and cash flow margins—smaller increases, in fact, than those found in the 1980s, both in the United States and Europe. At the same time, Hotchkiss found high investor returns at the portfolio company level. Acharya and Kehoe found similar results for public-to-private deals in the United Kingdom. These results suggest that post-1980s public-to-private transactions may differ from those of the 1980s and from leveraged buyouts overall.

Impact on Jobs

Critics of leveraged buyouts often argue that these transactions benefit private-equity investors at the expense of employees, who suffer job and wage cuts. Such reductions would be consistent—and, arguably, expected—with the productivity and operating improvements that private-equity firms' portfolio companies achieve. Even so, the political implications of economic gains achieved in this manner would be more negative. For example, the Service Employees International Union, in a 2007 report, questioned the effects of private equity on both job destruction and the quality of those jobs.

Whatever the reputation of private-equity firms as job cutters, the actual employment track record at companies purchased by private-equity firms differs from the slash-and-burn stereotype in the popular press. When I studied U.S. public-to-private buyouts in the 1980s, I found actual employment increases post-buyout, though they were less than for other firms in the same industry. Steve Davis and coauthors, in subsequent research that examined data through 2005, found similar results: employment at leveraged-buyout firms increased, but at a slower rate than at other firms in the same industry during the same time period. Davis' research also found, meanwhile, that firms purchased in leveraged buyouts also experienced smaller employment growth in the time period prior to the buyout transaction. The relative employment declines were concentrated in retail businesses, and there actually was little difference in employment in the manufacturing sector. In new establishments, employment in companies owned by private-equity firms actually increased at a faster pace than in those controlled by non-buyout firms.

Overall, then, the evidence suggests that employment grows at firms that experience leveraged buyouts, but at a slower rate than at other similar firms. These findings are not consistent with concerns over job destruction, but neither are they consistent with the opposite position that firms owned by private industry experience especially strong employment growth. I view the empirical evidence on employment as largely consistent with a view that private-equity portfolio companies create economic value by operating more efficiently. As a group, companies controlled by private-equity firms do not cut jobs willy-nilly, but neither are they likely to add unusually to payrolls, even as business grows, because of their emphasis on bottom-line efficiency.

The Crystal Ball Myth

Another persistent myth about private-equity firms is the idea that these investors as a group acquire superior information on the future performance of companies that may become part of their portfolios, as if, somehow, their investment techniques are tantamount to a crystal ball for corporate performance. While operating improvements and value creation consistently occur after a private-equity investment, the data do not support an argument that these investors have discovered an ability to develop superior information on target companies prior to making them part of their investment portfolios.

Critics of private equity often assign a sinister explanation to the supposition that private-equity investors develop superior information. Some claim that incumbent management is a source of this inside information. To some extent, supporters of private equity implicitly agree that incumbent management has information on how to make a firm perform better. After all, one of the justifications for private-equity deals is that, with better incentives and closer monitoring, managers will use their knowledge to deliver better results. A less attractive claim, however, is that incumbent managers favor a private-equity buyout because they intend to keep their jobs and receive lucrative compensation under the new owners. As a result, incumbent managers may be unwilling to fight for the highest price for existing shareholders, a tendency that, if true, would give private-equity investors a better deal.

Several observations suggest that it is unlikely that operating improvements are simply a result of private-equity firms taking advantage of private information. When I studied this issue in the late 1980s, I compared the forecasts the private-equity firms released publicly at the time of the leveraged buyouts with their actual performance results. The asymmetric information story suggests that actual performance should exceed the forecasts. In fact, actual performance after the buyout lagged the forecasts. Moreover, when Elie Ofek studied leveraged-buyout attempts that failed because the offer was rejected by the board or by stockholders, even though management supported it, he found no excess stock returns or operating improvements for these firms.

The argument that management has strong incentives to manipulate the release of operating information is belied by the simple fact that these managers are well aware that private-equity firms frequently bring in new management. Because incumbent managers cannot be sure they will be in a position to receive high-powered incentives from the new private-equity owners, they would have less incentive to distort how information about target companies is released.

A third factor that belies the truism about private-equity investors' supposedly greater insight into the future performance of target firms is the fact that, at boom times in the boom-and-bust cycle, private-equity firms have overpaid in their leveraged buyouts and experienced losses. For example, the late 1980s were one such time, and it seems likely that the recent private-equity boom will generate lower returns than investors expected, as well. If incumbent managers provided inside information, it clearly was not enough to help private-equity firms avoid periods of poor returns by lowering the offering prices for their purchases. In fact, in these periods, the private-equity investors did the selling companies a huge favor by buying at what turned out to be high prices.

The Negotiation Advantage

While the research does not support an argument that operating improvements result from asymmetric access to information, there is some evidence that strong negotiating skills help private-equity funds to acquire firms more cheaply than other bidders. A series of studies on post-1980s buyouts found only modest increases in firm operating performance, yet those same companies still generate large financial returns to private-equity funds. This suggests that private-equity firms are able to buy low and sell high. This finding is consistent with a notion that private-equity firms identify companies or industries that turn out to be undervalued, as proven by subsequent valuations of the companies in question. Even so, it is difficult to pin down exactly what accounts for such differences. Perhaps private-equity firms are particularly good negotiators. Or, perhaps target boards and management do not get the best possible price.

The results are consistent with private-equity investors bargaining well, target boards bargaining badly, or private-equity investors taking advantage of market timing and perhaps market mispricing.

In the end, the empirical evidence suggests that leveraged buyouts by private-equity firms create value, quite apart from any negotiating advantages or the vicissitudes of marketing timing. Whatever the reasons for their success, it appears that private-equity firms are not particularly generous when it comes time to share the fruit of their labors with their limited partner investors. First, because private-equity firms often purchase firms in competitive auctions or by paying a premium to public shareholders, sellers likely capture a meaningful amount of value, particularly in boom periods. For example, when Kohlberg Kravis Roberts & Co. purchased RJR Nabisco, KKR paid a premium to public shareholders of roughly $10 billion. After the buyout, KKR's investors earned a low return, suggesting that KKR paid out most, if not all, of the additional value to RJR's public shareholders.

Investment returns to the limited partner investors in private-equity funds are reduced by the simple fact that limited partners pay meaningful fees to their general partners who operate the private-equity firms. This implies that the return to outside investors, net of fees, will be lower than the return on the private-equity fund's underlying investments. In this, they are no different from investors in mutual funds who pay substantial fees but do not outperform the stock market.

When Antoinette Shoar and I studied the data in 2005, we found that limited-partner investors in private-equity funds earn slightly less than the Standard & Poor's 500 index, net of fees, ending with an average ratio of 93% to 97%. On average, therefore, we did not find the outperformance often given as a justification for investing in private-equity funds. At the same time, however, these results imply that the private-equity investors outperform the Standard & Poor's 500 index when their fees are added back. Those returns seem to indicate that private-equity investors actually do add value over and above any premium paid to selling shareholders—though the limited partners in their funds are not necessarily beneficiaries of this higher level of performance.

Not only do private-equity firms obtain above-market returns on average, but the good ones have also consistently done so. Historically, the performance by a private-equity firm in one fund predicts performance by the firm in subsequent funds. In fact, their results likely understate historical persistence because the worst performing funds are less likely to raise a subsequent fund. In contrast, mutual funds and hedge funds show little or no persistence. This persistence result explains why limited partners often strive to invest in private-equity funds that have been among the top performers in the past. Of course, only some limited partners can succeed in such a strategy.

Some Speculations

Overall, then, the empirical evidence is strong that private-equity activity creates economic value on average. The increased investment by private-equity firms in operational engineering should ensure that this continues to hold in the future. Because private equity creates economic value, private-equity activity has a substantial permanent component.

The evidence, however, also is strong that private-equity activity is subject to boom and bust cycles, driven by recent returns as well as by the level of interest rates relative to earnings and stock market values. This pattern seems particularly true for larger public-to-private transactions—the sort of transactions that typified the recent boom period that began in 2005 and wound down as leverage became scarcer in 2007.

So, what will happen in the near future? Is the private-equity explosion temporary or permanent?

Given that the unprecedented boom of 2005 to 2007 has ended, and as a result of the economic crisis that began at about that time, it is virtually certain that there will be a decline in private-equity investment and fundraising in the next several years. Consistent with the historical boom-and-bust pattern, the ultimate returns to private-equity funds raised during the recent boom are likely to prove disappointing.

Firms are unlikely to be able to exit the deals from this period at valuations as high as the private-equity firms paid to buy the companies. It also is likely that some of the transactions undertaken during the boom, particularly the larger deals, were driven less by the potential of operating and governance improvements and more by the availability of debt financing, which also implies that the returns on these deals will be disappointing.

This also suggests that performance will turn out to be less persistent than in the past. That is because the private-equity firms that became very large and did the large deals (that are likely to perform poorly) tended to be the better performing private-equity firms in earlier periods.

At the same time, limited partner commitments to private equity will decline for three reasons. First, the decline in the stock market and other assets necessarily reduces the amount of money limited partners have to invest. Second, limited partners are likely to respond to the poor performance of the private-equity firms and shy away from making new commitments. And, third, some limited partners, now having first-hand experience with the costs of illiquidity in private-equity investments, will want to reduce the illiquidity of their overall portfolios. It seems inevitable, therefore, that the private-equity industry will contract.

That said, a significant part of the growth in private-equity activity and institutions is likely to be permanent. First, the less fragile deal structures (higher coverage ratios and looser covenants) of 2005 to 2007 relative to those in the first wave give private-equity investors more flexibility to ride out the current downturn. Second, private-equity investors have expanded their operational engineering capabilities. This may help their companies through the current downturn. Third, unlike the hedge funds and investment banks, the long-term duration of private-equity firm capital matches the long-term duration of private-equity firm assets, making private equity less subject to bank runs or redemptions.

Finally, unlike hedge funds whose returns are compared to Treasury bills or absolute returns, private-equity investors benchmark returns relative to public equity returns. Hedge funds failed relative to their benchmark in 2008 when they declined by more than 20%. With public equities declining on the order of 40% in 2008, private-equity funds have a much better chance of outperforming such benchmarks.

Future of Private Equity

To modify Mark Twain's famous quip, the reports of the death of private equity are exaggerated. Although the private-equity industry will not be as large as it was as its 2007 peak, five years from now I fully expect private equity to have survived and prospered. The core private-equity firm skills of financial, governance, and operating engineering—the sorts of techniques described by the pioneers of private equity who share their experiences in these pages—are real and create real value. Private-equity firms will retain if not improve those skills through the current recession and financial crisis. At some point, financial markets will thaw, and we likely will return to a more normal or stable private-equity industry, one that adds value to portfolio companies and creates value for investors.

2

OPERATING PROFITS: USING AN OPERATING PERSPECTIVE TO ACHIEVE SUCCESS

Joseph L. Rice III

Founder and Chairman
Clayton, Dubilier & Rice

AUM: $10 billion

Years in PE: More than 40

Location: New York, NY

Year born: 1932

Grew up: Katonah, NY

Location born: Brooklyn, NY

Best known deals: Uniroyal Goodrich, Scotts, Hertz, Sally Beauty, U.S. Foodservice, Lexmark, Alliant, Brakes Bros., VWR, Kinko's, and Jafra Cosmetics.

Style: Understated, direct, intellectually generous

Education: B.A., Williams College, Class of 1954
J.D., Harvard Law School, Class of 1960

Significant experience: Has spent most of business career in the buyout business

Personal interests: Family, education, tennis

The lesson: "Nothing in the world can take the place of persistence."

Today, many private-equity firms extol the importance of "operating perspective," but Joe Rice and his firm, Clayton, Dubilier & Rice, were first to make that a point of focus. Today, the firm is recognized as the pioneer of combining operational and financial skills to improve the performance of portfolio companies. CD&R's unique staffing model has permitted the firm to take the operational private-equity investment model to high levels of achievement. CD&R's deep bench of proven corporate leaders—most of them former chief executives of major multinational companies—often take active roles in managing portfolio companies with an eye toward improving execution and resetting strategy. After General Electric chief executive Jack Welch retired in 2001, Rice recruited him to join the firm as a special partner, sharing his unique passion and vision across the firm's portfolio of companies.

Rice believes operating perspective is one of the essential elements that helped his firm achieve everything from the unprecedented carve-out of IBM's printing business to the purchase of Hertz from Ford Motor Co. The result has been one of the best long-term performance records in private equity. Over the years, Clayton, Dubilier & Rice has, on occasion, directed its operating expertise inward to improve its internal processes and address issues that had created challenges for the firm. As Rice notes: "You can't be in the corporate transformation business without a willingness to transform yourself."

Every successful private-equity firm excels in at least one particular aspect of the trade. Some are superb financial engineers, some specialize in turnarounds, and some focus on certain kinds of industries. Clayton, Dubilier & Rice is unique because it combines in a single organization both an operating capability and a financial capability. The firm pursues an "industrialist" approach to the buyout business.

An operating capability has been the essence of our firm from the very beginning. Three of our firm's four founding partners—Martin Dubilier, Gene Clayton, and Bill Welch—had extensive operating experience before they got involved in buyouts. My own father was the chief executive of Allegheny Power Company, and I suppose I picked up some insights into how companies operate from him. From our very first major deal, the $250 million spinoff of the graphics division of Harris Corporation in 1983 that at the time was the largest ever buy-out divestiture, we applied an operating perspective to achieve success. When we owned the Uniroyal Tire Company in the mid-1980s, one of our partners ran the business after we merged it with B.F. Goodrich. A few years later, our operating perspective helped us emerge as the chosen company to orchestrate the carve-out of Lexmark International from IBM. That investment was truly a landmark for the industry and became one of our firm's signature transactions.

The list goes on, but the lesson never gets old. Operating experience can project an investment, and an investment firm, into the upper reaches of success. I thought I knew this as well as anyone. After all, I have been in the deal business for nearly half a century now. But the lesson was brought home to me in a new way at our firm's 2008 annual strategy meeting by Jack Welch, a special partner of the firm.

It is fair to say that almost any partnership holding a strategy session in September of 2008 would have approached the event with a certain amount of dread. Transparency had reached all-time lows. Lehman Brothers, the venerable Wall Street firm, had failed. The U.S. government had been forced to bail out American International Group, AIG, the insurance giant; orchestrate giant banking mergers; and infuse some of the world's biggest banks with billions of dollars. The securitization of financial risk—collateralized debt obligations, mortgage-backed securities, and other now-infamous instruments—was coming under intense public and congressional scrutiny. The U.S. economy and much of the world economy seemed to be verging on a free fall toward an economic breakdown worse than any in our lifetime.

As our strategy meeting opened, several of the management teams of our portfolio companies were scrambling to prepare for quarterly operating reviews scheduled for the next week with the firm's operating partners. Word had gone out that this was a time to be cautious. With all that was going on in the financial markets and the rest of the economy, we expected a set of very conservative operating plans and financial projections from our portfolio management teams.

The economic circumstances had put many seasoned finance professionals into a defensive crouch. Certainly the dire environment had that effect on me. But Jack had another perspective. He took the floor at our strategy meeting and transformed not just the tone of the meeting but also the direction our firm would set through the tough economy.

"At a time like this, we want our companies to be aggressive," Jack said. "They are all market leaders. They are all well capitalized. We want them to take the appropriate defensive steps for sure, but we also want them to do something else—play offense, because they can. By virtue of their relative strength in the marketplace, each one is in the position to buy or bury their competitors."

Jack counseled us, and the partners agreed to have our portfolio businesses adopt forward-looking strategies, such as taking market share, offering flexible terms to strategic accounts, recruiting talent from weaker players, and considering acquisitions. Rather than advising the need to take a defensive attitude because the economy was going into a hole, Welch was saying, "Hammer them. Don't play defense. Play offense."

That is exactly the reason why we have proven operating executives deeply embedded into our firm's structure. Though Jack is a special partner and is not expected to roll up his sleeves and dig into the details of our portfolio the way our full-time operating partners do, the contribution he made had the same sort of catalytic impact that our operating partners have on our companies. They bring their breadth of experience, at the highest levels of business, to the problems that the management teams at our portfolio companies must address to take their businesses to higher performance levels. Operating partners have lived through business cycles before. They know how economic stresses can create winners and losers, and they know from experience how the right moves at the right times can mean the difference between success and failure.

Operating perspective is for us the single most important aspect of our investment model, and its importance will only grow in the aftermath of the economic crisis, as financial engineering becomes far less prominent in terms of driving investment returns in the private-equity industry. It will always be important to pay the right price for a company, to structure the financing appropriately and creatively, to have strong management and a powerful product portfolio. But, just as Jack Welch's aggressive view in the midst of economic crisis transformed our strategy meeting, an operations viewpoint can increase the chances of success by bringing a world-wise perspective to the work.

How Operating Perspective Works

An operating perspective also helps us, as buyers, make smart decisions about the investments we make. It's no accident that our firm reviews 100 offering books for every one deal we complete. Often enough, our operating partners spot something that our more financially oriented partners might never have seen. They have different insights based on what they have experienced in the day-to-day management of large global businesses. And, when we bring that operating perspective to bear on our assessment of management, it helps us quickly measure whether the existing team does or does not have the natural talent and the requisite experience to achieve our goals for the business.

Whatever the "it" factor is for operational excellence, our operating partners have it. People such as George Tamke, who spent many years at Emerson Electric before eventually rising to the top job, and Fred Kindle, former CEO of ABB, one of Europe's largest corporations, have demonstrated the ability to work closely with our portfolio company management teams to drive productivity, cost, and growth initiatives. Ed Liddy handled a complex transformation of Allstate's relations with its insurance agents, and his tough-mindedness and acumen as a financial manager certainly were as critical to our investment screening and decision-making processes as they were when then-Treasury Secretary Henry Paulson recruited him to salvage AIG when it was on the brink of failure. When someone has that operational ability, it becomes obvious because it emerges as naturally as a hair color or ability with languages. When someone does not have it, that shows up, too. People such as Welch, Tamke, Kindle, Liddy, and our other operating partners, who have proven they possess that sort of intuition themselves, can spot it—or, just as importantly, decide that it is missing—more quickly than the rest of us.

A Personal Perspective

I learned years ago the importance of natural talent as a prerequisite for success. After graduating from Williams College, I enlisted in the Marine Corps, then went to Harvard Law School, and ended up practicing law at Sullivan & Cromwell. At this great law firm, I had the good fortune to work for a born lawyer, John Raben. He had a very perceptive legal mind. John could see all the issues, turn them on their side, and view them in a way no one had thought of before. Clients respected him tremendously. He was a great lawyer, and everyone knew it. I recognized that my chances for becoming a lawyer on a par with John fell somewhere between slim and none. That motivated me to look for a field in which I, too, would have that natural ability.

One of Sullivan & Cromwell's clients was an institutional research firm named Laird & Company. Its corporate finance practice was the deal business: "bootstrap deals," we called them. Laird would find companies they wanted to acquire, then go out and raise the financing necessary to do the deal, "boostrapping" themselves into position to make the purchase. As I grew to understand that business, it appealed to me, so when a position opened at Laird, I left the law practice and went to work doing deals. Very quickly, I found I was a better deal guy than I was a lawyer.

Over time I learned the craft of dealmaking. I am not a great financial analyst, but fortunately we have plenty of partners who complement my weaknesses. When we are investing in a company and assessing its management, we look for all the ingredients that contribute to making a great company. If not all of them are there, we decide whether we can provide the missing elements. Our operating partners are essential in making these judgments, thanks to a sense of perception that only a former top executive with deep experience can muster.

The importance of an operating perspective was brought home to me relatively early in my buyout career. In 1969, I had started a firm with three other individuals whose skills, like mine, were chiefly financial. This made us proficient in reading financial statements but not adept at assessing the operating challenges that we might face in running a business. We had contracted to purchase a magnetic tape company together with an individual who was to become the chief executive. He believed that the company had a winning technology.

Our prospective partner was wrong about the technology, but none of us knew enough to challenge that assertion. Over time it became clear that we did not have a technically advanced product, but rather a commodity. The deal was a bust. That experience made me conclude that I needed somebody—every single time—on my side of the table who understood businesses and could evaluate markets, operations, technology, and, importantly, the ability of the business to respond to different cycles in the economy.

The importance of operational savvy as a way to avoid losses, if nothing else, was at the top of my mind when I decided to strike out in 1978 with Martin Dubilier and Gene Clayton. At the time, my new partners had a crisis management firm. Along with Bill Welch, they were hiring out their expertise on a day-to-day basis to manage troubled businesses on behalf of banks and insurance companies that had taken control of them. They were helping Jerry Kohlberg, and, after it was formed, Kohlberg, Kravis & Roberts, to evaluate deals. So, when we eventually came together as a partnership, each of them had some buyout experience. My new partners were not financiers. That was the furthest thing from their minds, but they wanted something more enduring than the consulting work they were doing, and my experience, when combined with theirs, permitted us to create a unique buyout firm.

Building the Pattern of Success

We started in the middle of 1978 and over the next 3 years completed a number of smaller transactions, but our 1983 purchase of Harris Graphics was our first really noteworthy transaction. Harris Graphics was the old Harris Intertype business. It manufactured printing presses: small ones, medium ones, large ones. But the business was not central to the corporate parent that was in the process of transforming itself into a technology company. Our job was to liberate Harris Graphics and provide it with the monetary and intellectual capital necessary to succeed as an independent enterprise.

The deal was remarkable in retrospect. We had no pool of capital that we controlled, so all the financing, both debt and equity, had to be raised by us from other capital sources. For our firm, relatively unknown at the time, raising $250 million was a challenge, but we plugged away at it and got the financing done. Interestingly, Harris Graphics was one of Drexel, Burnham Lambert's early transactions, and its success helped make Drexel a dominant force in the subordinated debt market.

The concept our firm was founded on was that if we combined within a single investment organization both an operating capability and a financial capability we would be more effective investors. Through the decades we have been true to that principle. We are constantly searching for individuals who can be operating partners in the firm. They are a hard resource to identify because, first, they must have established that they can successfully manage a multibillion dollar international business and, second, they have to want to continue to work very hard in a partnership culture, which can be quirky at times. Not an easy individual to find.

CD&R's operating partners are fully integrated into all aspects of our business, unlike some other firms that have former corporate executives as advisors. Our operating partners help to source new deals and analyze proposed transactions, but their most important value comes after the transaction is closed. We expect them to be very active chairmen and be sufficiently conversant with the portfolio business so they can assume the chief executive officer position if the need arises. Over our history, CD&R operating partners have stepped in as interim CEO in about a third of our investments. This was the case with our investment in Uniroyal.

We got involved with Uniroyal in late 1985 almost by chance. The maverick investor Carl Icahn had made a hostile offer for the company, and Uniroyal management had hired Salomon Brothers to find a "white knight" for the company. Salomon's investment bankers had just finished visiting with KKR, and as an afterthought called us to ask if we would meet the chief executive officer, Joe Flannery. Joe's presentation was sufficiently compelling that we decided to examine the opportunity in detail. After an extended period of due diligence, we were able to fend off Ichan and acquire the business.

A major part of Uniroyal was its tire operations. It was an intensely competitive industry, and when we were afforded the opportunity to combine it with B.F. Goodrich's tire business, we did so. The entity that resulted was a true joint venture owned in equal parts by Goodrich and CD&R. The executive positions were split equally: chief executive officer for them, chief operating officer for us; chief financial officer for them, controller for us; and so on. It was a recipe for disaster. So much so that we eventually went to Goodrich and said to them, "One of us has to go; either you buy us out or we will buy you out." We ended up buying them out and installing Chuck Ames, one of our operating partners, as chief executive officer. Chuck's enlightened leadership led to a revitalized organization and ultimately to a very advantageous sale to the French tire manufacturer Michelin.

Building an Operating Structure: The Lexmark Deal

There probably is no better example of our distinctive approach than our purchase of Lexmark, the office printing products business, from IBM in 1991. It is thought that John Akers, the chief executive officer of IBM, had decided that IBM had gotten to the point where it was unmanageable and needed to be broken up. Because the operations of the various IBM divisions were intertwined and were so dependent on the corporate staff for many functions, a sale to a private buyer was the only sensible choice.

The decision to carve out the office products business was made not long after the notorious battle for RJR Nabisco had wrapped up. The bestseller written about that deal, *Barbarians at the Gate*, painted an unflattering picture of all the participants. Supposedly, when Akers decided to sell the printing business, he dropped a copy of *Barbarians* on the desk of one of his subordinates and said, "I don't want to sell it to anyone whose name is in this book." In retrospect, that turned out to be a good thing for us. Our name was not in the book.

It was clear from the start that it would be impossible to auction the business. Lexmark as a stand-alone business existed only in IBM's mind. It was a product line and nothing else. It had no sales force, no technology to call its own, no dedicated production plants, and no corporate infrastructure. It was a collection of business lines—typewriters, impact printers, and suppliers. Even though the IBM Selectric was a workhorse of American industry at that point, it was clear that computer printers would soon put the Selectric out to pasture. And the one part of the operation that ultimately would become the backbone of the business we were buying was not even a commercial product yet: the laser printer.

Martin Dubilier had run a business products company at one time, and even held the original patent on the daisy wheel printer, so he had an intuition that, despite everything, we ought to be able to make it work. "We can do this," we said. "This will be a great business."

We knew that turning a stand-alone typewriter manufacturer into a dynamic developer of computer printers would be a tall order that required all of the firm's resources, both operational and financial. But, before we could transform the business, we had to complete the transaction, and that required infinite patience. Don Gogel, now the firm's CEO, painstakingly negotiated more than 80 transitional commercial agreements with IBM covering trademarks, intellectual property, and the like before we could complete the purchase.

There was something else that made this investment enticing for us. It's difficult to fully appreciate today, when IBM is no longer the standard in business that it once was, but for that company to reach out and choose us as the counterparty was huge. It was a turning point for us and for the entire private-equity industry. It was a sign that private equity was acceptable—and that we were a worthy counterparty to IBM.

A Harvest and Grow Strategy

Our business plan for Lexmark was simple: use the cash flow from the mature businesses to build the laser printer business. The IBM people believed, and we came to agree, that the laser printer market could become a significant one. Our chief concern was whether we could develop the products and the market quickly enough to rely solely on the dwindling cash flow from the mature businesses.

Negotiations over the transaction took months—almost a year—and of course price became a key issue. Public companies, in particular, are always sensitive about price, and IBM needed to show a big number to Wall Street. As the first transaction in what might be a massive corporate restructuring, they needed to set a high bar. Price was problematic, in part, because it was difficult to say with any authority what the earnings of the underlying business actually were. There were no audited financial statements for the group of product lines that we were buying.

Putting the pieces in place in a way that we could meet IBM's objectives was a challenge. We knew IBM would not show a lot of flexibility. But we also felt we could organize the transaction in a way that would enable us to pay a relatively rich price yet still build a profitable business. After all, Lexmark would not be completely independent of IBM. We would still be buying products and equipment from IBM, and they would be doing the same from us. By creatively negotiationg the contracts arising from this interwoven series of relationships, we could raise the purchase price high enough to reach IBM's price objectives yet still have a robust enough revenue stream to make the independent Lexmark business a success.

As negotiations wore on, we began addressing other challenges. Staffing was a key concern. It was pretty obvious we would need to pull the leadership team from within IBM. The IBM corporate culture was so strong that outsiders would be rejected as if they were some sort of biological antibody. We were fortunate to be able to recruit a well-regarded IBMer, Marvin Mann, to run the business, and we appointed as his deputy Paul Curlander, who had led the development of the laser printer.

If we were going to succeed, we knew we would have to create a distinctive corporate culture. The IBM culture was very strong—white shirts, dark suits, and a very regimented training system—but not very entrepreneurial. We focused on compensation, increasing the performance incentives built into the compensation scheme and reducing the fixed compensation. Most importantly, we gave every employee of the new company a direct or indirect ownership interest in it. When the new company went public, the value of the employees' investment interest was greater than $1 billion.

We also focused on the product development cycle. IBM had a 30-month product development cycle. Hewlett Packard's was 18 months. We needed to get to 15 months and at competitive price and performance levels. We succeeded by introducing the concept of pay-for-performance into the development lab.

The financing climate was very difficult in 1990 and early 1991. It was only because IBM let it be known that they really wanted to see this transaction done that the bank syndicate came together.

The transaction closed in March of 1991. By the end of the year, we had paid down $300 million in debt, well ahead of schedule. We had streamlined the manufacturing operations, cut the development cycle in half, and succeeded in motivating our sales force. We brought the company public in late 1995 and ultimately returned to limited partners over four times the original investment through a series of public offerings, the last of which was made in 1998. Lexmark still exists as an independent entity and is listed on the New York Stock Exchange. I have always felt our operating perspective helped this transaction develop in a way that this represented the buyout business at its best in creating a dynamic, independent entity where one had not previously existed.

After the Close: Operating for Success

All investments present opportunities and challenges. Two transactions with similar challenges—integrating and improving the performance of multiple-location businesses—produced results at opposite ends of the spectrum: Kinko's and U.S. Office Products.

With Kinko's, which we bought in 1996, we knew from the outset that we would have a challenge combining 127 businesses into a single entity and teaching them to function as one. The Kinko's outlets were scattershot all across the United States. Each operated as if unrelated to the other Kinko's units: different hours, different service offerings, different customer orientation. George Tamke, the operating partner who ultimately became responsible for Kinko's and actually ran the company on an interim basis, found that one of his most effective techniques in producing uniformity of performance across the portfolio was "quartiling." He would pick a particular attribute—revenue per employee, for example—and divide the Kinko's stores into four different groups, based on how each performed against that metric.

Once Tamke had "quartiled" the Kinko's stores, he then studied the top performers to determine why they excelled. He identified the attributes of success and then worked them into the system. He also drove the units in each quartile to perform at the level of the quartile above them. It was common sense, and it worked. We eventually sold Kinko's to FedEx. Tamke's by-now intimate knowledge of the company's metrics also had persuaded him and his management team to build a fast-growing document management business within Kinko's that became a logical and profitable adjunct to its retail business.

The turn of the century was a tough period for our firm, and U.S. Office Products illustrates one aspect of our challenges as well as any company in our portfolio at the time. U.S. Office Products was a roll-up of more than 100 business-products distribution businesses. It had outgrown the abilities of its founder to manage it, and as it turned out was beyond our capabilities, too. Our due diligence effort was not what it might have been, and we were unable to establish a control system that permitted us effectively to manage the business. When the business began to slide, we could not stop the decline, and the business was eventually restructured and our investment was lost.

Fairchild Dornier Corporation, a manufacturer of regional jets based in Germany, and Acterna, a leader in communications technology, both faced unprecedented—and unpredictable—shocks to their respective markets shortly after we acquired them. Fairchild, with a backlog of over $10 billion when we acquired the business, saw its orders dry up after the September 11, 2001, terrorist attacks, causing the business to fail. Acterna, acquired in 1998, suffered a severe revenue decline as customers cut back significantly on telecommunications spending in the face of the steep telecom industry downturn. The company ultimately was restructured.

Looking back on this period, I believe we suffered because we thought we were better than we really were. We thought we could do anything. "Pride goeth before the fall." But I also believe that it is a measure of our institutional resilience and the strength of the firm's underlying investment model that, even with significant underperformance of the investments made between 1998 and 2000, our overall performance continued to be strong.

Turning Operating Perspective Inward

These disappointments happening as they did in a very short period of time made us reexamine the way we were conducting our business. It became clear in retrospect that we had gotten too far up the risk curve. It served our firm well that during this period Jack Welch joined the firm. Given our firm's management orientation and Jack's reputation as one of the most creative and successful corporate leaders of our time, he was a perfect fit.

We did not expect Jack to be an operations partner. Rather, we wanted him to play a role that would span the entire portfolio. We looked to Jack for ideas that would help us focus, as a firm, on strategic objectives. From there, the individual companies and our individual transaction teams could focus on success. This is something that Jack had done well at General Electric, particularly in the latter years of his long tenure at that complex, global company. We hoped he could bring this sort of acumen to Clayton, Dubilier & Rice.

In an effort to improve our performance, we instituted two organizational and investment process enhancements: the operating review and an investment screening committee. We asked Jack to chair the first of these and to participate in the second. The operating review brings together all the operating partners of the firm with the management of our portfolio companies. In frank, detailed discussion, the management teams have the benefit of the collective wisdom of seven individuals, each of whom has been the chief executive officer of a major multiple-industry international business. The record demonstrates that their collective wisdom is of great value.

The screening committee imposes a system of quality control to our deal making. Consisting of the firm's senior partners, the committee meets with the deal team over the course of negotiations on a transaction. It ensures that the team considers each of the issues that the committee thinks is important to the investment and that the proposed transaction will have qualities that the entire partnership will approve.

In many respects, we as a firm did what we ask our companies to do: respond to changing circumstances decisively and effectively by making positive, strategic changes.

Acting on Operating Insight

Consider the case of our 2008 strategy meeting. We had no idea in advance that we would come to the collective conclusion that we needed to seize on the economic opportunity that would emerge out of a global economic collapse. But what was important to the firm, and ultimately should be important to our operating companies, is that the partners looked at the changing landscape and resolved to act.

When we took a break from the strategy session, we immediately got word back to the portfolio company management teams that they would need to prepare for an entirely different sort of operating review than the one they had expected the following week in New York. The deal teams from the firm all called the CEOs of their companies and said, "You know that presentation you were working on for the operating review? We are going to change the whole focus of it. It's now going to be, 'How do you play offense in the current environment?'"

It would have been more convenient to just stick with the original plan and merely talk about this changed focus in each of these operating reviews. But that would have been a wasted opportunity. Ultimately, it did our companies a lot more good to rip apart their plans, look at them from a different perspective, and come in with new ideas.

I have spent a lot of time explaining how operating partners affect our firm's success, at the risk of neglecting the important role played by CD&R's financial partners. That is because our operating partners are so clearly distinctive. There are, however, more financial partners in the firm than operating partners, and they remain the heart of the firm. Without them, there would be no deal flow for the operating partners to evaluate. This is, after all, an investment business. They are uniformly hardworking, driven professionals. Typically they are a generation or two younger than the operating partners. Importantly, because they are joined at the hip with operating partners, CD&R financial partners must have a level of maturity that extends beyond their years. Most of our transactions are divestitures, which are complex and demanding. They require tremendous intellectual capabilities and persistence, which our financial partners have in abundance.

The most critical element of the firm we have built is the human capital represented by our people. Just as we have developed an investment style that is distinct from most other private-equity firms, our balance in terms of operating and financial skills is what truly sets us apart.

LESSONS FROM JOE RICE

 Labor hard at the front end of an investment. Be patient and careful in transaction structuring and analysis. Study the operations as carefully as the finances, and shape the balance sheet to fit the character of the business with plenty of liquidity cushion for tough times.

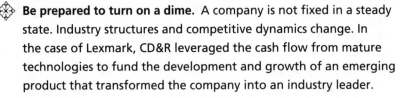

 Go beyond the numbers. Spreadsheets and balance statements don't tell the whole story. It's important to understand the operating challenges—and opportunities—when considering an investment, as well as the skill and drive of the management team.

 Be prepared to turn on a dime. A company is not fixed in a steady state. Industry structures and competitive dynamics change. In the case of Lexmark, CD&R leveraged the cash flow from mature technologies to fund the development and growth of an emerging product that transformed the company into an industry leader.

 Look in the mirror. Be prepared to transform your own firm or company. Insist on accountability, change people and processes as necessary, and get everyone moving together toward success.

 Be passionate about your vocation. Great lawyers, managers, and dealmakers may actually be born, not made. Follow your heart, and your natural talent, to achieve success. Do not remain in a profession that seems a poor fit.

3

SKIN IN THE GAME: INVESTING IN SERVICE BUSINESSES

F. Warren Hellman
Chairman
Hellman & Friedman LLC

AUM: $25 billion   **Years in PE:** Over 25

Location: San Francisco, CA   **Year born:** 1934

Grew up: San Francisco, CA   **Location born:** New York, NY

Best known deals: Levi Strauss & Co., Eller Media Company, Inc., Young & Rubicam Inc., NASDAQ, DoubleClick Inc.

Style: Investing in high quality business franchises

Education: B.A., University of California at Berkeley, Class of 1955 M.B.A., Harvard Graduate School of Business, Class of 1959

Significant experience: Investment banking at Lehman Bros. Private equity and venture capital experience

Personal interests: Banjo playing, endurance horse racing, skiing, and studying the Torah

The lesson: "All potential investments should be considered guilty until proven innocent."

Though he comes from an almost royal line in the history of California finance, Warren Hellman has a down-to-earth investment approach. The great grandson of I.W. Hellman, who built the Wells Fargo Bank, and son of a prominent San Francisco investor, Hellman forged his own path on Wall Street. By age 26 he became the youngest partner in the history of Lehman Brothers and later served as president during a tumultuous period for the firm.

After its co-founding in 1984, Hellman & Friedman quickly broke into the ranks of leading private-equity firms with the $1.6 billion management-led buyout of Levi Strauss & Co. Since then, Hellman & Friedman has put together a string of successful deals including: the recapitalization of ad giant Young & Rubicam, the demutualization of the NASDAQ stock market, and the acquisition of internet advertising manager DoubleClick. Hellman typically avoids heavy industry, preferring to invest in non-capital intensive people-oriented services businesses. He has developed an ability to work from a minority investment position yet still provide strong guidance that helps create value in Hellman & Friedman's portfolio companies.

⌒◯✕◯⌒

A defining moment in my life occurred in 1959 when I had just started my career as an investment banker at Lehman Brothers. My father was visiting from San Francisco and marveled at the ways of the "new" Wall Street.

We were in the midst of one of Wall Street's periodic booms in initial public offerings, and the team I was leading at Lehman was executing public offerings for companies with modern-sounding names and can't-miss technologies and products. Among them were Infra-Red Industries, Microwave Associates, and Gulton Industries—names that seemed important at the time but that almost no one would recognize today.

As we discussed the economy, my father confessed to me how troubled he was by the frenzied state of the markets. "I feel as if I don't understand the markets anymore," said Marco F. Hellman, my father. "The things that I have always believed in most implicitly—fundamental valuation metrics such as price earnings ratios, price to book value, free cash flow—none of them mean anything anymore."

"You are absolutely right," I told him. "You just don't understand at all what is going on. It's a whole new world out there!"

It wasn't long after his visit that the stock market crashed and along with it, my proud portfolio of high technology IPOs. In a phone conversation soon afterward, my father reminded me how much he had enjoyed our conversation in New York.

"Clearly one of us didn't understand what was happening and it wasn't me," he said.

Periodically, the markets go through a phase where the old economics seem completely outmoded. In the last decade alone, we have seen this happen twice. During the dot-com boom, profits themselves seemed a quaint way to gauge value. Rather, true value was all about "eyeballs" and "cost per click"—or so the thinking went. More recently, we experienced the leverage frenzy that came crashing down in mid-2007. These events led to the untimely collapse of my own Wall Street alma mater.

In the end, there is little new under the sun. Old-line measures of value continue to count. Companies that have lasting franchises, which meet a need or provide a mission-critical service, that are run by high-caliber managers whose interests are aligned with shareholders, that produce strong free cash flow and don't require significant capital investment to grow—those are the ones that will always last. My firm seeks to invest in companies that possess these traits.

For many, the tide has shifted, of course. Broad market corrections often force investors to refocus on fundamental value metrics, and that is where we seem to find ourselves again today. Investors are migrating back to basics in large part because they have no choice. With a challenging economic outlook and constrained financing environment, back to basics appears to be the way forward.

Back to Basics

For me, the move back toward value is a welcome re-awakening of investment principles our firm has tried continuously to respect ever since Tully Friedman and I founded Hellman & Friedman in 1984. This is not to say our investment approach did not change over time. In fact, it is not clear to me whether one of our first major investments, the $1.6 billion management-led buyout of jean maker Levi Strauss & Co., would still fit our investment approach today. Through time and experience, we have focused on companies with fewer physical assets and lower capital costs.

There are certain common denominators that define our typical portfolio company. We look for strong franchises with high barriers to entry, plenty of free cash flow, a strong and capable management team, and a persuasive case that our investment can help grow the business.

A key measurement in our cash-flow analysis relies on a concept called "return on tangible capital." It is a modification of the typical cash-flow model that takes capital expenditures into account. Stated simply, we prefer to invest in companies that can afford to operate and grow "inexpensively." If the business does require capital to grow, we expect the business to earn a significantly above-market return on that capital outlay.

I also believe it is impossible to overstate the people quotient in the investment decision. Even if a company meets all our firm's benchmarks, we can succeed only if the people running the company can make it work. We change management teams if we have to, but we prefer to invest behind and support an existing management team that we believe can execute a joint vision and will be motivated by their own significant equity stake in our deal. Often times, our investment serves as a catalyst to help management acquire, or meaningfully increase, their ownership in the business.

Major Successes from Minority Stakes

Unlike many private-equity firms, which insist on majority ownership of their portfolio companies, we have a wealth of experience taking minority stakes in companies and helping transform their strategies even though we cannot exert the typical majority ownership controls. This approach is somewhat unique in the world of large-scale private equity and has facilitated our ability to obtain stakes in the Young & Rubicam advertising enterprise and the NASDAQ stock market, among others.

Though our founding partners all got their start as investment bankers, we typically try not to rely on outright control or financial engineering to make the case for an investment. I have a saying: "Every potential investment should be considered guilty until proven innocent."

This is a shorthand way of saying that the fundamental business case for an investment must be proven sound through rigorous due diligence on the underlying industry and business.

As "recovering" investment bankers, we know that a smart financial person can find a way to construct an elaborate capital structure that will justify almost any investment. I do not believe that is the way to create lasting value, and only lasting value can deliver the kind of investment returns my partners and I expect.

Investment discipline is critical as well, and we hold that concept to mean more than just saying we apply certain metrics when we commit capital. To me, discipline means constantly re-evaluating investments. In fact, every one of our portfolio companies periodically goes through an in-depth evaluation process in which we re-assess our original investment thesis and re-underwrite the expected performance, at least on paper. This process has significant influence regarding our decisions on when to exit an investment.

Learning from Mistakes

We began developing our "hold/sell" strategy after experiencing our firm's most gut wrenching early loss, the bankruptcy of a paging network company called MobileMedia Corporation. Ironically, the MobileMedia investment got off to a healthy start. In fact, at one point in our ownership, the company was worth approximately three times our original investment. However, the company—and industry—soon began to experience significant pricing pressure, and MobileMedia wound up filing for bankruptcy protection before we had a chance to exit the investment.

We learned several key lessons from the MobileMedia experience. Among them were the vital importance of investing in high quality, defensible businesses and being proactive in determining when to exit an investment. Had we exited MobileMedia sooner than we did—as soon as the business fundamentals began to change—we likely would have avoided bankruptcy and made a healthy return. As it turned out, though, the MobileMedia investment was a seminal event for our firm and significantly contributed to our current investment philosophy. Irrespective of the type of investment, I believe it is important to be an active investor in the sense that we continuously reassess how we feel about the underlying business, its management team, and our prospective return on investment.

If this sounds carefully thought out and, to a point, almost regimented, let me tell you: It is. If it also sounds as if we had all these concepts figured out when we formed Hellman & Friedman 25 years ago, let me tell you this: We did not.

We brought a few inklings of what we knew with us from our careers on Wall Street and other work we did before landing, finally, in San Francisco's financial district. However, we learned much of what we now know about private-equity investment and the management of our portfolio companies through experience, through trial and error as owners or major investors in our portfolio companies. The errors have hurt, but without them, we would not have learned the vitally important lessons by which we have built a record of success. It is much easier to make a statement like that long after the mistake, after the hurt has died down—not that it ever completely goes away.

The Long Trail to Wall Street

For nearly as long as I can remember, my life seemed directed toward a career as a professional investor. Although to be honest, as memory serves, I did have some early years when it was not altogether certain I was going anywhere at all. This great revelation hit my dear mother when, at the age of eleven and without any prior permission, I decided one day to ride my horse on a 70-mile round trip excursion to Sacramento.

In retrospect, I like to think that, at some level, my mother appreciated my independent streak. After all, she was a unique personality in her own right. She had earned a pilot's license at the age of 16, and during World War II she volunteered for the service. The Air Force required every able bodied pilot to be flying bombing missions over Germany or the Pacific Islands, so dedicated female pilots such as my mother would fly airplanes around the country repositioning them for the armed services.

When I returned from my long horse ride—and this, by the way, was not the sole indiscretion of my youth—my mother responded in the manner of many aggrieved parents through the ages. She sent me to San Rafael Military Academy, otherwise known as reform school for rich kids.

My family had a long history in finance. In 1871, my great grandfather, Isaias W. Hellman, formed a bank in Los Angeles called Farmers and Merchants Bank, which helped Harrison Otis start the *Los Angeles Times* and orchestrated several other notable financings. Isias is best remembered as the person who bought Wells Fargo in a distressed sale in 1905 and greatly expanded its role as the bank that financed growth throughout California and the West.

As a private-equity investor today, I like to think that I inherited at least one trait from my great grandfather: The desire to own businesses outright rather than just work for them. As it was, Edward Harriman, the railroad baron who had gained control of Wells Fargo, had approached my great-grandfather in 1905 and asked him if he might be interested in running the bank.

Isaias had a simple response. "I don't run businesses. I own them," he said. He bought Wells Fargo, recapitalized the bank, and never looked back.

The Hellman family name and connections were useful to me by the time I finished my undergraduate studies at the University of California–Berkeley and Harvard Graduate School of Business. I was newly married to my wonderful wife, Chris, and we were anxious to strike out on our own. It seemed that I could best do that by heading east to Wall Street, rather than going to work for my father's investment firm, which was doing venture capital before anyone called it that.

Lehman Days

In 1959, my uncle Fred Ehrman was a high-ranking partner at Lehman Brothers and helped me land a job in the firm's investment banking division. I quickly started putting deals together. At the time, the firm was putting its own capital into deals, and I was drawn naturally to that part of the business. We put up the original capital to form Litton Industries and controlled Great Western Financial.

I rose quickly through the Lehman organization becoming, at age 26, the youngest partner in the firm's history. It was at Lehman that the asset management business first piqued my interest. The asset management division, which at one point reported to me, had incredibly consistent earnings quarter over quarter. This was in direct contrast to the highly volatile profitability swings among the investment banking and sales & trading departments. This interest in asset management would re-emerge years later after I co-founded Hellman & Friedman.

Lehman Brothers always had a well-deserved reputation for being a highly internally competitive firm. In fact, when Bob Rubin was a lead partner at Goldman Sachs, he often used to say to me that the main difference between Goldman and Lehman Brothers was not in the quality of people, but in the way people in the firms dealt with each other. The partners at Goldman Sachs understood that their real competition came from beyond the walls of the firm. Lehman's partners seemed to believe their chief competition came from the inside.

The internal tension at Lehman Brothers constantly boiled beneath the surface. Rivalries between factions—traders vs. investment bankers—had intensified in the years after the firm changed from a partnership to a corporate structure in 1970. Making matters worse, the old guard leadership team hoarded power, kept people in the dark about their chances for promotion, and paid themselves substantially more than lower-ranking members of the firm, regardless of their contributions. On top of it all was a lack of adequate controls.

The unhealthy dynamics at Lehman led to an outright crisis by 1973, just after I became president of the firm, when the fixed income desk made an outrageously risky bet on interest rates that turned against us. The fixed-income traders had purchased nearly $1.5 billion of long government bonds at a time when the firm had less than $20 million in equity, so the ill-advised trade was a huge problem, one that threatened the very survival of the firm. Pete Peterson had left his job as Commerce Secretary for President Nixon only a month earlier, and along with a small group of partners, I helped convince Peterson to step in and take charge. Once Peterson had agreed to the assignment, I personally had to walk into my uncle's office with Peterson and another colleague and fire my uncle. To this day, that conversation remains the most painful thing I have had to do in business.

The Lehman Turnaround

Once in control, Peterson and I worked as hard as we had ever worked to get the firm turned around and headed in the right direction.

The job ahead of us was just incredible. At one point we calculated that we had gone three straight months without eating more than a handful of meals outside the firm, including weekends. Obviously, there might be more physically demanding jobs, but it was extremely taxing, difficult work. We cut the workforce from 1,300 to 550 employees and many of those cuts included partners with whom I had worked closely for several years.

Among the many key decisions we made during that period was that Lehman could no longer afford to be active investing as a principal in corporate buyouts. An investment banking firm needed huge amounts of capital to operate its underwriting and brokerage businesses, and Lehman did not have enough capital available for it to act as a principal investor, too. Since my true interest was investing, not trading or underwriting, that decision more than any other probably prompted me to leave Lehman in 1977. I had run out of patience, too, with some of the continued infighting that went on despite Peterson's hard work. And since the rest of the firm was responding to his leadership, I no longer felt indispensable.

I have said for years that in my work at Hellman & Friedman I have a simple rule of thumb: I decide how the old guard at Lehman would have behaved, and then I do the opposite. It sounds like a throwaway line, but it is not. Hoarding of power, internal intrigues, lack of accountability and intellectual laziness are all unacceptable to me. I had so little patience with it all that from time to time I completely lost my temper. It happened frequently enough back then that I was given the nickname "Hurricane Hellman." The temper outbursts were another part of Lehman that I did my best to leave behind once I departed from the firm.

It was clearly time to go. After Lehman, I worked eight years in Boston, forming two different investment firms. The more substantial of the two, Hellman Ferri Investment Associates, was the predecessor firm to Matrix Partners, which still exists. At Hellman Ferri, my partner Paul Ferri and I invested mainly in venture deals, and even though Ferri and I had to go through a fairly bitter breakup with our other founding partner, the work in Boston provided valuable experience in principal transactions. By 1981 I was back to California, and it was there, while working on a project basis for Lehman Brothers to restructure the finances of Crown Zellerbach Corporation, that I first connected with Tully Friedman, a managing director at Salomon Brothers who was advising Crown Zellerbach.

Teaming with Tully

From the outset, Friedman and I knew we wanted to go beyond investment banking and eventually become principal investors in our own deals. However, we did not want to raise third-party money right away. Rather, we wanted to take some time working with each other and working with a younger group of incredibly talented people who joined shortly after us, Matt Barger, Jack Bunce, and John Pasquesi. Our view was, let's see how we exist together as a firm for a few years before we raise a fund backed by institutional investors. Until then, any investments we did would be on a one-off basis.

The investment that first put us on the map was the $1.6 billion management-led buyout of Levi Strauss & Co. Levi's came to us at first not as a potential buyout candidate, but because company executives were seeking advice regarding capital structure. At Hellman & Friedman, we were as much in the advisory business in those early days as we were acting as principal investors, and as we dug into the business in early 1985 we kept looking at each other and saying, "This company should not be public."

In our view, Levi's was one of the great global brands. This was in the mid-1980's when college students from the U.S. would travel to Eastern Europe and pay their expenses by selling Levi's jeans out of their backpacks. The company had huge market share and strong free cash flow—it was a veritable cash machine. But the public market valuation did not reflect that view. Since the family owned more than half the company's stock, there was no takeover play and Wall Street had seemingly lost focus on Levi's cash flow.

The investment case was simple. If we offered a premium to the market price on behalf of the family shareholders, we could probably succeed with a purchase. At the time, Levi's had no debt. To take control of the company, we needed to borrow approximately $1.2 billion, and roll approximately $400 million of the family's stock into the deal. After the transaction closed, the Levi's family owned approximately

93% of the equity, with Hellman & Friedman owning the remaining 7%, which we attained as payment for our advisory fee.

The Levi's deal was the largest leveraged buyout of a publicly held U.S. firm to that point. We proudly told anyone who would listen that we had just done the largest buyout of all time. Then two weeks later, Storer Communications was taken private and we were the kings of the buyout world no more.

Part of the formula for success when you're a principal investor is to have the right chief executive in place and to give him or her the right backing—or to replace the CEO if need be. Fortunately in the case of Levi's, the former was the case. Bob Haas, who actually is a distant relative, proved to be a tremendous CEO, and he quickly took advantage of his status leading a company that no longer needed to answer to Wall Street's obsession with quarterly earnings. Bob and his team generated tremendous operational improvements and quickly generated a series of impressive financial returns at Levi's.

Genuine Success

Prior to the buyout, Levi's had an odd mix of too many product lines that were not making money and too few in the areas that were profitable. Over the years, Levi's had acquired a bunch of cats and dogs. For example, they owned Resistol hats, which simply did not fit. After the buyout, we found ourselves in a seller's market for divisions of companies like Resistol and we took advantage of it. Among the other product lines Levi's divested was Oxxford Suits, whose Chicago-based buyer was represented by a young Goldman Sachs banker named Hank Paulson. Haas also shut down dozens of plants, cut redundant management and reduced the 38,000-person workforce by more than 15%. This was not easy, given Levi's tradition as a benevolent employer, but Bob did not completely lose focus on that tradition, either. For example, he created a systematic program for incorporating employee feedback into product and manufacturing decisions.

One of the clear advantages of operating as a private company is the ability to invest aggressively when opportunities arise without being second-guessed by Wall Street. Haas invested in a new product line—

Dockers—that launched with a $10 million advertising program. At the time of the deal, Levi's was considering withdrawing from foreign markets, where demand had fallen, in part due to the strong dollar. Instead, Bob redoubled efforts overseas, and within five years sales in more than 70 foreign countries were contributing more to profit than domestic sales.

By the mid-1990s, Levi's had paid off over two-thirds of the debt we had used to help the company go private. The company also was ahead of schedule with debt repayments, a condition that made possible a major recapitalization. Following the recap, we had approximately $3.5 billion in debt, and despite the tough conditions that began in the early 2000s, we pared that down to about $1.5 billion by the time I came off the board in 2008. I served on the Levi's Board for 23 years. The company proved to be quite cyclical, and it seemed Haas had to reinvent it every few years. However, even in its tough periods, Levi's cash flow and basic business remained strong.

Investment Banker No More

When Friedman and I first formed Hellman & Friedman, we had decided not to begin raising funds from limited partners until we convinced ourselves that we could be successful investing as principals. I always felt confident we would be successful. At Lehman, almost from the time I started, I had gotten involved in investing the firm's capital as a principal on behalf of the firm. Back then, only we and Lazard Freres were doing this on a regular basis. Then during the years in Boston, I had succeeded as a venture capital investor and the Levi's investment provided proof, right from the start, that we had the eye for a strong deal and the requisite knowledge to structure investments to the advantage of both the companies we bought and our own firm.

Even so, we still had plenty to learn. Another of our early investments from that time period, the purchase of American President Lines, taught us that we needed to change our mindset if we truly were going to transition into the private-equity business. We were advising the management team on a restructuring when they offered us a 9% convertible preferred security with a small conversion premium. We reacted as investment bankers would. We thought: "This is a great deal. Look at this incredibly lucrative security." We invested $50 million.

There was only one problem: At its core, American President Lines just wasn't a great business. The capital costs were too high, and it was an average company in a mediocre industry. Further, our investment was small enough that we did not have the clout to make much of a difference in strategy. A Singaporean company came along and offered to take us out at a 13% compounded return on our investment. We jumped at the chance to exit.

Guilty Until Proven Innocent

Though it did not result in a fantastic investment return, American President was another transformative investment for our firm, one that paid significant intellectual dividends. It became the turning point at which we changed from being investment bankers dabbling in principal investments to being full-fledged private investors. A lot of that transformation is about mindset. An investment banker will look at a prospective deal and say, "We have an opportunity to do something, so let's figure out how to do it."

As a principal investor, the mindset must be completely different. It bears repeating, so I will restate the core principle: "Every potential investment should be considered guilty until proven innocent." It is fundamental to what we do and if we behave that way, there is no way we end up in investments such as American President Lines. If someone came to us today and said, "This is a great security, you ought to take it," that alone would never get over our bar. As principals, we have to really understand and like the business, we have to be able to diligence the cash flow, and have a strong feel for the prospects to grow the business. We also have to like management and be able to work with them. The whole mindset is completely different.

This revelation in the aftermath of American President Lines hit Friedman and me at around the time our other partners were ready to change course, too. A group of the younger partners came to us not long after and said, "Look, we didn't leave investment banking careers on Wall Street careers to give financial advice. We left to act as principals."

In the early days, Friedman and I looked at everything first as an advisory opportunity and secondly as a principal opportunity. When we decided to get out of the advisory business, at the urging of those younger partners, it helped to further our thinking about how to invest. It marked the beginning of the end of our "Field of Dreams" style of investing. From then on, we would build opportunities ourselves.

Principles to Invest By

It was also the beginning of a period in which we concentrated on what, exactly, our management and investment styles should be. "Guilty until proven innocent" was just the start. The more investments we made, the more I personally concentrated on setting forward a series of principles to guide us. One of the most important principles for me personally was to ensure that our team's interests were always closely aligned with those of both our investors and our management teams.

There are several reasons why an alignment of interests is important for any investment firm, but first and foremost is that it is simply the right thing to do. It also is a very powerful internal management strategy, as the investment team is always motivated by and working towards the same goal. We always seek to ensure that both we and company management have a lot of skin in the game through meaningful personal ownership. In fact, every active investment team member at Hellman & Friedman invests in every deal. I also have made it my mission to share equity and not hog ownership at the top levels of the firm, as the Lehman old guard had done.

Another critical aspect of this principle relates to the practice of charging deal fees. We do not charge deal or advisory fees, as some general partners do, for transaction-related work and we do not charge monitoring fees to our portfolio companies. In the event that we are partnered with another private-equity firm that does charge deal fees, we credit 100% of our portion of those fees immediately back to our limited partners. To me, these are activities that we believe are already our responsibility as investors.

In recent years, the size of these deal fees, often charged as a percentage of overall transaction value, have become so enormous that they alone often represent a sizable payout to the general partner. To me, that presents a huge conflict of interest. I never want to have to look one of my partners in the eye and question whether they were being influenced at all by the sizable cache of fees, rather than the merits of the actual investment itself.

Purely from an investment perspective, one of the most important principals was our decision early on to focus on projected return on tangible capital in evaluating investments. We could not be successful if we continued making humdrum investments such as American President Lines. One that followed almost immediately, Great American Management & Investment, earned only an 8% return. If we were going to attract limited partners to trust us with their capital, we needed to improve our returns substantially.

Fortunately, it was during this formative period that as a result of thinking by Matt Barger, an incredibly astute investor who in 1984 was one of the first to join our firm, we came across the notion of return on tangible capital. This idea, which some of our other younger partners helped develop alongside Barger, became a second major revelation that transformed the future of our firm. Most everyone knows that cash flow is important in business, but how you measure that cash flow can be the difference between success and disaster. In measuring cash flow, we try to carry the cash flow calculation a step further, in a way that reflects the longer-term demands an investment will place on our firm. We take into account all the capital requirements needed for a business to operate and grow. We like to know the expected return on the tangible capital consumed and replaced through the normal business cycle.

An early investment made with our own money, before we began raising institutional funds, illustrates the importance of the adjustments we made to reflect return on tangible capital. In 1986, we invested in Genstar Rental Electronics and believed we paid about three times cash flow. This looked like a good price at the time. However, depreciation expenses were huge. In the real world of real cash flow, the Genstar investment was made at more like 20 times cash flow—a very expensive purchase multiple. The company eventually failed and taught us yet another huge lesson.

One other calibration that is vital to our measurement of return on tangible capital is our assessment of how much additional investment a company will need to succeed. When assessing a prospective investment we need to account for future capital expenditures, not just the cost of buying the company. To do otherwise is akin to buying a house without taking into account how much it will cost to replace the leaky roof.

The tangible cash flow calculation gives us an idea of what it will take to run the business successfully, and how high the hurdle might be for us to successfully invest. When measured this way, the typical U.S. business might have a return on tangible capital in the range of 10%. We typically look for businesses that return in the 20% to 30% range. Companies that have that kind of cash flow can fund growth, pay down debt, and make dividend payments to owners.

The Perils of Industrial Leverage

There is one more personal bias that I layer on top of this analysis. One of the things that I believe implicitly—at this point it's almost a prejudice—is that I and my partners don't like companies that have double leverage. Financial leverage is one thing, but industrial leverage is another. Companies with large amounts of physical assets, plant and equipment, have heavy industrial leverage, and if a company has industrial leverage, it is very hard, I think, to impose financial leverage on top of the industrial leverage. Such double leverage can severely constrain the business: If revenues shrink by 2%, you no longer have any free and clear cash flow to service the debt.

Our bias against industrial leverage, combined with our measurements of return on tangible capital, has led us away from investing in conventional manufacturing companies and toward services-oriented businesses. An exceptional company such as internet advertising manager DoubleClick holds up against these filters. Its cash flow is enough to support growth and pay down debt. Relatively weaker companies, such as American President, Great American Management, and Genstar, cannot. We try to rule out companies where only two cents out of every dollar are returned to us after running the business. In general, more finance- and service-oriented companies tend to fit our mold.

Tale of Two Investments

In the early 1990s, after studying the wireless sector extensively, we decided that we liked the industry and made two separate investments at almost identical times. Our first investment was in Western Wireless, which ultimately turned into two separate investments after VoiceStream was spun-off, and made us more money than I thought anyone could make on an investment at that time. Western Wireless returned 10 times our investment while VoiceStream, the predecessor to what is now T-Mobile USA, made us nearly eight times our money. In those days, in every small rural town or medium sized city, there were no more than two wireless operators. Western Wireless was one of the leading wireless operators. We found it to be a strong business with an absolutely fantastic CEO named John Stanton running it.

The second wireless investment was MobileMedia. For reasons that are no longer clear to any of us, we thought we should own a paging company. So we acquired one major and some other minor paging companies and created the second largest paging company in the world.

With customers migrating away to newer technologies, the paging industry began to experience significant pricing pressure. MobileMedia quickly felt the impact and management responded with several important missteps. The company ultimately went bankrupt. It was another revelatory moment for our firm, because as we rode that investment down, we sat down and talked to each other day after day about what went wrong. Being financially oriented people, we looked at the balance sheet; we looked at the company's acquisitions; we looked at the problems in the back office and the call centers and wherever else the company may have erred.

I recall asking our team, "What if we put another $5 million into it?"

I also recall Matt Barger's response, "Over my dead body we will invest another $5 million. I wouldn't put twenty-five more *cents* into this investment."

Matt was tired of the meetings and tired of analyzing what went wrong with MobileMedia. He kept saying he did not even want to talk about it anymore.

Some time later, when looking back at the investment, someone asked, "By the way, what's happening with PageNet?" PageNet was the largest paging company in the industry and had very modest financial leverage.

It turned out that while MobileMedia's stock had once sold at $29 a share, and was by then worth zero, PageNet's stock had decreased in value from $30 a share to 25 cents. We finally determined that Mobile-Media's problems were not unique to it. The industry was the primary culprit, and we had done a poor job of industry analysis.

In retrospect it sounds as if anyone could have or should have thought of this. Regardless, I think that has been one of the most important analytical experiences in our firm's history. Nothing we could have done—changing the capital structure, consolidating the industry, changing the management team, back-office improvements—would have made a difference. We were in a dying industry, and our investment was not going to bring it back.

Away from Industrial Assets

There was one certain way of escaping industrial risk, and that was to invest in companies that were less heavily invested in physical assets. One of our earliest such investments was in 1989, when we helped Brinson Partners, an asset manager, spin out of its parent in a management buyout. We later invested in Young & Rubicam, the advertising agency, in 1996, another company that was light on tangible assets, but rich in "elevator assets." Elevator assets refer, of course, to the people who walk in and out of a company's doors—and ride up and down the elevators—every day. Over time, this approach led us to focus on firms in the advertising, new media, financial services, software and asset management industries.

With such investments, we need the people running the companies to be hugely motivated to be successful. Y&R is a perfect example of how this works. When we invested in Y&R, in terms of pure arithmetic, we could have controlled the company. In fact, that is what the Bear Stearns investment banking team had in mind when they originally approached us with the deal. Senior partners of Y&R wanted out, and rather than selling to one of the big firms—WPP or Omnicom—CEO Peter Georgescu wanted to recruit a new, financially oriented owner.

We had a different view from Georgescu's initial inclination of how to approach the situation. I said to him, "Peter, I don't want to control this company. The key to success with this company is you and the management team. We are not advertising people. I think there is a lot we can do to help you, but we need you and your team to be fully invested, too."

We were investing $240 million in the firm, enough to demand total control, but I told Georgescu we wanted to put 10% of the voting stock of Y&R into a voting trust, voted by management, not us. We wanted them to understand that they controlled their company. We might still try to force difficult or awkward decisions on them: strengthening management or cutting overhead, for example. But we hardly were going to drive discrete advertising decisions and say, "Gee, we really don't like the Ford campaign."

The Impact of Working Capital

One of the single greatest contributions we made to Y&R was introducing a greater appreciation of working capital. The firm's biggest financial problem was excess working capital, mainly in the form of accounts receivable. Their net working capital was positive, while both Omnicom, and WPP had anywhere from 0 to negative 20% working capital.

This disparity in working capital had a big impact on the company's operational flexibility. Y&R was one of those firms that had plenty of assets, but because the assets were in the form of accounts receivable, not actual cash, the firm had an impaired ability to pay down debt. When it came time to pay their current liabilities—the other main part of working capital—they would have a hard time getting the cash to do so.

We spent a great deal of time educating and focusing the Y&R management team on how to manage the working capital and pay down the firm's debt. They responded well and went at it aggressively, eventually paying down 100% of the acquisition debt over two years primarily through changes in their working capital. In some cases, it was as simple as calling a client and demanding timely payment. Once clients stopped letting payments drag out for 90 days or longer, working capital improved considerably.

Alongside the change to their balance sheet came a high-charged operational turnaround engineered by the company's talented chief executive, Georgescu. Born in Romania, and separated from his family during World War II, Georgescu and his older brother were forced to dig holes and clean sewers all day for the Nazis. That sort of life experience stuck with him even after he reunited with his parents in the United States, attended Phillips Exeter Academy, then Princeton, and then Stanford Business School.

Georgescu's turnaround began soon after he was promoted to chief executive in 1994, two years prior to our investment, and accelerated afterward. The firm won over $1.5 billon in new business in 1995. They brought back lost clients, squeezed more business out of existing clients, and recruited entirely new ones. I believe the increased activity was generated in part by the fact that employees on the creative side had a greater stake in results. A new pay-for-performance method of charging clients yielded a more results-oriented compensation at the firm, and with equity in the picture, many of the firm's employees had a new motivation to help the firm succeed. By 1998, the firm went public and was acquired two years later in a transaction that returned us more than four times our investment.

The Y&R transaction illustrates how we were able to take a minority position and leverage that position into an outsized result in terms of strategic impact and financial results. Part of the result, I am convinced, arose from the fact that we had left such a large portion of the ownership in the hands of employees who then became exceptionally motivated to deliver results. As word spread of our approach, we began to get access to other management-led buyouts in which our willingness to take only a partial share of professional services firms gave us a competitive advantage. That advantage helped us prevail over other firms for the right to invest in the carve-out of Delaware International Advisors Ltd. from Lincoln National Corp, which was later renamed Mondrian Investment Partners.

The decision came as a result of an unorthodox approach to accepting bids. Mondrian's management team had issued a request for proposals, similar to what a city does when asking for bids on a construction project. Mondrian requested, among other information, for firms to list their experience investing as minority investors in asset management deals. Our willingness to have management control a majority of the firm, with the possibility of a larger future stake should results improve, won us the deal.

Outsized Influence

To some, it may seem counterintuitive that a minority investor would be able to wield the control needed in order to bring about strategic change, but our experience has been quite the opposite. One of the most powerful cases in point is NASDAQ, the stock exchange and automated trading system, where in 2001 we made our initial, $245 million investment.

The most we ever owned of NASDAQ was about a 19% stake. Despite that relatively small ownership position, we still had significant skin in the game—more than any other investor. That meant that from the outset I was the director whom the others looked to when a difficult question arose. "What do you guys at Hellman & Friedman think we should do?" someone would always ask. This investment amounted to roughly 10% of our Fund IV's committed capital, a large stake for a single investment, but our firm has always preferred to run a concentrated portfolio as opposed to a diversified portfolio approach.

Once we were invested in NASDAQ, we brought plenty of ideas into play. At the time we invested, NASDAQ was on the cusp of significant, strategic change. It was transforming from a regulation-dominated, almost bureaucratic system to an entrepreneurial venture. At every board meeting, there was a common interest in commercializing NASDAQ, yet most of the people there didn't have the time or the personal wealth at stake to really look at it every day, as we did.

As we got to know the company, it became obvious why other board members were so willing to defer: The place was a mess. For example, the NASDAQ was trying to form relationships with little stock exchanges all over Europe, but virtually none of these deals made any sense.

"If we pay $20 million for one of these exchanges, it will likely result in a $20 million per year reduction in operating income," I told the board.

The Greifeld Effect

Many of the problems turned around, though, when we went through a new CEO search and eventually found Bob Greifeld. We had gotten down to the wire and were deciding between a handful of candidates when Bob surfaced as an innovator in the industry who had created one of the earliest market-based electronic communications networks, called ECNs.

I ran Bob's name by Arthur Rock, one of the great private investors of our time, who had an immediate, positive reaction. "This guy has successfully done exactly the job you are looking for in nearly an identical business," Rock said. "He'll simply have to do again what he has done before."

On his first day in May of 2003, Greifeld laid off the top layer of management. He killed a long list of foreign ventures, including that $20-million-a-year sinkhole effort to expand into Europe. Within weeks, he had axed the investment designed to replicate the NASDAQ system on the other side of the Atlantic, NASDAQ Europe.

However, cutting costs was only part of the job. Greifeld had big growth ambitions and with our support considered an initial public stock offering. But before we could register for a sale, the IPO business ground to a halt. Making matters worse, the exchange's closely held stock dropped sharply in value. NASDAQ members who had obtained shares during the exchange's demutualization in mid-2002 began selling, and the market capitalization dropped from just over $1 billion to under $600 million in less than six months.

In my mind, the stock sales engendered near flashbacks of early days, when we still had not cleansed our investment banker thinking. In NASDAQ, Hellman & Friedman owned a preferred stock that was convertible at $20 a share, but NASDAQ common shares were selling at $4. Still, "We own a great security!" I kept murmuring. It was a sardonic riff on the lesson we had learned years ago that no matter how good a trade may seem it's not a good investment if the underlying business is not sound.

Greifeld seemed to see the problem the same way, and the exchange was having problems that went beyond the stock sales as the NASDAQ demutualized. The company's debt level in 2003 when Greifeld took the reins was high. And three years after the dot-com boom went bust, the NASDAQ was still hit hard—far harder than its rival the New York Stock Exchange. The NASDAQ took years to recover in the new listings market.

Instead of panicking, though, Greifeld focused attention on the real value of the business. Greifeld improved NASDAQ's performance.

He also saw that we needed to maximize revenues by increasing margins on each trade. It was a return on tangible capital analysis, plain and simple.

Greifeld's solution: Instead of fighting ECNs, and their lower transaction costs, he would acquire one of the biggest of them and export its technological expertise throughout NASDAQ system. He targeted one of the most successful electronic networks, Instinet, and in December 2005 we invested $60 million in new capital to make the deal possible. From the start, Greifeld had pushed the company to get costs below Instinet's, and now we owned this important rival. It would not be long before Instinet's expertise in low-cost transactions would spread throughout the rest of NASDAQ system.

Pouncing on Transitions

Transition periods tend to create investment opportunities, as the NASDAQ experience showed. In recent years, we have focused on the major transitions and taken investment positions that comport with our standards but might seem risky to outsiders. For instance, at the time we acquired DoubleClick in 2005, the one-time dot-com darling had undergone a somewhat painful transition in the aftermath of the 2000 dot-com crash. However, we had a unique view: Digitas, a prior H&F investment, had been a large customer of DoubleClick's services, which gave us differentiated insight into DoubleClick's business.

We believed there were certain strategic and operational enhancements we could make that would help renew the company's focus on its core business. For example, we structurally separated DoubleClick's two primary businesses, promoted operating management to run those businesses, and realigned management incentives accordingly. We sold the Abacus division to a strategic buyer and strategically refocused the Tech Solutions business profile through divestitures and acquisitions. These actions not only served to reshape the business, but also dramatically increased new product development initiatives. Two years later, Google agreed to acquire DoubleClick from us for $3.1 billion, which returned over eight times our original investment.

Staying in the Race

At the end of the day, we all can only do our best—not just in investing decisions, but in the way we manage businesses and develop ideas for success in whatever industries we address. We need to be confident, but not overconfident; aggressive, but not foolhardy. I believe that an investment and management style such as the one our firm abides by is the best hope for success, and our track record would indicate I am getting that statement mostly right.

Still, we must all guard against self-satisfaction, or perhaps satisfaction of any sort. For me, that point was driven home at the unlikeliest of times, in the unlikeliest of places, during my time as an ultra marathon runner.

Bluegrass music, running, and endurance horse racing are perhaps my most important personal avocations. It was my passion for Bluegrass music that inspired me to personally underwrite the annual Hardly Strictly Bluegrass Festival. As many as 700,000 people attend the free concert festival each fall in San Francisco, in the shadow of the Golden Gate Bridge.

Then there is running. I run every day, beginning at 3:45 in the morning, and there was a time when I participated in ultra marathon events. Twice, for example, I ran the Western States 100—a 100-mile race through northern California.

My wife, Chris, has a saying: "Nothing exceeds like excess." The point is that we achieve our greatest successes only when we push ourselves to an excessive degree.

Even so, no matter how hard we push ourselves, it is likely that someone better will come along. Whether it's in deal making, investing or corporate management, or whatever we might do, there is always someone else who does it better, faster, longer, and with more intensity. I learned this lesson the last time I ran the Western States 100 race. A couple days after the race, Chris and I were at Crissy Field in San Francisco, running out the lactic acid in my legs, when two frail women approached.

I was proudly wearing my t-shirt, "Finisher, Western States 100," when one of the women approached me and said, "Did you run the race Saturday?"

"I sure did," I said, the words puffing from my chest.

She said, "Gee we were crewing at Green Gate," which is one of the water and rescue points. "That race really looks great," she added. "My friend and I are thinking about running it next year."

I was flabbergasted. "Look," I said, "you can't even begin to understand what it takes to run a 100-mile race. You have got to be in shape like you have never been in your life. You can't even imagine how difficult it is!"

"My friend and I ran across the United States last summer," the woman responded. "I think we can handle a 100-mile race."

Yes, our firm is made of good investors, good strategic counselors, and good people. We have a focused and disciplined approach, and we have put billions of capital to good use for our investors.

But, lest we get complacent about our success, it's helpful to keep in mind that, much like ultra marathon running, the race goes to those who persevere, no matter how long the run or how unexpected the competition. In the end, to finish is to win.

LESSONS FROM WARREN HELLMAN

⬦ **Guilty until proven innocent.** No investment theory, management hypothesis, or corporate strategy should be accepted simply on face value. Test all relevant scenarios before acting.

⬦ **Always align interests.** Ensure that you, company management, and investors are always working toward the same goal.

⬦ **Have skin in the game.** Investors with meaningful capital at risk care more, work harder, and get more respect than those with less at stake. Likewise, giving management a stake in the company increases both the desire for profit and fear of failure. Nothing empowers and motivates people like a share in the outcome.

⬦ **Avoid the "good security" fallacy.** Invest in companies with strong cash flow that can grow over time. Do not invest just because the security offered seems to promise a good return. The health and prospects of the underlying business count far more.

⬦ **Listen to your partners and associates.** Surround yourself with smart people and listen intently to their views—they often are smarter and often better investors than you. Reward them accordingly.

4

THE PARTNERSHIP PARADIGM: WORKING WITH MANAGEMENT TO BUILD TOWARD SUCCESS

Carl D. Thoma
Founder Thoma Bravo,
LLC and predecessor firms Golder Thoma & Co.;
Golder Thoma Cressey Rauner, LLC; and Thoma Cressey Bravo, Inc.

AUM: $2.6 billion   **Years in PE:** 35

Location: Chicago, IL   **Year born:** 1948

Grew up: Boise City, OK   **Location born:** Roswell, NM

Best known deals: Paging Network, Inc., Global Imaging, Inc., American Income Life Insurance Company, IMS International, American Cable, Tyler Refrigeration

Style: Skeptical, focusing on what can go wrong; anticipatory

Education: B.A., Oklahoma State University, Class of 1970
M.B.A., Stanford Graduate School of Business, Class of 1973

Significant experience: Very fortunate to have gotten involved in private equity early on; truly appreciate the difference strong management can make

Personal interests: Winemaking and modern art. Owns Van Duzer Vineyards in Oregon and investor in Eight Modern Art Gallery in Santa Fe, NM.

The lesson: "Private equity is about superiorly managed and performing companies, not being an investor. It is about being proactive."

Over the years, Carl Thoma and his partnerships have become known for a "buy and build" strategy that requires patience, industry-specific knowledge, and an unrelenting focus on performance. Key to Thoma's best deals is a focus on management as the key to success, especially the chief executive, an approach summarized in his firms' longstanding motto, "partners with management."

Thoma, who has operated from a Chicago base for more than 35 years has adapted to changes in the economy and in the industry by developing an approach that more actively exercises the powers of ownership. Part of the reason for this is Thoma's belief that time is of the essence. Before a purchase even closes, as a condition of the deal, he insists on changes that must be made and metrics met at or before the close of the transaction. An investment firm can deliver its best results only when decisions and actions are taken quickly and effectively by the management of portfolio companies.

I am a world-class worrier, and, as much as anything, worrying—effective worrying—is responsible for my success. In fact, I think anyone in this business needs to be an effective worrier in order to be successful.

I came upon this vital skill as a young person growing up on a ranch in the western part of the panhandle of Oklahoma. Agriculture, whether raising crops or raising livestock, is a business where worrying is a major part of your work. You worry about blizzards, rain, lightning or grass fires, grasshoppers eating your forage, and, always, the price of cattle—both buying and selling. There is always something. Agriculture is a great industry to teach you to worry because something can or will always go wrong.

That is how we try to run our companies. You just have to anticipate things, especially the things that can go wrong. Worrying is one of the most effective means of doing that, but worrying alone is not enough. That's why the word *anticipation* is my favorite business term. Anticipation starts with worrying and leads to thinking about and preparing for taking action to mitigate business risk.

I think private-equity groups do a very good job of that—worrying about and anticipating problems—in working with their companies. It is important to be an effective worrier. Just wringing one's hands and fretting about what could go wrong is not enough. But if you're someone who anticipates troubles and acts before they happen, then you can be an effective business leader. And at the speed of business today, timely mitigation of risk is more important to what we do than it has been at any other time in the 30 years I have been in this industry.

For worrying to be worth the trouble, it has to be accompanied by effective action. This is something I learned from my mother. She always emphasized that, once you think you know what you want to do, don't sit there: Do it.

Our industry has evolved over the years, and the opportunities and challenges today require a different set of skills than when I started out in private equity in the late 1970s. Yet, at the same time, there are essential tactics and skills that do not change. Effective worrying is one. So is a sense of urgency: the need to reach good decisions quickly and execute them effectively in order to succeed. Of course, in private equity, we're not always the ones who have to execute. In almost all cases, we rely on managers we hire to actually implement strategy, and dealing with management is not just a source of considerable worry, it is the key to success—or the cause of failure.

Making Management an Asset

Perhaps one of the most important, and most difficult, aspects to master as conditions change is the way we deal with management. There are times when management can seemingly do no wrong and other times when the economic crosswinds are so great that it seems almost nothing management does can make any difference. A chief executive who is a star when building a business can lose his way when it comes time to operate a more mature company. For the private-equity investor, such turning points are key moments of decision. We have to decide whether to stick with management and help them mature or make a change and hope for better performance.

The essential element for success is the mindset that we as private-equity investors bring to our investments. In short, we need to adopt an ownership perspective and treat each investment not as an engagement for short-term profit but as an asset we have invested in and one that we must work to improve over time. The most important work we do in this regard is select, work with, evaluate, and improve management. Our roles and responsibilities have changed, too, due to changes in the economy, increases in leverage that leave less room for error, and the growing sense that cycles of investment keep growing shorter.

I jokingly tell colleagues that the only position that is more senior than the CEO is the owner, and so when we take on the role of an owner, that defines a lot of the relationship with management. It's a paradigm shift, one that is easily felt by everyone involved. If you ask who controls the Dallas Cowboys, is it the quarterback or the owner? I think there's not much doubt about who has control. Or, consider the Yankees when George Steinbrenner was in charge. Nobody ever mistook him for just an investor. Steinbrenner clearly viewed it that way, and he felt free to make a change, even with managers who had brought him a World Series ring, if their results slacked off.

As we exercise the prerogatives of ownership, we also become more accountable for results than we had been in the past. In fact, I think we as investors share the same responsibility for the performance of our companies as the CEO does. We bear responsibility for making certain that the right people are in place and that we have the right mix of operations and sales people and the key technical expertise. It means setting up the right compensation and incentives. It means creating a culture of accountability. We have to have an involvement in and understanding of the business at levels of detail that were not necessary before.

Carried to its logical extreme, this change in orientation really has had an effect on our role with our companies relative to the one played by the managements who operate them on a day-to-day basis. In some cases, we are asking the CEOs of our companies to act more like chief operating officers once did. We ask them to focus less on setting strategy and more on execution. That's because the times are forcing us, the owner–investors, to assume part of the leadership role that once was exclusively held by the CEO.

The Platforms of Success

My observations about dealings with the CEO and management may be particularly acute because of the sort of deal my firm is best known for. Literally since our first investment, in a paging services company called Paging Network, better known as PageNet, we have specialized in buying small, multi-unit companies and building them through acquisition into major national players. The technique came to be called *platform investing* or *leveraged buildups*, but regardless of the name, it seemed to us a sensible way to use leverage, our ability to work with management, and our strategic vision to create great return on our investments.

We have executed a platform strategy in industries as varied as funeral homes, golf courses, and copier dealerships. At times, we have actively identified industries in need of consolidation and then worked to recruit a chief executive whom we think can execute a consolidation plan. We did this, for example, with Kevin Rogers, who made the equipment rental company National Equipment Services a national power in less than three years. The economic downturn in the early 2000s and reduced rental rates from excess equipment ultimately forced NES into bankruptcy, but his initial run was a remarkable bit of execution.

A CEO running a consolidation strategy can be particularly effective if he has the ability to assess the leadership qualities at the firm's target companies. We learned this through experience at companies such as Global Imaging Systems, which was successfully sold to Xerox in 2007. In that case, an assessment of the people and culture of acquired companies proved to be just as important as a close reading of their financial statements. Costs can be cut and systems streamlined, but changing culture or improving management is not always easy to do.

When I first came out of First Chicago along with Stanley Golder to set out on our own as investors, we did venture deals as well as buyouts, and in most of those early deals we got a number of investors together to spread the risk and the upfront investment. I think the investing approach we used then, the economic environment, the lender attitude, and everything else allowed us to be a little less demanding of management than is necessary today. There was room for error and less competition for deals, so purchase prices did not climb as high, and there was time to recover if we made a mistake.

No one has that kind of luxury anymore, and there are other, somewhat more subtle changes at our firm and throughout the private-equity industry that are affecting how we deal with the managers at our portfolio companies. These days, we are typically the only investor, so it is our capital—our investors' capital—on the line. We typically have made a large investment, which means we likely are using significant leverage. The higher leverage means time is of the essence. To get the rate of return we need, we have to move quickly. Information flows a lot faster than it once did, and there are about five times as many firms out there competing for deals compared to when we started out. The competition has a tendency to test our discipline when it comes to negotiating our deals.

The CEO Factor

Given all these changes, we can no longer afford to work with any except the very best chief executives. But, we are less inclined to change CEOs today than we might have been years ago, in part because any management change costs valuable time, something we cannot afford. This means that, quite often, we find ourselves coaching and encouraging the CEO today more so than in the past. The economic crisis that began in late 2007 has also taught us, in new ways, that there are some problems no management can solve. We have to see far enough ahead to avoid companies that just are not going to make it in tough economic environments, no matter how good management might be.

In many ways, too, all of these changes have forced us to learn new ways to work with, coach, and encourage management. For starters, in cases where we are more involved in setting strategy, we have to make certain before our investment that the CEO will be comfortable with such a close working relationship. Then, once we have made our investment and begun facing challenges, it does not work any more to just sit a CEO in the board room and berate him for missing goals or making mistakes. That approach does not yield better management. It might even make things worse.

This doesn't mean we have to coddle ineffective executives, either. It means that, from the start, there has to be a shared understanding of our objectives, a clear path toward meeting them, and an agreement about what will happen if we fall short. Accountability is the essential element: if someone says they will deliver certain results, they need to do that.

If we find that a CEO cannot deliver, there are times we must act, even though we know a change at the top will cost us, because the lost time will hurt our investment rate of return. If ever there were a time for "just do it," it comes at the moment that the board of directors concludes a management change needs to be made. Often, just after there is a consensus that the CEO must go, someone on the board will suggest that perhaps the person deserves just one more chance to change or improve. Take my word for it: By then it's too late. Unfortunately, in 35 years, I have never seen a situation where it worked out to give a second chance to a CEO who proved incapable in the first place.

The Ticking Clock

Time is crucial. In today's competitive environment, where companies are selling for higher multiples of cash flow than at any time before, time is the enemy. The difference between delivering outstanding returns to our investors and falling short is all related to how long we own the company. It's a lot easier to hit that higher number if we can improve performance in a shorter period of time. With that in mind, there is no room for mistakes, little room for management changes, and an absolute premium on accountability.

While some of the time parameters and other pressures have changed, other key components of success have not changed since our first deal, nearly three decades ago, for the paging services company PageNet. At First Chicago, we had carved out a business doing what today would be called both venture capital and private-equity investing. At the bank, we had won considerable attention for our decision in 1970 to back Frederick Smith, who was investing his $4 million inheritance to start up Federal Express. Leading a group of venture investors, we raised another $91 million in seed capital for an exceedingly capital-intensive business.

On the private-equity side of First Chicago, the orientation was far more prosaic. Similar to the prevailing approach at other banks and buyout shops at the time, we focused our attention on engineering buyouts of companies that were undervalued, had strong CEOs in place, and had promising growth prospects. At First Chicago, we mostly focused on the manufacturing sector, but Stanley Golder and I started to develop a theory that our impact might be just as good in the service industries. Rather quickly, a couple of deals we did in cable television and health care convinced us that we were onto something.

Eyeing Target Industries

I felt we could add more value by first identifying industries in need of consolidation, where there were great disparities between top performers and weaker players and where we could recruit at least one key leader and then a management team to operate the company. The setup was simple. While we would scour the market for any acquisitions that might fit into the company we were building, the CEO and management would operate the companies. They would take care of integration, which is always difficult, and improve the operations of the acquired units. For many of the companies we added to our platform investment, chances were that they had become available for us to buy because they were poorly managed in the first place.

PageNet is a good example of how this process worked. This was the early 1980s, before people had cell phones. Pagers were the best way, really the only reliable way, to instantly reach people on the go. We came across the paging industry almost by accident. We were investing in a cable television company, and someone made the comment, "Here is a sleepy industry that most people don't know exists. It is primarily doctors and plumbers who carry these devices all the time."

When we looked into it, paging fit the profile of the sort of industry that made sense for us. Industry revenue was growing 20% a year. There was no dominant national player. There were plenty of locally owned and operated, entrepreneurial companies that we could roll into one larger operation. That done, they could share costs, distribute best practices, and have greater purchasing power—all the benefits of size in any marketplace.

Profiling for Success

Finding the chief executive was, of course, our first key task. We did not yet have a company to operate, but we needed to put the right CEO in place before we started stringing together the enterprise. We were brand new to the industry—remember, we had first come across paging as a possible investment only a few months earlier—so we did not have the connections with or knowledge of the top talent that we sometimes do in industries where we have more background knowledge. We retained a search firm to reach out to all the leading executives in the industry and found George Perrin, who proved to be a remarkably good fit for what we were trying to accomplish.

It is instructive to look at Perrin's profile when we hired him, not just because he proved to be a particularly strong hire but because our experience in this case demonstrates the sort of thinking that goes into matching a CEO to the task at hand. Perrin had been the number two person at Communications Network, Inc. the leading paging company at the time. He had worked for the industry's best company, with margins superior to those of everybody else. Literally, their margins were twice what the other public companies were, so it was obvious he knew how to run a company and knew how to do it better than anyone else.

Now, here is something that is easy to overlook. If you are going to back management, especially someone you are recruiting into a challenging situation like a start-up, you've got to make sure that they have also had experience at the better companies. Management has to be a big difference maker, and if they are going to make a difference they have to know what the tools are to do that. A leader of a company that operates pretty poorly is probably going to bring some of those poor practices into the new job. A leader who has achieved extraordinary returns has a better chance of achieving that kind of performance in a new setting. It's common sense, but it's sometimes not fully appreciated.

Of course, one can never tell how much of a firm's success is due to the top leadership and how much comes from other factors, but Perrin brought to us other factors that clearly he could call his own. Communications Network had grown through acquisitions, and Perrin himself had worked many of their deals. Because acquisitions were a key part of our strategy, this was a big plus. He would know all the would-be sellers out there, they would know him, and he clearly knew how to negotiate a deal.

What's more, Perrin was available. You're not going to get the CEO of a public company to come join a start-up for a private-equity firm. For that sort of person, the risk doesn't make sense. Even the number two can be tough to recruit out of a going concern. Perrin, though, had moved to Boston to run a company for a private owner, and sometimes people learn that working for a private owner is not always as attractive as it sounds. Perrin had not been there long, but he was ready for a change.

He had just the profile we needed—the sort of profile that would fit in any start-up, platform investing scenario—so Perrin was our man.

The Power of the Team

Over time, Perrin proved to be an even better fit than he had first appeared to be on paper. Why did we succeed? First and foremost, of the first 13 people we hired in the company, 11 had worked for Perrin at Communications Network.

With a team that cohesive, Perrin was able to operate a company where there were few surprises. The management team knew that was important for him from their past experience. For us on the board, this was important, too. It is far easier to set a strategy when the CEO knows, from day one, that the people working for him can execute.

Perrin had a philosophy that people could lose their bonuses just as fast by beating budget as by coming in under budget. If one of his team forecast a $2 million profit, that's what he wanted: not $1.8 million, not $2.5 million.

"You need to know what you are going to do because I need predictability," Perrin would say. "It's kind of like a quarterback throwing to a wide receiver. You can't be two yards further down the field than where you are supposed to be or two yards short. You've got to be exactly where you are supposed to be."

The incredible discipline of Perrin's management team gave us a competitive advantage in the industry. To put it bluntly, the industry just was not that professional. That was one of the reasons we had found it attractive as an investment. If you have a team that can hit budgets, that can set a good plan, that can execute as you want, in an industry where the competition has a hard time doing all those things, you're bound to make money.

Perrin was able to decentralize decision making, so we were able to move more quickly than anyone else. His people were versatile enough that we could plug them in, very quickly, if problems developed somewhere. If one of the acquired companies wasn't doing well, we could drop a regional vice president in to start running it themselves. They would stay for six months or so, get all of the standardized systems set in place, then move out. The tactic was a bit unusual, but it just absolutely worked. It also was just the kind of mindset that we encourage as the owner–investors: do what you have to do to make it work.

Tactical Execution

With Perrin and his team in place, and our investment hypothesis proved out, we soon found we had to make adjustments as conditions changed. We all saw that as this industry grew and the cost of the equipment came down, prices were going to drop. As a major player, we felt we could lead prices down. We would come into a new market, build a state-of-the-art system, introduce new technologies, and lower our prices. Within two to three years we could have 60% of the market and then just sort of start running the competition out of town.

We quickly did seven acquisitions at PageNet, but then the prices got too high. People knew we were buyers, so we decided to try start-ups. There was no reason to buy somebody for $10 million when you can start a company for $5 million, spend two or three years, and wind up with the same size company, a lower cost basis, and probably a more efficient operation because it wasn't started by an entrepreneur who may have introduced some inefficiencies along the way.

We stayed in PageNet for 10 years. Our aggressive market entry, with a very outstanding group of people, new technology, and an effective management structure, gave us the momentum to eventually become the largest company in the industry. We invested $8 million in the company and netted about $800 million for our limited partners when we ultimately sold. That was 100 times their money, which makes everyone happy, of course. And it was a big enough return to put our firm on the map.

Of course, you jump forward 10 years and the company got wiped out by cellular, but that was several years after we liquidated our position. Cell phones pretty much killed the paging market. Entire industries get wiped out sometimes. In others, major economic dislocations can overwhelm the efforts of management. Airlines are that way. There are times when the differences between the top performers and the also-rans are not that great because management, no matter how good, can just get run over by industry fundamentals.

Refining the Strategy

Even so, as you do this kind of platform investing, there are lessons you pick up as you go along that can apply in many kinds of industries. Over the years, we have jumped in and out of the funeral home business several times. We built up Paragon Family Services in the 1980s, sold it, and then built Prime Succession in the 1990s. In that deal, we bought up 40 funeral businesses in five years and sold the company in 1996 for about five times the $29 million we put into it. We got in a third time earlier this decade, too, with Meridian Mortuary Group.

Our key insight with Meridian Mortuary, one that applies to other industries, is that there is a certain minimum scale that makes sense for investment. We bought up a few small operators—ones that would do, say, 60 funerals, or "cases," as they're called, a year. We also had several that would do as many as 800 cases a year. The small ones could never keep up with the performance of the big ones, and the small ones were vulnerable because if the funeral director left you might just have to shut down the operation altogether. It can be very difficult recruiting good funeral directors. Ultimately, with our funeral home investments, our strategy would run its course. We got out each time because prices for the acquisition targets got too high. It was better to sell the businesses than to keep buying at those levels.

We made two forays into the golf course business. With golf courses, it was shockingly simple to bring operating efficiencies. For example, in the late 1980s when we first got into golf courses, many of them did not even have cash registers, so it was almost certain there was a gap between reported revenues and the larger figure the courses actually took in. The most important lesson for us as a firm, though, was that it can be hard for a CEO to repeat his success.

Our golf course CEO did a marvelous job for us the first time, but the second time we worked with the CEO, just a few years ago, it was difficult for him to bring the same intensity. He might argue it was the weather, in that it rained too much, but the business did not quite achieve the same levels of performance. We as a firm felt that part of the problem was it was more difficult for the CEO to invest himself totally in the business a second time. He possibly was not quite as hungry for success.

What we learned from the experience is that it probably is best not to bring a CEO back in the same role he has already performed.

If we want to work with him again, it ought to be in a different role, as a board member, maybe, or as a mentor to management of one of our portfolio companies. At the same time, we want to make certain the industry in the second instance is the same or similar to the one the CEO worked in the first time around. We do not subscribe to the great athlete theory, that a great CEO in one industry will automatically succeed in another one. The skill set may be transferable, but the industry knowledge and contacts are not. And in private equity, where time is of the essence, we cannot afford to give the CEO time to develop the connections needed to be successful in a new industry.

The Focus on Management

In all of these platform businesses, the management-centric approach is extremely important. As we developed and refined our techniques over the years, not just in paging, funeral homes, and golf courses but also in health care and software, we always asked ourselves how much of a difference management could make. We answered that question using a simple technique. We would look at an industry to see what sort of performance gap existed between companies in the first quartile of the industry and the third quartile.

In some industries, the differences would not be that great. In others—the industries we picked—management can have a big impact. The leaders might have 25% margins, while the third quartile margins are 10%. That 15% gap is where we could make our money, bringing the average or poor performers up to or above the standards of the top performers. Once we identified the opportune industries, it was up to us to recruit, motivate, and incentivize the sort of management team that could give us a competitive edge.

We got to the point in the late 1990s where two-thirds of our investments fit this model. Other firms adopted the approach, too. Go recruit a great management team and give them capital. Go out and buy companies, and then they run them for you.

We as board members stay very involved. We've got to watch for the pitfalls as well as the strengths of our managements. For example, we must make sure that an aggressive acquisition pace does not become an excuse for failing to achieve better margins and revenue growth.

We must also make sure the acquisitions we make meet our standards and that the leaders of the companies we acquire as part of our platform strategy understand the expectations as to performance. As directors we may also need to be the governor on the pace of acquisitions, as we must make sure management depth and systems stay in sync.

A Changing Relationship

This balancing act between the investor and the CEO is never easy, and it is changing over time. In the early years, we developed a slogan that reflected our mindset: "Partners with Management." That worked for us for a quarter century, but in more recent years the relationship has changed. We used to be able to operate with the notion that 20% of the time we would hit a home run, 60% of the time results would land in a the middle, and 20% of the time things would just not work out.

The industry has changed now. Prices are more competitive. There are more firms chasing the deals. We have adopted a new strategy where we in effect are trying to bat 100%. No more 20/60/20. We especially are trying to get rid of that bottom 20%. In the old days, we used to buy companies at four or five times cash flow. Now, we often have to pay upwards of eight times. It's just a different game, and the old investment process no longer works as effectively. Execution is critical as we need to lower the effective purchase price as fast as possible by increasing earnings. We or the board have to take on some of the strategy-making role that CEOs traditionally play because there is just not enough time for the CEO to oversee both execution and long term strategy.

The upshot of all this is that the decision on hiring the CEO has become less of a final point in our success. These days, we tend to look for companies first. We look more at the complete management team and less just at the CEO. We want strong operators or teams at these companies who are competitive and want to improve and grow. We will accept a "good" executive with a team that we feel we can coach and develop into an "excellent" or grade-A manager versus an A+ CEO and no team. There's a company in our portfolio now whose management team really had not done anything special prior to the time we bought the company, but with some encouragement and training, they quickly went from producing limited earnings two years before to producing excellent earnings—in a very tough economy. That does not happen unless you can coach, inspire, and discipline the capability of your people.

While we are investors with an ownership mindset, we still do not want to be in the position of managing the companies we own. As a board member of PageNet, for example, I worked closely with George Perrin, but I never wanted to take charge of the company personally or crowd Perrin out in areas where he could manage capably on his own. With the company now in our portfolio, our firm got involved in enhancing the management tactics of the executives, but we expected and wanted them to implement and refine to fit the needs of their specific company.

The Worrier's Rewards

Because we have to take our hands off the controls, we by definition wind up worrying more about what might happen at our companies. It's tempting just to step in and fix every problem yourself, but once you decide you cannot do that you've got to grow comfortable with letting the management team handle most of the challenges they face. This means, by definition, that you wind up doing a lot of worrying.

My parents were ranchers, raising cattle, on about 12,000 acres or so near Boise City near the New Mexico border. Twelve thousand acres is a small ranch in that part of the country. My dad died when I was a sophomore in high school, and my mom took over the ranch after that. She had a great influence on me, obviously, as did an uncle nearby who was a great rancher and a good business man.

I did a lot of things as I grew up. I was one of a handful of kids in my class who went to college. I attended Oklahoma State University for undergraduate study and then Stanford University for business school. My wife and I both got our M.B.A.s from Stanford in 1973. She took a job at Quaker Oats in Chicago and I went to work at First Chicago, whose primary asset was the First National Bank of Chicago. But, probably nothing affected my career as much as growing up on a ranch, watching my father, my mother, and my uncle raise their cattle and learning to worry.

As I said earlier, though, worrying alone is not a secret to success: Effective worrying is. By "effective worrying," I mean the sort of fretting that leads to anticipation and from anticipation to smart and strategic action. My uncle was an effective worrier and a good cattle rancher because of it.

"If it might not rain, then let's not have too many cattle," my uncle would say. Then he would figure a bit and say, "If one feeder cattle really needs 10 acres to live on in grass, well, in case it doesn't rain, we better always just have one animal for 12 acres. That way, we've built in a buffer for where things can go wrong."

This sort of mindset—anticipating the worst possible outcome and taking steps to avoid it—is one of the reasons I typically do not expect salespeople to become CEOs. Salespeople simply do not worry enough. In fact, it's quite the opposite. They are born optimists.

For salespeople, every person they meet is their next prospect. In real life, the one that looks like a prospect could actually be a rattlesnake that bites you. You just never know. If you have 10 salespeople, and each can make $2 million in sales, they will budget for $20 million in revenue. But, in the real world, one will get sick, one will quit, something will happen to another. You've got to say, "I know something will go wrong so I guess I better put a 10% or 15% cushion in there."

Farmers and ranchers also learn how to measure people and insist that they deliver what they promise, and these traits, too, are essential to success in private equity. If you hire somebody to truck your cattle to market but they show up late, you just don't use those people again. You go with people who are reliable. Some people are just accident prone or tear up the equipment, and you just don't get those people on your team. And, if you're a good worrier, all that worrying should cause you to anticipate the problems.

Beating the Clock

One way to minimize risk is to shrink the time that you are exposed to any one company or industry. Over the years, I have really grown to appreciate the fact that time in our business is the enemy. We have to create value very quickly. The way to get in the upper quartile of all private-equity funds is to give investors a 32% return instead of a 22% return.

The simplest way to do that is to make an impact quickly and then get out of your investment just as fast, in three years rather than five years. Each company has performance targets, and the faster you reach them, the better.

To do that, you invest in industries you understand. You try to work with a CEO who can maintain a stable management team. You do plenty of upfront work before investing in a company. In fact, we have made it a practice to insist on changes that must be made before or at the time of the close on our transaction. That jump-starts our push toward a fast, profitable turnaround. Beyond that, we agree ahead of time on performance metrics with management of the target company. This is another way of making certain there are no surprises.

It's not easy getting in and out of companies as fast as you need to, but one way to make it happen is to do a lot of the work up front, before the money is invested and the investment clock starts ticking. Tom Johnson at Global Imaging was one of the very best at this. He did more than 100 deals for that company before it was sold to Xerox for $1.5 billion. Only one deal, the first one, didn't work out as expected, and that probably was our fault.

Tom's secret was to always buy a good corporate culture. Before the investment, he would have someone go in and interview all the key people in the company. It was always amazing what people would tell an outsider or consultant as opposed to their boss or new boss. After interviewing, say, ten people, we'd have a pretty good idea of that company's culture and whether it would fit into Global Imaging.

Tom also believed very strongly in benchmarking. Before a deal, he would sit down with the company's numbers, compare them to the results he was getting in some of his best operations, and then say, "OK, how are we going to hit those numbers?" He did all this before we decided if we wanted to buy the company. We have further refined this process today by bringing in operating executives we know, with industry expertise, and having them look at the target company's metrics, too. If, for example, margins at a top-tier company in the business are 25% and our target company is at 20%, we want to set a path toward reaching a 25% return before we close on our purchase.

A lot of times in our purchases, we have to downsize staffing in an organization. When we approach a purchase with all this upfront work in hand, as with Global Imaging and other companies, we insist that, as part of the transaction, at the closing these adjustments are made. This makes for a lot better process all the way around. We maybe are able to persuade the seller to pay the severances instead of making this a cost born by the buyer.

We also can potentially pay a higher price if we know the seller has streamlined the company before we own it. That way, when we are welcomed in as the new owner, we don't have people worrying about their jobs. We can tell them we are going to focus on growth, and it just makes for a lot better transition. From the day we own the business, we want to start growing the business.

We can use this upfront approach particularly effectively in the industries where we have deep knowledge—software, for example. Over the years, we have bought and sold many software companies and today would be among the nation's top ten software companies if you total the earnings of all the companies in our portfolio. We know, for example, that when times are tight it makes sense to reduce or slow development of new products as customers are slowing their upgrades; however you must keep your sales force fully staffed so as to take market share. Many times your competitors who might be lead by someone with an engineering background will do just the opposite. With one of the companies in which we made an equity investment, we insisted that a facility be shut down and sold before we invested. Thank goodness we did, because we could not have given it away once the economy broke down in 2008. In that business, it was pretty hard to justify having $20 million tied up in a single building.

Starting Larger

A recent change we have made is to start with larger platform companies than we once did. This gives us a deeper team that can then build the company faster. When starting from a small platform, it takes too long to recruit a CEO capable of operating a larger company and then stringing together a number of smaller deals. The CEO who comes along with a larger platform already knows how to run a large company, and we're working from a base that we can leverage, quickly, to build a big business.

Prophet 21, which develops software for distribution companies such as electrical or pumping supplies is a good example. We bought the initial platform company with $7 million in earnings before the $2 million of profit improvements which were implemented at closing. By comparison, when we acquired Global Imaging years earlier it had only $800,000 in profits at the time we bought it. In less than three years with Prophet 21, after a string of acquisitions, an improved operational focus and emphasis on sales growth, cash flow more than tripled, from $7 million to $25 million. We like to think our coaching and operating discipline contributed to the company growing faster than it historically had—and with better margins. After we sold the company, Chuck Boyle, the CEO, started mentoring another company we recently acquired, called Manatron, which provides property tax software to local counties and cities.

Right from the Start

We as investors feel we can make a difference. We bring a lot of expertise to the table with our industry perspective, contacts, best practices, and outside consultants or operating executive relationships. Probably most important is that we bring high expectations and a disciplined mind set, which we feel helps a company grow and helps explain our investment success. At the end of the day, though, it is the CEO of our portfolio company and, to a lesser extent, the management team around that person who are key to making the investment work.

Stan Golder used to kid me and say I had a tendency to try to wish a deal to success. This would happen, in particular, when the industry fundamentals and the company's products or services were strong, but management's ability to successfully execute was weak or in doubt. I've learned over time that, when we're looking at a company, we have to avoid wishing for the CEO to be a success when, in fact, it might be better to just pass on the whole opportunity. In about half of the companies we look at, this is the case. Spending time with the company and management before the deal can give us a good view as to whether there is something worth investing in.

While we hustle hard to get an investment and can spend significant time working with a management team, we have got to have that discipline to say no. This is not easy. No one likes to think they have spent six months looking at a deal only to say no. It's difficult to walk away. You've got, hopefully, not millions but hundreds of thousands of dollars of due diligence invested and it hurts to throw that away. We just had a deal like that. Thank goodness we didn't do it. The sign that finally soured us on it was that we spent so much of our time arguing with this CEO, who was obsessed with whether his old bonus program would remain intact.

It is important to learn to trust your gut. If the deal doesn't feel right at the end, at the time you are ready to close, it's going to be awfully tough to make it work over the long haul. You will wind up feeling frustrated that you were not more decisive before it was too late.

When you're looking at a deal and considering the management perspective, you've got to always be paying attention to the question of whether you can really work with that manager and the management team. In the old days, there was the idea that if this person doesn't work out we will just fire him. I think that today, there's no time for a mistake like that. We are going to be stuck with this person, so if we think we might have to fire the person then we shouldn't make the investment.

Although we must continue to improve, I feel very good about how we have evolved in working with managers. It starts with picking the right companies to acquire. We now have great people running our companies whose sole job is to make sure they are better run and growing. We may lay people off initially, but at the end of the day, we have more people working at our companies when we sell them than when we bought them. The best way to make that happen, consistently, is to develop a plan for partnering with management and serving as the supportive coach, cheerleader, and disciplinarian while being adaptive as markets and the economy change.

Once we set up a strategy that way, there's little reason to worry about the outcome. That doesn't keep me from worrying, of course, but it helps me worry a bit less to know that, really, I have little reason to be fretting so much.

LESSONS FROM CARL THOMA

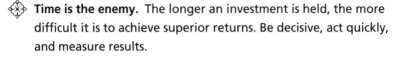 **Time is the enemy.** The longer an investment is held, the more difficult it is to achieve superior returns. Be decisive, act quickly, and measure results.

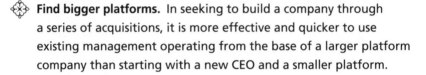 **Develop industry-specific expertise.** Contacts, sector-specific knowledge, and a sense of industry history are keys to achieving timely success. Hire CEOs who know their industries.

Act before the deal closes. Do enough upfront research and negotiation to have performance and "best practices" metrics, optimal organizational structure, and other targets set in place. This makes it possible to grow the company from day one.

Find bigger platforms. In seeking to build a company through a series of acquisitions, it is more effective and quicker to use existing management operating from the base of a larger platform company than starting with a new CEO and a smaller platform.

Worry, worry, worry. The time spent nervously pondering all possible negative surprises—and how to respond to them—is time well spent. Think ahead, plan ahead, and act on your "gut" so as to prevent calamity.

5

BEYOND THE BALANCE SHEET: APPLYING PRIVATE-EQUITY TECHNIQUES TO NOT-FOR-PROFIT WORK

Jeffrey Walker
Managing Partner and Co-Founder
JPMorgan Partners/Chase Capital Partners

AUM: $12 billion   **Years in PE:** 25

Location: New York, NY   **Year born:** 1955

Grew up: In the South until 17   **Location born:** Knoxville, TN

Best known deals: Office Depot, Jet Blue, Guitar Center, AMC Theaters, House of Blues

Style: Integrative

Education: B.S., University of Virginia, Class of 1977
M.B.A., Harvard Graduate School of Business, Class of 1981

Significant experience: Worked in the investment banking and finance divisions of Chemical Bank, predecessor to today's JPMorgan Chase

Personal interests: Bungee jumped from Victoria Falls bridge in Zambia, Africa; music (played tuba and bass in junior high and high school); four great kids and amazing wife

The lesson: "If you think you are on the right path, you are on the wrong path because there is no path. You are creating your own unique path every day."

When veteran private-equity investor Jeff Walker was approached by Jeffrey Sachs, the noted economist and poverty fighter, he was faced with a simple question: Could the disciplines that work in private equity also apply in the not-for-profit world? The answer is an affirmative yes, as Walker has found through his work at Millennium Promise, a nonprofit working with Columbia University and the United Nations in an effort to cut extreme poverty in half by 2015.

Walker began his private-equity career a quarter century ago, when he persuaded Chemical Bank to invest $100 million in a new private-equity fund. He soon found that active boards, strong chief executives, and effective growth strategies were key to success. He is exporting those notions to Millennium Promise while also helping to build a model that may be of use to the promising new field of social entrepreneurship.

W e live in a time of great inequities, of mind-boggling wealth, and heart-wrenching poverty. In the world of private equity, we operate near the top of the global economic pyramid. Financial pressure and the weight of worry increase as one moves down the economic levels. An entire middle class scrambles to pay the bills, to put the children through college, or to buy even the simplest luxuries. There are several billion more in the bottom strata of society for whom survival is a struggle. Food and shelter are not a given: they're a daily challenge.

It is this lower level, the level of daily survival, that has become the focus of my current work. I spent almost my entire career as a leader of the private-equity operation of Chemical Bank and its successors, the last one being JPMorgan Partners. Today, as chairman of Millennium Promise, I am helping to lead the work of many exceptional colleagues by applying the techniques of private-equity investing to the effort to make good on the goal of the United Nations to cut poverty in half by 2015. I have not entirely left the private-equity world behind. Rather, I am using the tools I worked with during a career in private equity to help ease the pressures of survival for people half a world away from my mid-town Manhattan office building.

This is a humanitarian effort that also is serving as a test case in applied economics: taking the disciplined, performance-oriented methods of private investing from the capital markets of the United States and applying them to address poverty in the villages of Africa. Through our experience so far, we have learned that the management techniques and business skills are remarkably transferable, even while addressing poverty-related issues in some of the most deprived places on Earth. There also is an element of social entrepreneurialism at work, as we, in essence, conduct field research into the use of venture and private-equity methods in a much broader realm.

The challenges we address while building an effective charitable organization—one operating on a multinational scale and addressing some of the most vexing health, environmental, and social issues of our time—parallel those we often face while building a successful for-profit company. There are certain questions we have to ask in both circumstances. How do I organize people? How do we build partnerships? How do we manage the board? What is our strategic vision? Where are the market opportunities? What can we do that is not redundant? What's our unique niche?

From Private Equity to Not-for-Profit

These were all questions I had dealt with, time and again, during a career in private equity that began in the early 1980s. I had founded the private-equity operation at Chemical Bank in 1984 and had overseen some $12 billion of private-equity investments by the time I decided to retire from the firm in 2007. Over the years, I had been through incredible ups and downs. In 1999, we invested $2.3 billion and took out $2.5 billion in capital gains. Then, in 2000, we had to take a $1 billion write-down of assets in a single quarter. This was in the aftermath of the dot-com meltdown, and we took our dot-com losses alongside many other investors. Still, in the time I managed the private-equity operations for JPMorgan Chase and its predecessors, our operation posted a 30% compounded annual return on invested capital. At the time I left, we had just spun off the firm and became CCMP, an independent private-equity firm, and had just raised $3.4 billion from outside investors. It seemed like a good time for me to focus on the nonprofit world.

Even as my responsibilities and our investment portfolio had expanded beyond anything I could have expected, I had taken an ever-greater interest in not-for-profit work. I have been involved at my alma mater, the University of Virginia, practically for as long as I can remember, as president of its undergraduate business school foundation, and I have chaired the Thomas Jefferson Foundation, which operates and preserves Monticello, his home. Jefferson is one of my personal heroes, so Monticello really is a passion for me.

I have done substantial work on the board at the Quincy Jones Musiq Consortium and Big Apple Circus, and I've particularly enjoyed being involved with nonprofit start-ups. One of those start-ups is NPower, a not-for-profit that provides technology services to charitable organizations and also teaches inner-city kids how to become computer technicians; it is really having an impact. As I became more involved in NPower and other organizations, I realized that they bear so many similarities to start-ups and growing private firms I had worked with in my day job that I really felt I could bring proactive, private-equity skills to bear.

The key to success in the nonprofit world, just as it is in business, is to have a powerful idea backed up by sound management. The Robin Hood Foundation here in New York City has set a standard, applying management metrics to everything it does and demanding results from any partners it works with. That process is similar to managing a private-equity portfolio. The Robin Hood Foundation explicitly states that it takes a private-equity approach to philanthropy. It even borrows a page from Jack Welch's management practices at General Electric in that it reviews performance results of all the entities in its portfolio each year and stops funding the bottom 10%. It is a very bottom-line approach, obviously, but it seems to work.

My own work in private equity gave me plenty to draw from as I began looking for techniques to apply in charitable work. As an investor in Office Depot during the 1980s, for example, we had helped a company start with a couple of prototype stores, and it became a national operation. At Doane Pet Care Co., a private-label pet food manufacturer, I had seen the transformative effect of charismatic leadership. At a variety of our portfolio companies, I had learned the importance of management metrics, planning and execution, and holding people accountable.

The Call to Service

The timing was fortuitous, in other words, when I received a phone call in 2004 from a friend of mine, Ray Chambers, one of the visionary pioneers of private-equity investors. I had known Chambers for twenty years, first as a partner with former Treasury Secretary William Simon in one of the most successful private-equity firms ever, Wesray Capital, and later through our shared interest in philanthropy. Chambers had done great things for his home town, Newark, N.J., establishing a performing arts center there and creating the public entity that helped bring a professional basketball team to town. Nationally, he had funded the Points of Light Foundation. The list goes on.

Lately, Chambers and I had begun talking about the problem of poverty in Africa. Discussing the UN led effort to drastically reduce extreme poverty in the world by 2015—the "Millennium Development Goals," as they are called—Chambers and I had begun wondering whether it might be possible to bring a private-equity approach to such a seemingly insurmountable effort. On this particular phone call, Chambers informed me that Jeffrey Sachs, the noted economist and pioneer in addressing the health and economic needs of the world's poorest people, had some ideas he thought I should know about—a new effort to fight poverty in Africa.

"I think this is something that you would really be interested in working on," Chambers said. "Come meet with us."

I would like to say I was hopeful, but frankly, I was fairly skeptical. I had not been to Africa, but I had read enough about the problems there to know how tough it would be to have any impact. There wasn't enough money to cure Africa's problems, and even if there was the widespread corruption in many countries on the continent meant much of what was spent would be stolen anyway. There were tribal wars, HIV/AIDS, famines, and droughts. To me, it had always seemed the United States was the place to focus my efforts. The systems were in place for me to have the most impact, I thought. I had always thought Africa would be the next generation's problem.

The dinner with Jeff Sachs and Ray Chambers changed that perception. At the time, Sachs was finishing his work drafting a blueprint for meeting the Millennium Development Goals. Then Secretary General Kofi Annan in 2002 had asked Sachs to write a report focusing on the approaches to addressing the UN goals of cutting poverty, hunger, and AIDS; educating people; reducing environmental threats; encouraging development and so forth. Sachs' studies had led him to a humbling assessment of the daunting labors at hand. With a decade to go before the Millennium Development Goals deadline, little progress had been made. Sachs at this point felt that we needed to prove the community driven, holistic strategy to poverty elimination was the best way to go.

While we talked over dinner, Sachs and Chambers said they were searching for new strategies for attacking the entrenched scourges of extreme poverty. I asked all the hard questions I could muster. Money in Africa just seemed to disappear into the hands of the cleptocrats or the inefficiencies of aid distribution. National programs had been tried before, but virtually all failed. The UN apparatus might be too unwieldy and bureaucratic to make much progress.

As we discussed all this, I began to appreciate the desperate need for new approaches. Chambers and Sachs were exploring a new idea of setting up a separate, privately financed entity, outside the UN, to help improve execution and accountability. This struck me as a classic private-equity solution to the problem. If this separate entity could take charge of a failing enterprise, bring in new management, rationalize operations, and push toward measurable outcomes, it might make progress. In the efforts so far, under the direct oversight of the UN, the Millennium Development Goals were just one of many important items on a complex and demanding global agenda, and the goals seemed out of reach. Addressed under the care of a separate organization, perhaps more progress could be made.

From Field Research to Start-Up

The more we talked, the more interested I got. This was an opportunity, if I could find a way to contribute, to have a huge impact in an area of urgent human need. Sachs and Chambers made it clear they wanted me to get involved. The least I could do, I agreed, was to visit Africa and see the challenges at ground level. To help make the issues more real, I brought my 17-year-old son, Ryan.

Our trip took us to Kenya, Malawi, and Tanzania, all countries with existing UN programs, all in dire need of more help. One village we visited, Sauri, in western Kenya, still sticks out in my mind. Eighty percent of the population survived on less than $1 a day. Three-quarters of the families went to bed hungry, and the harvest never lasted between rainy seasons. Starvation was common. More than a third of the children had lost both their parents, often to HIV-related diseases. More than 60% of children were affected by malaria.

Everywhere we went on the trip, we saw signs of breakdowns in philanthropic efforts. In Malawi, at a feeding station for the UN's World Food Program, my son and I saw babies literally dying in the arms of parents who were waiting in line for food. The difference between life and death for some of those children was a failure to distribute food that was literally within their reach.

In one country, we saw how local politics can get in the way. We met with a high government official responsible for a malaria-fighting program. He showed little interest in the details of the program to distribute bed nets impregnated with a mosquito-killing insecticide. This politician's top priority was to make certain he was in front of the television cameras when the plane landed in Nairobi and the bed nets came out.

When we got back to the United States, I realized that the existing approach toward the Millennium Development Goals, relying on governments to roll out national programs, was not going to work. An approach modeled on private enterprise seemed our best hope. With the Millennium Development Goals seemingly out of reach, it was time to start the Millennium Promise Fund. The idea, after the launch in 2005, was to open pilot programs in 10 African countries, "Millennium Villages," we called them, which are clusters of villages, 80 villages in total, in shared geographic areas. Sachs proposed a holistic approach in which we would work to improve agricultural practices, health, education, and infrastructure simultaneously at the village level. Working with the villages over five years and applying Sachs' program, we would work to prove that we could move the villages toward a sustainable, self-supporting state. Then, after obtaining external verification of our results, with the support of the national governments and the UN, we could scale these proven models to reach over 100,000 villages across Africa and other continents.

The questions I started asking were a variation on the ones I would ask in a private-equity setting. What is the five-year plan for a village?

Is our distribution system for malaria bed nets up to the job? What is the schedule for bringing lunch programs in? How many water wells are supposed to be built? Where are they? Where are the red flags to warn us if we are falling short? Are we watching the impact on the health system? The education system? What measures are we using that the schools are actually achieving? Who is going to manage this on a day day-to-day basis? How can we use the strength of Columbia University and the UN without being slowed down by their bureaucracies?

Rather than simply asking these questions and dutifully noting the answers, we developed a comprehensive means of notating each answer and tracking it over time. This way, we would keep track of what had been done and what needed to be done. Over time, we would be able to track cause and effect from our efforts. Using this information, we could invest more aggressively in those initiatives that had positive impact and reduce our expenditures of capital and effort in areas that had less impact.

Management by Inquiry

This iterative process, sort of a management by inquiry, is something I had developed during the course of my for-profit work. I began to see how all my work experience could be put to good use in the villages of Africa. For example, going back as far as our very first deal at Chemical Venture Partners in 1984, I quickly learned the importance of partnering in order to absorb risk and share expertise. When Merrill Lynch first approached us to buy a group of television stations in 1984, the deal was too big and the risks too great for us to go it alone. Once we brought in Wind Point Partners and First National Bank of Chicago's private-equity unit, though, we felt comfortable taking on the challenge. The strategy worked. We purchased for eight times cash flow and sold, fairly quickly, for 12 times cash flow. We shared not just capital and back-office resources, but also expertise in how to structure the deal, how to work with management, and when to exit the investment.

The partnering approach—shared risk, shared effort—has been an essential strategy for Millennium Promise. In fact, it is built in. Millennium Promise brings resources of the Earth Institute at Columbia University, Jeff Sachs' operation, which has primary responsibility for managing the on-the-ground programs. The UN Development Program has been helpful, too. They are in the field throughout Africa, and can draw on decades of experience activating local programs that have a national impact and support global development goals. We also rely on corporate partners, turning to Ericsson AB, the telecommunications giant, for example, to bring phone and Internet capability to the Millennium Villages. We also have partnered with 62 wealthy individuals to help fund our five-year experiment.

A further refinement is the way we rely on experienced operating partners in the same way that a private-equity firm uses consulting partners for expertise. At JPMorgan Chase, we hired general partners with very specific areas of knowledge—a financial specialist, a human capital specialist, someone experienced with workouts, and so on. These people, six in all, served as a universal resource for our portfolio companies, and the chief executives loved having them to draw on. One of them was an experienced executive recruiter, Dana Ardi, who worked with our investment professionals to find the best talent and search firms for our portfolio companies. She was key in helping us find numbers of great chief executive officers, chief financial officers, and other senior talent for companies such as 1-800-Flowers.com and AMC Theaters. We've done something similar in the Millennium Villages. The Earth Institute alone has more than 100 sociologists, biologists, engineers, and public health experts who have specific, world-class knowledge in their subject areas. Their talent has given Millennium Promise access to incredible resources that other nonprofits in Africa lack.

In the not-for-profit world, we can take this consulting approach to an even deeper level by asking corporate partners to provide resources and know-how that goes beyond anything we would be entitled to expect from, say, a board member or an informal advisor in the private-equity setting. In Millennium Promise, for example, we are working with a potential corporate sponsor, Tyson Foods, to offer expertise in raising poultry. In our villages, there are chickens present and some basic understanding of how to raise them and propagate them, but there is virtually no notion of how to turn those chickens into a profitable business on any kind of scale. Working with Tyson, we developed a plan to send their people to our villages for three-month stints. They would provide technical advice to the villages and nearby towns, help build processing centers, and equip them with machinery. Incidentally, Tyson would benefit, too. This work will give their people exposure to early-stage markets and a chance to do something that really has an impact on the lives of people on the other side of the world.

There is one other aspect of running the firm at CCMP and its predecessor companies that really set the framework for how we approached the set-up at Millennium Promise, and that is the international partnering. Almost from the time I started at Chemical Bank, through eight bank mergers in all, we always were focused on developing our international contacts. Chemical Bank always had a strong presence in Asia, but over time we established private-equity efforts in a number of places: London, Hong Kong, India, you name it. This gave us the capability to analyze deals and execute strategies around the globe. When putting together the boards for our portfolio companies in our international deals, we always added people from the local market as well as Americans. We don't know all the answers. Local knowledge tied to a global network is key to a successful investment.

Looking for Two-Way Benefit

It turns out that international exposure can be one of those things that brings benefits to everything it touches. At CCMP, we saw how this played out when we backed the buyout of Parker Pen, the London-based unit of Manpower, Inc., the Wisconsin-based temporary services firm. Our role was to help spin out Parker Pen from Manpower, and soon after we got involved, we worked with a London buyout firm named Schroeder Ventures to bring in new management and refocus the brand. With its local savvy, the new management team was able to increase the rate of new product offerings and push toward an upscale market.

In the process, we did more than just grow Parker Pen's business. We also learned that international experience was good for our own firm, too. Parker Pen had a global presence, including a decent business in Asia. This was the mid-1980s, and we in Chemical Bank's private-equity practice really had done nothing in Asia to that point, so we learned a lot about how to operate in Asia from our involvement with Parker Pen.

For me, it was one of those ah-hah moments: If we were smart, we would learn to use knowledge from our brethren in other areas of the bank, with their on-the-ground expertise, as we rolled out Chemical's global private-equity strategy. We could draw on their insights as we partnered with private-equity shops in relatively unfamiliar places. It was essential that we recruited and worked with the best professionals on the scene, a point Parker Pen underscored for us with its success, not just in its home base in Europe, but in Asia, too. It was not just a one-way exchange, I would add. We introduced expertise to non-U.S. deals that we had developed in working with management and boards at hundreds of portfolio companies here in the United States.

That international perspective and the focus on a two-way benefit, are pretty much baked into everything we do at Millennium Promise. We take advantage of the global connections at both the Earth Institute and the UN. Then, on the boards of each country's operation—whether it's our work in Malawi or Kenya or Tanzania or the seven other countries—we mix local know-how with world-class expertise. We also make a practice of sharing experiences from one country with another, aiming to replicate what works and avoid what does not. This, too, is an adaptation of an approach we developed as an investor in hundreds of companies.

Back to the Roots

For me personally, having an impact on lives on the other side of the world is the culmination of a life's work that I never expected while growing up. My father was a computer engineer for General Electric, working on the space program. We moved about eight times before I graduated high school. Dad programmed the first computer GE used in Louisville, Kentucky, in the mid-1950s, and later, I saw all the space launches in the 1960s. I wanted to be an astronaut until I got glasses and realized that would never happen.

My uncle, Bill Franks, was the entrepreneur in the family and a role model for me. He started a landscaping business, then built hotels and a race track, bought some radio stations and some fast food restaurants in Illinois and Florida, and finally purchased a very successful coal mine. If there was anyone who gave me the notion that I could buy and sell businesses for a living, it was him.

As a college student at the University of Virginia, I took a course of study that split liberal arts and business classes. For a while I wanted to be a corporate lawyer, because I just loved the contracts course I had, but I realized I would be bored with the rest of the things a lawyer does, so I decided to focus on business. It was at Virginia, too, that I came to love Thomas Jefferson—all of the founding fathers, really. I joined a group called the Jefferson Society, which helped me develop a deep understanding and love for Jefferson and his ideas about the importance of the well-rounded life. Jefferson probably has had as big an impact on me as anyone. Until Millennium Promise, I probably have spent more time working on behalf of Monticello and the University of Virginia than on any of my other not-for-profit work.

After graduation, I was admitted to Harvard Graduate School of Business, but on a deferred-admit basis, so I went to work for two years as an accountant at Arthur Young. Some of that experience still sticks with me. I ran across a Foreign Corrupt Practices Act violation while auditing a company that was doing business with PEMEX, the big Mexican oil company. One of the company's executives was borrowing money from the Las Vegas mob. Finding a bribe and deciding how to handle it and reading FBI wire taps as I followed up on it was quite a unique experience. After Harvard, I got a job at Chemical Bank, and I went to work for the CFO, Alan Fishman, who was head of investment banking.

At the time, investment banking was a new line of business for commercial banks like ours, and I helped develop business plans for different investment banking units. After working on four of those start-up units, I told Alan I wanted to write up a plan for a venture capital unit operation that would do what today we would call private-equity investing, particularly focused on small- and medium-sized companies. This was 1984, and the term "private equity" had not been coined just yet. Alan and I brought the idea to the CEO, Walter Shipley, and then to the board, and in the end, they decided to fund us with $100 million.

Chemical Bank had tried to start private-equity groups of various types before, but they never were successful. Chemical and other banks at that point had begun to realize they were losing good people to private-equity firms because the compensation was better and autonomy compelling. In 1979, Patrick Welsh and Russ Carson had left Citicorp to form Welsh, Carson, Anderson & Stowe. Later, John Canning left First National Bank of Chicago to start Madison Dearborn Partners in the early 1990s because he felt he could operate more independently on his own.

Part of the reason Chemical was willing to put $100 million into Chemical Venture Partners and let us operate as a fairly stand alone unit was that my colleagues and I were only paid when the bank also got a good cash return. This gave the bank assurance that they would get a good deal, and it gave us the ability to operate independently, to build our own book of business, earn our money, and not worry about micromanagement from the corporate side. One of the reasons why we were able to retain our staff and our franchise over the years was that when we started the group, we structured the compensation as if we were an independent private-equity fund paying a share of the profits to the investment professionals through a carried-interest format through a formal partnership agreement.

Building to Scale

Perhaps our most important early deal was our investment in Office Depot, which quickly became a hit and brought us a lot of support at the highest levels of the bank. We built a huge portfolio of businesses over the years, and also went through a series of bank mergers: the purchase of Manufacturer's Hanover, the merger with Chase Manhattan, and eventually, the merger with JPMorgan and the purchase of Bank One.

The deals kept adding breadth to our portfolio and talent to our team. The most impactful acquisition, not in the best way, was Hambrecht & Quist, which had a big portfolio of technology investments we inherited that went bad with the dot-com bust of 2000. We bought trouble, but we also compounded it with our own exposure to the wireless and telecom sectors. We made, in 1999, almost $3 billion in profit and accounted for about 25% of the bank's total earnings. Then, in 2000, we lost about $1.5 million. Our CEO at the time, Bill Harrison, stood by us, though. He knew we had gotten caught in a position where our investments were illiquid and losing value, and because of the accounting rules, there just wasn't anything we could do except write them up when they went up and down when they went down. His support of us was appreciated and we paid the organization back with excellent returns and performance over the twenty-five year period.

Looking back on the 25 years I spent at the bank, I realize that one of the most valuable attributes I have taken away, for purposes of my not-for-profit work, is the ability to take a good idea and build it to scale—adding resources and support where needed and just letting organic growth occur where it has not. That idea of building from small scale to large, literally from the villages to a continent-wide effort, is built into what we are trying to accomplish at Millennium. If anyone is going to make the kind of dent that the Millennium Development Goals require, they're going to have to leverage everything they know in order to be successful.

From Small to Huge

While we were building the partnership infrastructure at Millennium Promise, the real challenge that surfaced was how to move toward large-scale implementation of any poverty-remediation efforts. There, too, we were able to draw on experience from private equity that had a direct bearing on what we could do at Millennium Promise. Office Depot served as a case study of how to build a new, national enterprise, starting small but expanding rapidly once a successful model was found. We helped start up Office Depot in 1986, first with a store in Fort Lauderdale and pretty quickly a second one, experimenting with a new retail concept—office-supply sales, something that previously was dominated by catalog merchants or large-scale distribution to national accounts.

From the start, we had tough competition: Staples had started a few months ahead of us, backed by some smart consulting work from Bain & Company. By starting small at Office Depot, though, we could experiment with the merchandise mix, with pricing, with all the details that go into running a successful business. There were surprises, of course, as there always are. The founding executive, F. Patrick Sher, was diagnosed with leukemia soon after the first store opened, and he died the next year. But the concept was strong enough, though it took nine months to find a successor to Sher, David Fuente. We were able to take Office Depot public in 1988, two years after start up, and today the company has some 1,700 locations worldwide and sales of more than $15 billion.

The idea of prototyping and testing a concept, then rolling it out big, has caught on in private equity. Petco is another company that started that way. El Pollo Loco did it in 2005, changing the face of an existing chain after trying prototypes of a new concept in several of its southern California stores.

I also have seen this approach work exceptionally well in the not-for-profit world. NPower is a good example. We created a way to roll out technology to small-scale not-for-profits. We started in New York City nine years ago and teamed up with Microsoft, Accenture, JPMorgan Chase, and the Robin Hood Foundation to fund its growth. After hiring an entrepreneurial chief executive, Barbara Chang, we began rolling out NPower offices around the country. Within three years, NPower had 12 operational locations, a really remarkable growth record in the not-for-profit world. NPower, in turn, is helping hundreds of nonprofits operate with modern technology that expands the reach of their work.

NPower has been successful in leaning on corporate backers to help build itself up. There is another step, though, that not-for-profits need to take: They need to get better at sharing experience and expertise with each other. Too often, it seems, they are competitive with each other when they should be cooperative. They seem to fear that there is only so much charitable money available, only so many good executive directors, only so many volunteers. More often than not, charities operating in the same space—conservation groups, human rights groups, even poverty-fighting groups, perhaps—act as rivals when there might be opportunities to get more done as partners.

The Networking Effect

Competition can be healthy. There's no mistake about that. But in private equity we have learned the art of competing against someone on one deal only to partner with them on the next. Take Thomas H. Lee Partners, a big private-equity player. At JPMorgan Partners, we competed against T.H. Lee for Dunkin' Donuts, and they got that deal. But then, when we got a chance to invest in ARAMARK, the food service company, Lee was our co-investor and fellow board member.

We shared resources to ensure success. We also share and compare our views. Working with them and other groups over the years gives you a chance to ask, "How am I different? What makes us be someone people want to partner with?" Over time, we can decide whom to partner with because we know how they operate and whom we can trust.

The networking effect in the private-equity industry can be powerful. At Millennium Promise, it has been one of our key strategic insights. At the time I joined the Millennium board in 2005, we still were struggling with how to develop the best model for implementing the Millennium Development Goals. National programs seemed doomed to fail. There was too much exposure to corruption, to inertia, to all the problems that have caused philanthropy in Africa to run aground for years. We decided to start small—with 80 villages in 10 African countries—and develop models that we could then scale. The idea was similar to the experiences we had at Office Depot or NPower. We also could build networks and amplify our best practices just as we had at JPMorgan Partners by partnering with other firms.

The crux of the Millennium Promise model was for us to start with clusters of small villages in geographically compact locations. Similar to what we had done with Office Depot or even NPower, the Millennium Villages would rely on a home office—the Earth Institute and the Millennium Promise office in New York City—to provide the essential resources common to all of the field operations. The difference between this effort and prior, national efforts, though, was that our approach was to start very small, find out from our pilot programs which methods worked, and then replicate them on as broad a scale as possible. We wanted to build a solid foundation at the village level and grow from there to a national level. Again, this was the Office Depot model, applied in Africa. We wanted experimentation according to local needs and opportunities, and we wanted to create affordable, repeatable models in four key sectors: agriculture, health, education, and infrastructure.

Putting Pieces in Place

We set reasonable spending plans, a subsidy of $80 per villager each year, just what was promised by the Group of Eight countries at the Gleneagles Summit in 2005. The start-up costs were higher than that, though, around $110 per person in the first couple of years of our program. Even so, we figured we could get those numbers down as we focused on simple, repeatable interventions, such as introducing fertilizer and seeds to boost crop yields, giving out mosquito nets impregnated with insecticide, and providing lunch meals at schools, all of them designed both to provide nutrition and to get children to attend classes.

Just as a powerful business idea will attract private-equity backing, the Millennium Promise approach began to draw financial support. George Soros gave us $50 million to set up prototypes over a five-year period. That helped us raise another $70 million from wealthy individuals and corporate foundations—again, a parallel with what happens in private-equity fund raising. Once you get those first commitments, which always are the most difficult, more is sure to follow, especially when the first mover is a name like Soros.

With the Soros commitment in 2006, we were able to operate in 80 villages in a dozen countries, directly affecting the lives of 400,000 people in all. One of the most successful interventions has taken place in our agricultural program in Malawi, a small country in east-central Africa south of Tanzania. Before we got to the seven villages where we operate in Tanzania's Mwandama district, the villages often ran out of grain in August and had to do without for six months of the year. We introduced a program of vouchers for fertilizer and seeds and provided training on farming techniques.

The impact was practically immediate and very real. The Millennium Promise money is helping the community to build a large grain bank, which will enable the village to store grain so it can be marketed when prices are high. The program has been so successful that the president of Malawi rolled out the fertilizer voucher program throughout the country, and Malawi has now become self-sufficient. In addition, we have five other countries that have asked us to help them raise funds to roll out the village models across their countries.

Going by the Board

One of the reasons why Soros backed us, and a big reason for our success, I am convinced, is the strength of our board and our eye for managerial talent. In private equity, building a board is not all that complicated.

Each of the firms with an investment stake gets a board member, and management has a couple of seats. There are always a few outsiders with relevant industry experience or specific knowledge: international operations, financial, or legal expertise, for example.

In the not-for-profit world, it is a bit more complicated. Because fund raising is such a crucial part of the enterprise, you need people who can bring in money as well as give it. You need knowledgeable experts, and most of them, if you pick right, should be willing to work.

The board we had at Parker Pen was one of the best I have seen. Its members had vision, industry knowledge, and geographic expertise. Richard Winkels, who represented the investment money from the Schroeder Ventures of London, had been at Dr. Scholl's, the foot products company, before he went into private equity. He brought all kinds of European retail insight. At another of our portfolio companies, 1-800-Flowers.com, the board found one of its essential tasks was to support the vision of a remarkably gifted founder who had a vision for the company, a strategic vision, that no one could match. Jim McCann was the first to use a telephone number as the company name, among the first to recognize the power of the Internet, and quick to see the need for add on investments such as The Popcorn Factory.

There are mistakes that not-for-profit boards make that they likely would avoid if they took a closer look at private-enterprise boards. Board size is one of them. You can't get anything done with a board of 32 members—a feature all too common on the boards of not-for-profit entities. Board attendance has to be as close to mandatory as possible, which is the case in private industry these days. The celebrity board members at nonprofits, if you have them, have to carry their weight. At Millennium Promise, Quincy Jones gets on the phone and calls people he knows to help us get things done. Angelina Jolie, another board member, has funded two of our villages and makes herself available to help.

Management Leadership

The ultimate predictor of success, in the end, is the quality of the person at the top. Doane Pet Care, one of our portfolio companies at CCMP, is a good example of this. We had invested $20 million or so in Doane, but after three years we had the chance to change chief executives. The company had succeeded in becoming the largest private-label dog-food supplier to the big-box retailers: Wal-Mart, PetSmart, and others. But, in mid-1997, commodity prices started going up and the company's profits were being squeezed. Most people thought, "Good luck raising prices with Wal-Mart, the toughest customer on the planet. It's just not going to happen."

We recruited a guy I had known for a long while, Doug Cahill, to be the CEO for Doane. I said, "Doug, what would it take to make you really join Doane?" Cahill said the answer was simple. He wanted to run Doane with the team he selected, and he wanted the team to have a chance to make a lot of money.

Cahill had worked for Olin Corporation and sold pool chemicals and Winchester products into the Wal-Mart system. He brought six or seven of his team from Olin. Cahill visited all the factories, worked the midnight shift, and had seen what the line people go through. Most importantly, he got Wal-Mart to trust him and to share in the financial risk of the commodity cycle, so when corn or soy prices went up or down, Wal-Mart shared the impact. He convinced them to accept this deal because Doane was making Wal-Mart's house brand of dog food, Ol' Roy. It's named after Sam Walton's dog. Cahill convinced them that we were a strategic asset to them. He put in a great hedging strategy, too, and the company's results just took off. We sold Doane to the Canadian Teachers' Pension Fund for a solid return on our investment, and Cahill and his team made a lot of money—just as he had wanted right from the start.

In not-for-profits, the chief executive officer factor can be tricky. Sometimes you've got a founder with a vision, but that person can carry the operation only so far. Or they get very proprietary and don't want to stretch the organization. Then there are the people like Jeff Sachs. I would compare him to Jim McCann at another portfolio company of ours, 1-800-Flowers.com, who is a passionate visionary but also listens well to others and takes their good ideas in as his own. You're lucky to have him, and as a board member, your job is to just do whatever you can to support him and his team.

Turning Philanthropy into Profit

The next stop for us at Millennium Promise, and for the not-for-profit world generally, is the move toward social entrepreneurship. This notion of the hybrid mix of for-profit techniques with charitable objectives really is the ultimate move toward sustainable philanthropy. At Millennium, we have worked with the Acumen Fund, which is one of the leaders in this new field. One of our people, Rustom Masalawala, runs our business development strategy and joined us after working at Acumen. He has identified a number of business opportunities that will help our Millennium Villages create jobs and significant cash flow for themselves. We have teamed him up with several of our investors, people with private-equity experience, and board members who can help him structure deals so that other investors would be interested in funding them.

When some of the agricultural experts out of the Earth Institute at Columbia University suggested that the area in eastern Ethiopia where we have a village cluster is a potentially rich area for bee keeping, Masalawala was able to help us recruit investors with a background in foodstuffs and food products to help make that happen. They will not have to invest much—$1 million, maybe $1.5 million in seed capital—but once they get started, we can start setting up a loan system to help the local people raise crops that they can then market to the food service partner, who is also an investor. It's a virtuous cycle.

If that model succeeds, then we've got something that could work in other villages, with other natural resources. We can then start moving some of our operations into the cities where some of the products would need to be distributed. Integrating into the cities is part of the Millennium Promise plan. We make a village sustainable by helping to start businesses, then continue to make them sustainable by marketing some of those village products in the cities.

I can't really say if poverty will be cut in half by 2015, in time to meet the Millennium Development Goals deadline. By the same measure, I never would have predicted, coming out of Virginia, that I would wind up running a private-equity firm that managed $12 billion in assets invested around the world. The experience doing the private-equity work has given me a chance to contribute to the effort to assist in the fight against poverty. I feel fortunate that the work I did for a quarter century gives me something to offer to one of the most important pursuits of our time.

LESSONS FROM JEFF WALKER

 Private-equity techniques have broad application. The financial disciplines, accountability, and growth strategies of private equity apply in multiple settings, including the not-for-profit realm.

 Pilot small, build to scale. The same technique of proving concept that worked for Office Depot applied in Millennium Villages, and can work in building many businesses.

 Turn competitors into colleagues. Just as private-equity professionals share insights and practices with colleagues, competitors can become colleagues in the right not-for-profit circumstances.

 Learn across borders. Instead of seeing organizational, geographical, cultural, or other differences as barriers, look at them as opportunities to gain knowledge, experience, and competitive advantages.

 Leverage early successes. Agile, scalable projects with the right people attract attention. The Chase board backed the author's private-equity unit, and early progress with Millennium Promise drew support from George Soros.

6

THE INSIDE GAME: MANAGING A FIRM THROUGH CHANGE AFTER CHANGE

John A. Canning, Jr.
Chairman
Madison Dearborn Partners

AUM: $18 billion

Years in PE: 29

Location: Chicago, IL

Year born: 1944

Grew up: Long Island, NY

Location born: Tucson, Arizona

Best known deals: PayPal, Cinemark, Nextel Communications, Ruth's Chris

Style: Fair, straight, unpretentious

Education: A.B., Denison University, Class of 1966
J.D., Duke University, Class of 1969

Significant experience: 11 years practicing law and 29 years as head of a private-equity firm

Personal interests: Own part of Milwaukee Brewers and four minor league teams

The lesson: "My leadership and influence are predicated on my being seen as fair."

With four decades of successful private-equity investing to his credit, John Canning knows all about getting deals done. He has seen the private-equity business change from small-sized transactions in the early 1970s to the leverage-fueled frenzy of the early 21st century. In 2007 alone, his firm put together a string of five deals with a total price tag exceeding $25 billion. The economic crisis, though, means the big-deal era is in eclipse, and Canning has called for a reassessment of strategy and an adjustment to a new, low-leverage future.

Through years of economic change, Madison Dearborn has remained remarkably stable. Eight of its founding partners remain at the firm today, where a flat compensation structure and careful recruitment contribute to success. So does an exacting management of the firm's investments, both before and after deals close. The Madison Dearborn experience shows that management of the firm can be as important to success as investment know-how and strategic vision.

⸺∞⸺

Private-equity investing has gone through certain distinct phases. A handful of venture investments in the late 1950s set the stage for what we know of today as private equity. In the 1970s came bootstrap deals, in which private-equity investors raised money for buyouts on a transaction-by-transaction basis. Late in that decade, the major banks and investment banks began developing an expertise in using leveraged transactions to buy companies, while relying on improved performance to deliver investment returns.

During the 1980s, when the term "private equity" first came into common use, certain partnerships that began expanding their deal size and the use of leverage drew major public attention—and some criticism—for the first time. The contentious bidding over tobacco and food giant RJR Nabisco led to a $25 billion purchase by Kohlberg, Kravis, Roberts & Co. that remains the biggest leveraged buyout ever. The 1990s saw the industry mature and a dramatic increase in the number and size of deals. The first decade of the 21st century started with the dot-com and telecom bust that hurt many firms and is ending with an economic crisis unlike any before. The crisis has challenged many private-equity investors to scale back on the size of deals and the use of leverage and made it more difficult for many firms to raise money from investors.

Through all of these changes—the growth and retraction, the booms and busts—there has been one constant: the firm. The partnership form of investment is at the heart of the way we do business, and management of the firm is perhaps one of the least discussed but most important aspects of our trade. It is through the firm that we, as general partners, raise capital from our limited partners. As a firm we evaluate investment opportunities, make investments, interact with our portfolio companies, and decide on exit strategies. As members of our firms, we distribute the wealth created by our activities. We distribute to the limited partners who make our investing activity possible while also distributing investment proceeds and bonus payments among our partners and associates.

Management of the firm is essential to success. While no one can succeed in this business without investment know-how, industry knowledge, negotiating abilities, and strategic vision, effective management of the firm helps sustain and enhance the deployment of those skills. When a firm is well run, the professionals can concentrate on their chief purposes of deploying and managing the limited partners' capital. The fewer distractions from that essential activity, the better.

A firm that is well run avoids falling victim to the factionalism, conflicting and shortsighted interests, and disruptions that occur at those that operate without paying attention to such potentially divisive practices. Well-run firms retain their key partners, take advantage of the skills they develop, and have little to fear from seeing a partner or group of partners take their experience, contacts, and investment know-how to some competing operation. For an industry in which we spend so much of our time advising executives how to manage their businesses, I believe we sometimes do not spend enough time focusing on how we conduct our own affairs.

No firm is without its troubles, and any firm that has lasted as long as my firm, Madison Dearborn Partners, likely has gone through periods of robust growth and occasional difficulty. Although difficulties may be inevitable, we can work our way through them more effectively and get back to the investing and other work we enjoy if we are operating from the strong base of a well-run firm. In fact, issues that might sink or splinter some firms become quite manageable challenges at those that are effectively run. Firms that keep compensation disparities, decision making, interdisciplinary rivalries, and generational differences well in hand can survive and prosper. The best private-equity firms make their mark through a mix of savvy investing and a keen sense of corporate strategy, but none can reach its potential unless someone in the firm's leadership has an ability to direct the firm toward long-term prosperity.

The Roots of a Firm

Madison Dearborn Partners today is one of the larger, longest lived private-equity firms, but what is not as well known is that eight key people in our firm have been together for an average of 25 years. Our roots trace to the early 1970s, when I began work as a lawyer advising the venture capital arm of the old First National Bank of Chicago, which over time transitioned into more of a private-equity approach. My predecessor, Stanley Golder, beginning in 1970 had taken a small, money losing activity of the bank and turned it into a substantial business. In 1971, he provided funding that enabled Frederick W. Smith to found Federal Express, one of the greatest venture investments ever.

I had played a small role in helping Golder get the First Chicago venture operation started. As a young lawyer out of Duke University Law School, I helped provide the legal underpinning for the bank as it set up an operation to move into direct equity investments. My job was to make certain the bank's new private-investment operation complied with the Bank Holding Company Act amendments. Golder's successes in his years running First Capital Corp. of Chicago showed that changes in the law can create expansive new opportunities, but only those who—like Golder—are ready to seize them will fully benefit.

By 1980, Golder became restless at the bank and decided he could expand his business more aggressively operating on his own. Along with Carl Thoma and Bryan Cressey, he raised $65 million, an astounding figure at the time, second only to Kohlberg, Kravis, Roberts & Co., which had raised $100 million. Ironically enough, KKR actually had helped First Chicago Capital build a profile in bank-owned private-equity investing by inviting First Chicago to participate in some of their early deals. When Jerome Kohlberg, Henry Kravis, and George Roberts started their firm, and before they raised their $100 million, they would come to us, Security Pacific, Mellon Bank, and a few others who were dabbling in direct investment at the time. They would take our capital and give us preferred equity or subordinated debt, and this helped us all because our banks began building experience and a reputation in private equity even as KKR became perhaps the best-known firm of the early era.

At the time Golder left the bank, in 1980, I had seniority over anyone else at First Capital, so I was the logical person to take charge of the bank's venture and private-equity business. It was hardly an auspicious moment in terms of the broader economic environment. Conditions were not on the order of the crisis that began in 2008, but they were extremely difficult. The prime interest rate hit 18% in 1981, and we used to joke that it would be cheaper to fund a buyout with a credit card than to borrow the money from a bank.

Still, we persisted, and we strung together several large deals, including the buyout of household metal products company Norris Industries, and car parts makers PT Components and Imperial Clevite. Their markets were all hard hit by the economic conditions, but the lowest result we got on any of the early deals was a 20% rate of return. This underscored an insight that has proven useful to us over the years: Solidly run companies, even in bad economic conditions, can still be profitable, successful investments.

Our biggest success at First Chicago was the investment we made in Nextel, a company that bought up radio frequencies that had been used to dispatch taxi cabs and turned them into a successful wireless communications company. Jim Perry, who remains one of my partners today, was contacted in 1987 by two somewhat unlikely entrepreneurs. One was Morgan O'Brien, who had represented taxi companies and other users of special mobile radio frequencies before the Federal Communications Commission. The other was an accountant named Brian McAuley, who had experience at the cell company Millicom. These two would-be entrepreneurs wanted to collect all these 900-megahertz licenses—held by the taxi company, the pool guy, other very local companies—and build a national phone service. Perry thought it made sense. Without any real leverage, O'Brien and McAuley strung together a company by picking up mom-and-pop outfits, hundreds of them, literally, and we had our biggest success in the time that I was running First Chicago Venture Capital.

Carry and Confusion

I finally left with my team of 13 other people to set up Madison Dearborn in 1992, and it was in this transition period that I learned a good deal about how to manage a firm. When Golder had left First Chicago more than a decade earlier, he had taken with him all but a couple of the best people. That meant I needed to hire the team who would work for me at the bank. This made for a tough transition, but it served me well over the years. I had gotten to hand select some of the brightest young people in the business, and right from the outset there was no question about who was in charge. That helped streamline our operating style at the bank, and it helped when the group of us decided to go out on our own. I was at least 10 years older than everyone, and I was going to be the boss; there was no question about that. To have that clarity, right from the start, was good for our firm.

As we began laying plans for the new partnership, there was a question about how we should allocate the carried interest—or share of profits—in our funds. I felt it was important to be fair to everyone and suggested that perhaps we should vote on the matter. That turned out to be a spectacular mistake. We took a blind vote, and when one of our partners tallied it he discovered all kinds of shenanigans had gone on.

Everyone gave me the biggest percentage, but after that it was a free for all. We had already decided to set up the firm according to a number of teams who specialized in certain industry sectors, and the teams were smart enough to figure out that, for pay purposes, they were in competition with the other teams. When I looked at the vote results, it was clear we had a mess on our hands. I immediately tore up the results and just decided that I should allocate the carry according to what seemed fair based on the work that was expected from each team. I announced this at a strategy session in Kohler, Wisconsin, and some people were shocked, but before any discussion could get going one of our founding partners said resolutely, "Next item. That one's done." And that was it.

Incidentally, that first fund was the only one in which I had more carry than the other senior partners at the firm. By the time we raised our second fund in 1997, my carry was set at the same level as about five other senior partners. It has been that way ever since. I think it's important, for the good of the firm, for people to feel that at a certain level we're all in it together. We want people concentrating on putting good deals together, helping their companies perform, developing good exit strategies—the important elements—and not on who has a slightly higher percentage than someone else.

There was a more important point being made by this relatively flat compensation structure. There is an element of basic fairness, of equity, among our partners that is reflected in the fact that we do not sanction large disparities in compensation. In a larger sense, our partners and associates have to believe that we operate our firm according to basic notions of fairness. The minute I am seen as unfair by the people I work with, I can no longer lead them. I am out of a job. That is something I can never allow to happen, and keeping compensation on a relatively even footing is one way to make certain that everyone sees our firm as being essentially fair minded.

Dry Run to Start Up

With our compensation levels set, we began raising money to launch the firm. I was the chief fund raiser, along with Kent Dauten, who was my most senior partner. The fund raising process itself taught me an important lesson about how our firm might look to outside investors. A chief issue, one I had never anticipated, had to do with our succession plans. Around the time we had decided to go out on our own, I had briefly considered retirement. Only a few people knew this, Dauten being one of them, but given the high profile I was assuming with the fund raising, it was inevitable that the succession issue would come up. It did, in fact, even before we hit the road to raise what turned out to be $550 million from a group of limited partners.

A private-equity investor in Chicago named Bon French, who had been a great friend and supporter of us at the bank, offered to sit in on a dry run of our fund raising pitch. So we went through our presentation: How much we planned to raise, the industry sectors we thought we would target, the experience of the partners in the firm. As we wrapped up, I turned to French and his partners in the room for questions.

"Now, what are the succession plans?" French asked.

Dauten and I looked at each other. Everyone else looked at us. We had no answer. It was just something that had not crossed our minds.

"I think this needs some work," French said.

By the time we delivered our presentation to someone less familiar with us than French, we had decided Dauten would be the successor if anything happened to me. The irony of that decision is that Kent wound up staying with the firm only a little longer than it took to raise the first fund. A year after we closed on fund raising, Dauten realized he could not commit himself over the long haul. He had come from an entrepreneurial family, and he wanted to set out on his own. He struggled with the decision. After all, Dauten had been out on the road with me, the only other guy pitching to investors, and I think he felt conflicted about leaving. He felt loyal to me and to the other partners. In the end, though, there was no fighting his desire to be on his own. Fortunately, he has been spectacularly successful, so he made the right decision.

One last step before we set up shop was the meeting in which I had to tell Richard Thomas, who was president of First Chicago at the time, that I was leaving along with 13 of his other top equity-investment people. Of course, I handled the conversation with a bit more finesse than that. After all, there were strong business reasons behind our desire to leave. One was that we were running up against the legal limits on a bank's ability to invest in unrelated businesses. The other—and the more important element in terms of First Chicago's future—was that mark-to-market accounting was coming.

Mark-to-market accounting was going to be bad for First Chicago Capital, because it would change how our activities were treated on the bank's balance sheet. Before the accounting change, the bank could use us to help level out its earnings. The bank's lenders were always stepping in holes somewhere around the world, creating a need for earnings on the income statement. We had a portfolio of unrealized gains, of course, so when they needed earnings they could ask us to sell assets, book those gains, and offset the losses elsewhere in the bank.

With mark-to-market, we were going to become a liability, because as stock prices climbed, the value of our portfolio would rise, too. That would be reflected on the bank's income statement. But, if the market went down, we would suddenly have to call up the chief financial officer to announce the bad news that we were delivering a large loss he had not expected. Beyond that, mark-to-market would erase our ability to help the bank log asset sales in a timely way that helped level its earnings performance. I could see we were going to become worse than not useful to them. We were going to be a problem. And this meant it was time to get out.

When I walked into Thomas' office, though, I did not put the emphasis on mark-to-market. I painted a scenario that showed that the bank could have the benefit of our investment work but without the costs of our salaries and operations. I showed him how much money he could save. Investing has a long tail on it, and the earnings do eventually come in, but on the front end, as the bank put on the investments, it was expensive. We were getting paid and investing the bank's capital, but there were no gains for several years. After all, the bank did not book gains back then until it realized them through a sale or a public offering or some other event. The bigger the portfolio got, the more costly our operation looked to the bank's investors. I explained that it would be cheaper for them to have us on our own and give us a cut of the upside.

"We would like to do this," I told Thomas.

He had a simple response. "OK," he said. "But once you make the decision, you are gone."

We left, but we did not completely sever the relationship. We continued to manage the bank's $2 billion portfolio of equity investments. In addition to Nextel, the portfolio had a stake in Fortune Computers, which got very hot before it crashed. It also invested in U.S. Windmills, a company that was a generation ahead of its time. These investments looked good to the bank at the time, and Thomas made certain that the bank was a participant in our first fund.

First Funds

It was a very tough year to raise money. We were one of only a few firms out there trying to do so. Our first commitment came from Williams College, where an old friend and private-equity investor, Joe Rice, was on the board. We had been good to KKR, and the KKR guys individually put in money and gave us a full list of investors whom they said we could call. We lined up meetings with some Japanese banks, Shell Oil, and pension funds from General Motors, General Electric, and AT&T. None of them said yes, but we did get the California Teachers'

Pension Fund and California Public Employees' Retirement System to make large commitments. Then we got the commitment of some highly regarded endowments such as MIT, Princeton, and Yale and we were off and running. The only local money we got, besides First Chicago, came from Aon, the big insurance company.

First Chicago initially had committed to 25% of the fund, but after seven months of fund raising we realized we could not take the entire amount. One of the reasons we had succeeded with the limited partners was that we had agreed not to raise more than $550 million. But, if we gave First Chicago a quarter of that, we would have needed to turn away other limited partners who wanted in. Accepting all of the bank's money would have put us over the $550 million limit. Quite graciously, Thomas agreed to limit the size of First Chicago's investment so we could bring the other limited partners into our fund.

Path of Surprises

I have to admit there was some exhilaration, along with a certain air of suspense, for me personally as we set up shop at the corner of Madison and Dearborn streets in Chicago. Since my days as a freshman in high school, I had wanted to make a lot of money. My father was a doctor on Long Island where I grew up. He was an artist and sculptor, too, but making money in itself was not a major focus for him. My life was pretty sheltered. I had 70 kids in my high school class and played all the sports, so money was not a chief focus for me, either, during those early years.

That perspective changed quite abruptly one summer during high school while I worked at a gourmet food store owned by the father of a friend. Investment bankers, lawyers, stock brokers, and doctors would come into that store, and there was something about their lives that seemed so comfortable. I was on the other side of the counter but did not want to stay there all my life. I decided then that I wanted to make a million dollars. That would be a measure of success.

In those early years, I had a hope that I might be able to play professional baseball. I was a catcher, and between high school and college I had a week-long tryout with the Atlanta Braves organization. It turned out I couldn't hit minor league pitching, and exactly how that contributed to a feeling of homesickness I developed, I do not know.

I was slow and couldn't hit, but I still had an arm that was strong enough for me to play college ball at Denison University. Fortunately, the colleges did not check into amateur status very carefully back then, so when I enrolled at Denison I was still able to play. Much has been made of my baseball career, because today I own a stake in the Milwaukee Brewers and also had bid to buy the Chicago Cubs from the Tribune Company, but to imply that I was a superstar ball player is an exaggeration.

When I was 20, my mom and brother both died within a week of each other. My brother died in a car wreck, and my mother choked to death while eating in a restaurant. I was a senior at Denison and on my way to law school. It's hard to put into words how tough that was. Let me just say it taught me I could survive anything. Failing in business is not the end of the world, and as long as we have our health and our loved ones, life can be okay.

One irony of my life is that I had never intended to go to law school. I had always planned to go to business school and had taken the entrance exam. Meanwhile, I had a friend who needed a ride to Columbus, Ohio, to take the law boards, and I figured, as long as I was driving him there, I might as well take the test myself. It turned out that I bombed the business boards, but I got the highest score ever in Ohio on the law boards. The Vietnam War was getting started, and the only way to skip the draft was to stay in school, so law school suddenly sounded like a great idea.

I wound up at First Chicago almost by happenstance, too. In my last year at Duke University Law School, a First Chicago lawyer visited, and I applied for a job. The Vietnam War was still escalating, and I listed my draft status as 1-Y, which meant I could be drafted. But the recruiting lawyer didn't know what that meant, so he offered me a job anyway. The lawyers back in Chicago were not happy about that, especially when I wound up with No. 12 in the draft lottery, which meant I soon would ship off for Vietnam. When I went for induction, though, I flunked the physical, so the law department had its newest associate after all. I started work, in fact, on the day the First National Bank Building opened. The building is a landmark in Chicago, with its sweeping, curved, white exterior walls, and I have always enjoyed having something in common with that great building.

The Firm Is Flat

I had wanted to be a principal investor since a time early in my career when I was a young lawyer representing First Chicago Venture Capital. One day we were working on an investment with KKR in the offices of the buyout boutique Simpson Thacher & Bartlett when Henry Kravis told another attorney and me to draft up some documents while he and the other principals went to dinner. I said to myself at that point, "I want to be the guy who goes to dinner."

Now, at long last, I and my 13 partners were setting up shop as principal investors. One of our first major successes was in a company called OmniPoint. It was a wireless phone company in which we invested $30 million, and like many telecom startups it went through about four different boom-and-bust cycles. We were always living by FCC limits on our expansion and who would let the company put up cell towers. It was a precarious ride.

OmniPoint was a no-leverage deal, but that was not the norm. We set a course early on such that about 60% of our deals would be growth equity investments, like OmniPoint, and the remaining 40% would be buyouts, which by definition were bigger deals. OmniPoint ultimately became T-Mobile, and they were acquired by Deutsche Telekom. As a firm, we took $600 million out of that deal. The people who sold their Deutsche Telekom stock are happy with what they got, but that company has fallen on hard times, so the ones who held onto their shares probably regret it.

The end result of the investment for the partners in our firm always boils down to the share they hold in the form of carried interest. Over the years, we have learned to develop a very flat carry system. In our last two funds, no one person has more than 10% of the carry, so the gap between individuals at the firm is not great. Now, if you don't have this sort of flat setup, you are not going to be able to govern a partnership, because there will be too much infighting. Sooner or later, the partners will storm the castle and try to take over to show they can do it better.

A flat compensation system also has the effect of making a point within the firm that we do not operate under a star system. We do not view our firm as groups of people, operating from silos of expertise and all competing for the same resources. Equitable distribution of carry is a persuasive way to make this point.

Hot, Cold, and Sitting on Hands

From time to time, each of our industry groups is going to be playing a hot hand. Telecom gets hot and then turns cold; the manufacturing sector rises and falls. It is the job of these sector groups to jump on such opportunities, but by retaining a relatively even approach to compensation we make it clear that no individual group is responsible for our success. Likewise, when conditions change and results turn against a particular group, everyone tends to be more tolerant of those conditions, as well. These broader points are made, too, by the way we evaluate deals, the way we manage our ongoing investment in companies, and through a variety of other methods. It is an intrinsic part of our firm and one that contributes to our even-keeled style and our success.

We keep the partners aligned with the firm's objectives by distributing carry at the start of a fund. We do not allocate based on deal flow because we do not want to build in a volume incentive for people to do deals. Given the choice between doing no deals and doing bad deals, I'll take no deals every time. We don't want to penalize our people for not doing deals, especially if they are focused on an industry that is just not attractive at the time. We do not want any of our people to feel they are not going to get paid because they are sitting on their hands, especially in tough economic times when perhaps that is precisely what they should be doing.

Everyone has meaningful investments in the funds, too. Many of our partners and associates have to borrow money to make their investments, particularly the younger professionals. That way, they are fully committed. There is no temptation to throw in the towel when things go bad. After all, the firm has guaranteed their loans. They know we will hunt them down in the night if they do not pay.

We use a compensation structure to provide incentive for management at our portfolio companies, too. One of the reasons why private equity is a better approach than hedge funds or public companies, in our view, is that we can align with management by requesting that they put a meaningful amount of money into the deal. When things do get tough, they can't walk away. They can't say, "Well it didn't work out, but I just had options, so it's no big deal."

Growing Pains

Every deal we did in our first fund turned out well, not just OmniPoint. We got four times the total amount invested. By 1997, we were ready to raise a second fund, targeted for $900 million. Some of our limited partners thought that was too big a step up—nearly double our first fund—but the second fund turned out to be very successful, so we quickly raised a third fund, which capped at $2 billion.

That fund became the source of some of our firm's biggest mistakes. Part of it, I think, was that we were taking in the returns from our first fund, so we probably were acting with some overconfidence. After all, we were cashing checks for $600 million for OmniPoint, so nobody was going to say we did not know what we were doing with our new round of investments. We were investing in 2000, at the height of the dot-com bubble, and because of our experience we weighted very heavily toward the telecom sector. After the telecom bubble burst, we had to close down 25 companies. Some of them were hitting their plans, but we had to close them down anyway because the lenders had no patience with anything in the sector.

We had never known much stress before. We had only known success. Now we were facing a lot of stress. In one of our companies, Focal Communications, we had invested $15 million, and at its height the investment was valued at $1.4 billion. We never got a nickel out of it, though. The stock topped out, but we could not sell because that would have undermined the whole market for the company. As we looked back on it, the mistake we made was that we concentrated too much in one sector, telecom, which had been so hot.

The blistering experience with the telecom boom and bust taught us a few lessons about managing a firm under changing market conditions. Mainly, we learned that it is a mistake to get too excited about inordinate success. It is equally an error to overreact when the markets turn against us. At the height of the telecom bubble, those of us in leadership of the firm spent a lot of time deciding how to compensate our telecom group. After all, they were doing most of the deals, and they were having remarkable success. At one point we considered launching a sector-specific fund that our telecom people would manage. We changed our hiring so sector groups—the telecom group, in particular—could hire associates without having them interview throughout the firm, as had been our practice.

Confidential Compensation

We did not change our carry structure. That was sacrosanct. But we did make certain that the telecom group received hefty bonuses. It was important, though, to make certain that the bonuses remained confidential. We published the bonus pool each year, so everyone in the firm could estimate how large a share they had gotten. Our own experiences told us, though, that it would be corrosive to let everyone know exactly how much a particular team received.

In the end, we did not permanently change the structure of our firm, either when telecom was on its way up or on its way down. We never launched a separate telecom fund, and we decided, after experimenting with new hiring practices, to return to our old style.

Our decision to continue with our traditional hiring approach is having an important impact on the firm. Letting one industry team take responsibilities for hiring had the potential to have a corrosive effect on the firm's sense of cohesion. Instead of feeling loyal to the firm, we thought that our young people over time would develop that commitment only toward the particular group that hired, trained, and mentored them. Their commitment inevitably would be to the group, not to the entire firm. This, in turn, might create a sense of competing fiefdoms at the firm rather than the notion we prefer—that we all contribute, from our different disciplines, to our shared success.

We now believe it is important that everyone in leadership at the firm meet every new person we hire, and we work to make certain our new associates also develop this firmwide perspective. We make clear to new associates that it is the firm, and not a particular team, that hires them. We assign our new associates to a pool from which they might be called to any industry group, depending on the firm's needs. Only after about three years of experience do we allow the new associates to pick a specialty.

Giving Back Fees

Ultimately, the most dramatic impact on our firm from the telecom bust that began in 2000 was the decision we made to quit taking management fees. We had finished raising our fourth fund, $4 billion, and with the telecom sector collapsing we had our hands full monitoring our portfolio. We were focused on ensuring that our third fund's relative performance would be as good as possible. I raised the idea of foregoing our management fee, which would mean giving up a $15 million revenue stream that arose from our .75% assessment against the fund's $2 billion of capital commitments.

We did not even send out an announcement. Word got out when we started getting calls from the wire rooms of our limited partners. They had expected invoices, telling them they owed us so much money, but the notices never came.

Soon after that, we decided to cut the amount of our fee for our fourth fund. In this case, the reasoning was different. The buyout market was dead. After the telecom bust and the dot-com bust, deal flow had just dried up. It seemed difficult to justify collecting our full fee when there was going to be so little deal flow.

We cut our fee on the fourth fund from 1.5% of $4 billion to 1.5% of $3 billion. With the cuts from those two funds, we were giving up $30 million a year in fees. I told our partners that I believed we were not the only firm being hit by these conditions and that, before long, all the other firms would follow suit. Venture firms had already begun giving back money to investors. I figured private-equity firms would match, in their way, by cutting management fees, and we wanted to be the first firm to do so.

As soon as we announced the cut in our fees, I got a call from the CEO of a major buyout fund. "What are you guys doing?" he wanted to know. "Everybody in the world is talking about this. They're all angry at us because we're not doing it."

The call was hardly a surprise. Our cut in fees breached a long-standing protocol of the industry and was controversial at the very least. We simply felt it was the right thing to do for our limited partners.

As it turned out, I had misread the situation in the industry. No other major firm followed our lead and cut its own fees. Still, to this day I think the move was a good one. We earned all kinds of good will with our limited partners. Until that point, some of our limiteds had raised questions about the size of our newest fund. They told us they were concerned about "style drift"—the tendency to change investment style when a firm raises too much money. What they really meant, though, was that they were concerned about paying such large fees when there was so little action in the marketplace. Once we cut the fees, the questions about style drift went away.

Style Drift and Vintage Risk

Style drift was not accurate in describing what happened during the telecom bust, but some think it is fair to apply the term to what happened during 2006 and 2007, when our firm and many private-equity firms began doing extraordinarily large deals. This was the height of the deal frenzy, when credit was cheap and money just flowed. Heading into this period, we were raising a $6.5 billion fund and had to turn down a $500 million commitment from a large pension fund because it would have put us over our cap.

The deal flow and the price tags were just incredible. At one point, we had three different teams in our firm, in three different industries, working three major, multi-billon-dollar deals. The size of the deals had gotten larger. We invested 45% of our $6.5 billion fifth fund in just three companies.

As it turned out, we were not facing industry concentration risk, as we had with telecom, but what we and the industry were facing more than anything else was vintage risk. In other words, the bulk of these deals all were getting done around the same time, with similar debt profiles, and they would respond similarly if the economy turned against us.

Before 2006, the entire private-equity industry had done only one deal larger than $10 billion—KKR's $25 billion purchase of RJR Nabisco, the infamous "Barbarians at the Gate" deal. Beginning in 2006, 18 deals were $10 billion or larger. Because many of these deals had similar debt profiles, the entire industry would be facing vintage risk, especially once the economy tightened in late 2008 and it became challenging to comply with debt covenants as the economic performance of companies declined.

An Uneasy New Era

The easy credit was creating an uneasy amount of leverage the likes of which our industry had never seen before. Total debt during this period was 6 times cash flow, nearly double what it had been in 2001, when leverage multiples fell to a 10-year low of 3.5 times cash flow. Money was easy. Loans were offered with liberal amortization schedules, without restrictive covenants and with the ability to pay interest in kind. Some of the best financial minds in the world had been asked to create innovative new products to help fund the financing frenzy, and they did not disappoint.

The deals that have gotten into trouble are in industries that were most adversely affected by the economic downturn and have done so because the extraordinary amounts of leverage left them little room for error. Prices ran to remarkable levels, in part because the availability of cheap credit tended to drive prices skyward. The bankers were so anxious to lend, they were offering us more than we were willing to take.

Protective Measures

The experience from this period has taught us the value of extreme stress testing when we are evaluating an investment. Like most firms, we have always conducted tests of how a potential portfolio company might perform under tough economic conditions. Over time, we have refined this into what we call a "waterfall analysis." The term is meant to reflect what can happen when a stream of bad news cascades, like a waterfall, on any given company.

Before investing in one retailer, for example, we looked at how the company would operate even in the face of a series of extreme occurrences. We looked at how they would do if the company signed no new accounts, if wholesale margins fell by 1%, if sales in new stores fell dramatically, if same-store sales growth flatlined for four straight years, if the company failed to open more than 10 stores a year, and other factors. The company expected to sign an important new customer, but we estimated the impact of what would happen if the deal would fall through. Then, we added all those negative occurrences together and looked at the numbers.

We learned from experience that reality sometimes might be tougher than even our worst-case scenarios. The economic assumptions we made prior to the economic crisis of 2008 clearly were not severe enough. From this recent experience, we have extended the duration of our worst-case assumptions by several years, to take into account the possibility of an economic downturn that persists for five years. Perhaps we did not take into account the more global effects of an economic downturn—a lack of credit, a dysfunctional banking system, 10% unemployment, and so on. Previously, our assumptions had focused more at the internal nature of the business than at any potential for a collapse of the global economy. From this point forward, we know we need to give particular emphasis to the impact of the world economic situation, too.

The careful calibrations do not change once we close on our deals. On an ongoing basis, we reassess our investment decisions. Each year, as we review the performance of our portfolio companies, we treat each one as if it were a new investment. The deal team that was responsible for the investment has to justify sticking with the company, as if keeping our money in it is no different than committing the capital in the first place. They have to set out a timetable for when they expect to get liquidity on the investment—in other words, when and how we expect to exit—and then that goes on a big master schedule. These timetables are reviewed quarterly, and any delays have to be explained.

We look at stress tests on an ongoing basis, too. If the stress test shows that a default may occur on any of the company's loans, the team is required to create a scenario for how we will prevent that from happening or, if necessary, how we will deal with the problem. As a matter of practice, we generally do not put new money into a company that is running into trouble. We did that once, early in Madison Dearborn's history, when the chief executive of the company came to Chicago and laid out his case for additional investment. We had invested $50 million in the company at the start, and the chief executive felt he could get out of trouble if we put in $10 million more. It was an extraordinary circumstance and a good presentation, and we went against our gut and contributed new capital. That additional investment actually turned out well. We just distributed some of the company's stock. But let's just say that this case was the exception that proves the rule that we do not believe in putting in good money after bad.

An Altered Economy, A Changing Business

As the crisis that began in 2008 extends and expands into historic proportions, the private-equity business is changing and presenting new challenges for us as managers of our firms. For me, personally, the change has coincided with the transition, beginning in March 2007, from my day-to-day role as chief executive to becoming chairman of

Madison Dearborn. My partners, Sam Mencoff and Paul Finnegan, now share the CEO duties. The industry is in transition, too. The days of easy credit are over, and we are experiencing a return to smaller deals, virtually all of which must be funded without the use of leverage.

There literally is no leverage available. I do not expect leverage ever will return to the levels we just experienced, at least, not while I am around. Leverage will return, though, once banks feel more comfortable with their capital structure and once a market recovery gets the capital markets flowing again. Regardless, we have adjusted to this new era of low- or no-leverage deals. We have said internally that we are going to limit ourselves to investing no more than 10% of the fund in any one transaction. We prefer to keep the average investment lower than that, if possible. Even though we have raised over $4 billion we expect deal size to remain relatively small.

For the time being, deal flow will be rather thin. For more than a year we did just one deal. Right now we are saying our current fund will last us for a good, long time. There is nothing on the horizon to suggest that broad economic conditions will change any time soon, and our business tends to reflect the underlying economy.

Private equity is entering a distinct new phase. We are back to basic values and growth-oriented investing. Leverage is out of the picture for now, but will almost certainly make a comeback at some point. Much will depend on how and when the economy regains its strength. The new phase has a familiar look, one that harkens back to the conditions that prevailed when I was first getting into the business.

What shape our economy, and our business, will take in the future remains to be seen. As ever in private equity, uncertainty creates opportunity. It is up to us to find opportunity where others see only trouble—and make the most of it.

LESSONS FROM JOHN CANNING

Use leverage prudently. The days of runaway borrowing, with few loan covenants and seemingly endless access to debt, fueled a flurry of large highly leveraged deals. A growth investing approach is not only necessary but also leads to more careful investment decisions.

Assess risks carefully. Before investing, take into account all the negative contingencies. Add up their impact, over an extended period of time, to see how the investment would hold up under the worst of circumstances.

 Get skin in the game. Management should have a substantial personal investment in a deal. Partners of a private-equity firm should also be heavily invested in the firm's funds.

 Avoid large pay disparities. Large inequalities in pay can cause friction in a firm, and rewarding a hot deal team can backfire if economic conditions change. Use bonuses to recognize extraordinary performance but keep base pay relatively flat among partners.

 Adjust to economic conditions. The economic downturn is sending clear signals that investing styles will have to change. Experience shows, too, that it is best to use caution when money and credit are easy.

PART II

VENTURE CAPITAL

7

THE ENTREPRENEUR AND THE VENTURE CAPITALIST

Garth Saloner
Philip H. Knight Professor and Dean
Graduate School of Business, Stanford University

Garth Saloner has both studied and practiced entrepreneurship, leaving Stanford University business school in 2001 for a two-year stint working at start-up companies. An authority on the role venture capital plays in spurring economic activity, Saloner has researched and written about e-commerce, strategic management, organizational economics, and competitive strategy. Named in early 2009 as dean of Stanford's business school, Saloner has focused his recent research on advancing our understanding of how start-ups and established firms set and change strategy.

Training his eye on the complex ecosystem of venture capitalists, entrepreneurs, and investors, Saloner here explains how all these groups work together, despite some inherent conflict, to promote innovation and create new industries. Venture capitalists must make risk-reward calculations that drive their decisions, while entrepreneurs often lack such an objective appraisal because they have so much of themselves invested in the commercialization of their ideas. Recent, historic stresses in the financial markets and economy have added to the complexity of these relations.

The venture capital industry is an important part of the engine of growth in developed and, increasingly, in developing countries as well. As the stories in this book illustrate, many of the largest companies formed as new ventures in the last several decades emerged from an ecosystem in which angel investors, venture capitalists, entrepreneurs, and university research all play a role. Yet the relationship among these participants is not always easy. Despite the enormous benefit to society and the substantial creation of wealth arising from the relationship between venture capitalist and entrepreneur, each tends to consider the other as a necessary evil for the success of the venture. To better understand this complex love–hate relationship, it helps to understand the goals and incentives of the typical venture capital firm.

Clearly, the goals, incentives—and ultimate returns—of venture capital investment are desirable enough that legions of investors forego other possibly lucrative pursuits to devote their careers and substantial pools of capital to entrepreneurial start-ups. Since 1970, venture capitalists have invested $466 billion into more than 60,700 companies, according to the National Venture Capital Association. In that same time, as the venture capital industry has become more institutionalized, total assets under management have grown from $1 billion in 1970 to $197 billion. At its height in 2000, before the collapse of dot-com and telecom companies scared substantial capital away from the venture sector—the figure reached $225 billion. All told, companies formed as a result of venture-backed investment today account for 10.4 million U.S. jobs and 18% of the U.S. gross domestic product (Table 7.1).

Year	Total Cumulative Funds	Total Cumulative Firms	Capital Managed ($ Billions)	Avg. Fund Size ($ Millions)	Avg. Firm Size ($ Millions)
1980	186	117	4.1	31.8	44.6
1985	539	320	17.9	33.1	60.3
1990	1,055	457	29.2	39.8	74.3
1995	1,527	615	40.6	57.4	94.6
2005	3,677	1,428	271.4	152.6	265.0
2008	4,273	1,648	197.3	144.4	223.7

Table 7.1   Source: National Venture Capital Association/Thomson Financial.

In the midst of the current economic turmoil, with both the credit markets and the economy under significant stress, it is hardly surprising that venture capitalists are particularly selective in the companies they choose to support these days. In prior times, cycles of venture capital tended to rise and fall with the ebb and flow of the market for initial public stock offerings. As the initial public offering market seized up beginning in 2008, broader economic conditions and the availability of credit tended to become the overriding factors.

This is not to say that venture capital investors have left the field altogether. Rather, they are merely more careful than ever about their investment decisions. Venture capital investors are ever more vigilant to ensure that the companies they do support have enough cash and "runway" to manage the rate at which they spend—or "burn"—their way through capital or spend and burn through a difficult period.

Likewise, venture capitalists themselves are finding that their own access to capital is limited in ways few have seen before. Fundraising from limited partners typically is taking longer and yielding less than in prior periods.

Over the long term, venture capital funds have generated a net internal rate of return in the range of 15% to 20% each year to their limited partners, but those rich and reliable returns no longer seem quite so dependable to their limited-partner backers who have suffered economic loss due to recent market and economic conditions. Chastened by losses in the stock market and other forms of investment, the limited partners are putting pressure on venture funds not to make a call on their capital. In short, the limited partners are asking the venture capitalists to avoid demanding that the investors actually produce the capital they promised at the time the fund was formed, unless such a capital call is absolutely necessary. Venture capitalists are now much more solicitous of public pension fund investors whom until recently they had often dismissed in favor of more sophisticated endowment funds. Indeed, endowments these days frequently are retreating from the business of meaningful venture exposure, as they recover from significant equity market losses and move toward a more conservative mix in their investment portfolios (Table 7.2).

Fund Type	Net IRR to Investors for Investment Horizon Ending 12/31/2008 for Venture Capital Funds				
	1YR	3YR	5YR	10YR	20YR
Seed/early venture capital	–20.6%	1.7%	3.7%	36.0%	21.8%
Balanced venture capital	–26.9%	4.6%	8.4%	13.5%	14.5%
Later stage venture capital	–6.8%	9.5%	8.7%	7.5%	14.5%
All venture capital	–20.9%	4.2%	6.4%	15.5%	17.0%
NASDAQ		–38.1%	–10.3%	–4.6%	–3.2%	7.3%
S&P 500		–36.1%	–10.0%	–4.0%	–3.0%	6.1%

Table 7.2   *Source: National Venture Capital Association/Thomson Financial*

Thanks, but No Thanks!

These are the novel and stressful market conditions under which venture investors and entrepreneurs are undertaking the age-old courtship by which both hope to find a way to build a successful and profitable enterprise. No matter how robust or weak the market conditions, the rituals undertaken by investor and entrepreneur remain essentially the same. One of the most frustrating experiences for an aspiring entrepreneur is a meeting with a venture capital firm that goes splendidly in all respects except one: no investment comes forth! The presentation went well, the discussion was lively and engaging, and it seems as though all the bases were covered. The technology is sound, customer satisfaction with the beta version is high, there are more customers hungry for the product, the unit economics of the business are promising, the team is well qualified, and the financial projections all make sense. Yet, in a polite but firm way, the venture partner delivers the news that this is not a venture that is suitable for this venture firm at this particular time.

What went wrong? To understand what probably went wrong, the aspiring entrepreneur needs to understand the financial model of the typical venture firm. That model begins with the risk–return aspirations of the limited partners who invest in the venture fund in the first place. Whether made by a pension fund, a university endowment, investment fund, or other investor, the venture investment is a dicey proposition.

Yes, many venture investments have been wildly successful, but venture capital is a risky investment class, one in which one's money will be tied up for a long time and in which there will be limited visibility into how the investment fares along the way. In exchange for tolerating this risk and uncertainty, the limited partner requires a risk premium over and above what it expects it could obtain by simply investing in, say, an equity index fund. If, for example, they expect U.S. equities to return an average of 12% over time, the limited partners in a venture fund might expect a 10% premium for the risk and illiquidity associated with venture investing. All told, the limited partner might be looking for an expected 22% return.

As if that 22% expected return is not steep enough, the capital allotted toward venture investing has even more demands placed upon it. The typical venture investment must return more than that 22% on average, because the economic return to the venture firm itself must be factored in. In a typical 2/20 fund, the firm takes an annual management fee of 2% and also shares in the upside of the investment by taking 20% of the return on investment—an allotment referred to as "carry" in the trade. Venture firms with extraordinary track records can demand carry rates as high as 30%. Taking into account the additional demands on the capital invested in a typical 2/20 fund, then, the actual investments must deliver nearly a 30% return in order for the limited partner to receive the expected 22% rate of return.

It is hardly surprising that the economics of the typical venture fund have a substantial impact on the investment strategy of venture capital firms. Imagine that the venture firm thinks the typical life of its fund will be five years. In order to average a 30% return on investment, $100 invested on day one must within five years yield almost $400. Although many simplifying, and sometimes unrealistic, assumptions have been made here, that is a daunting prospect for many new ventures—the enterprises that must create the actual economic activity that creates the outsized returns that the venture funds need in order to meet the expectations of their investors.

The real-life picture actually is a bit grimmer than the basic numbers relate. After all, many of the investments that are made by the venture firm are not going to pay off anywhere nearly this handsomely. Some will go bust altogether, while others may exceed expectations and deliver substantially more than expected. It is fair to expect that of $100 invested, roughly 40% will return nothing to the venture firm.

One of the great virtues of venture capital is that it is willing to take risks where a significant number of ventures simply will implode. For argument's sake, let us suppose that another 30% return the amount invested and a further 20% do quite well and return three times the amount invested. At that point, $90 of the $100 that was invested has returned a grand total of $90. But remember that the $100 invested has to return a total of $400. That means that the remaining $10 that was invested must return a staggering $310, or 31 times the amount invested!

Tough to Predict

Of course, the venture capitalist cannot tell which of the many opportunities that cross his or her desk will be the one that is a "30 bagger"—in other words, the big payday. By the same turn, it can be nearly as difficult to predict which of the investments will return zero. These uncertainties—and the almost irresistible allure of the 30 bagger—drive the typical venture investor toward a home-run model of investing. Such investors put their money down knowing that the glowing average return they expect from their portfolios likely will stem from a small number of very spectacular successes.

But, matters do not end there: There is more bad news for the typical investor. Not only must the venture firm's partners identify entrepreneurs whose ideas deserve financial backing, but they also must maintain and monitor those investments over time—all the while scouting for new investment opportunities coming around the bend. Let us suppose, hypothetically, that our venture firm with $500 million in committed capital is composed of eight venture partners. That means that over the life of the fund, on average each partner will invest a little more than $60 million.

This may sound like a lot for a single individual to control, and it is. In fact, most venture partners feel they cannot adequately oversee more than about eight portfolio companies at a time. One of the most important things that the venture capitalist brings to the entrepreneur is risk capital, but as the pages of this book make clear, they also bring advice, networks of potential customers, and potential team members or employees. The venture partner also likely will sit on the board of the portfolio company and take a leading role in helping to move the company along its natural growth curve, from start-up, to success, to potential candidate for an

IPO, or—in these more stringent market conditions—to a buyout by a larger, more established corporation or group of investors.

It is difficult to do that effectively while fulfilling the fiduciary responsibilities of oversight and monitoring if a single venture capitalist is responsible for many more than eight portfolio companies. What this means, of course, is that an average venture must enable the partner to put $5 million to $10 million to work over the life of the venture.

Every venture firm differs from every other with respect to each of the elements in this hypothetical example that I have drawn largely from an analysis that my colleague Mark Leslie, the Veritas founder, presented when we taught a venture class together at Stanford University's graduate school of business. The required rate of return, the size of the fund, the number of partners, the target distribution of returns, and so on are drawn from our research and experience. Regardless of the precise numbers, though, the basic structure of the economic argument holds.

The bottom line is that a typical investment must, on average, be quite large and must have the potential for a very large rate of return. A new venture for which a $7.5 million investment returns 30 times its money, where any venture firm may be only one of several in the deal, and where the venture firms collectively may only end up with 50% or 60% ownership of the company, must have the potential to have a very large final valuation indeed. Historically, most of the companies successful enough to achieve such rates of return to the venture investor did so through an IPO. As the IPO market enters an extremely constrained period during the late 2000s, the barriers toward success seem to rise even higher.

Whose Side Are You On Anyway?

Now we are in a position to return to the disappointed aspiring entrepreneur with whom we started this section. In many cases, the entrepreneur emerges extremely disappointed from this initial exposure to the venture marketplace because the basic economics of venture investing were not clearly understood. The business plan might indeed be completely sound and may even be the basis for a perfectly viable new venture, but the potential market may not be big enough or the expected rate of return too difficult to achieve. Fortunately, a mismatch between the size and expected return of the venture and the requirements of the venture capitalist need not spell doom for the nascent venture. A variety of other sources of risk capital are available to fill the gap—with friends, family, and angel investors often being the most likely source.

For the entrepreneur who does obtain venture capital, the fundraising phase is only the first of many sources of possible conflict between the entrepreneur and the venture capitalist. At the heart of the issue is the fact that, while both the entrepreneur and the investor meet their respective goals when things go well, there are many respects in which the parties' incentives are misaligned. These misalignments often cause friction along the way.

For many entrepreneurs, financial success is only one—and often not the most important—source of their passion for their ventures. Their commitment to the idea itself and to seeing it to fruition is often what compels them. For the venture capitalists, on the other hand, as proud as they may be of the successful companies they have helped spawn, their fiduciary responsibility is to their investors and the return that they expect. This difference often manifests itself at inflection points where there is a choice between a low-risk, moderate-return alternative and one that requires "hitting for the fences."

The typical venture investor has every incentive to play long ball, while many entrepreneurs will be happy simply to see their product come to market, even if there is little hope of achieving substantial scale. The venture capitalist may often be more aggressive than the entrepreneur when the venture investor begins to suspect that this particular enterprise is a low-probability, high-return investment. On the other hand, once the venture investor believes that the enterprise likely will never hit it big, the interest in the investment may wane—regardless of whether or not the entrepreneur still believes in the business.

This disparity in perspective is rooted in two concrete aspects of the entrepreneurial opportunity. The first is that a venture investment is usually structured so that the investors hold preferred stock whereas the founders and employees hold only common stock. This means investors get their money back before the founders can. If the outlook for a typical, $30 million investment is such that continued investment is unlikely to return much more than that amount, the investors would typically be motivated to exit as soon as possible, almost regardless of any marginal extra return. They want to sell and get their money back. The entrepreneur, meanwhile, may prefer to keep going in the hopes that this particular venture might yet turn into something big.

The second reason for the difference in perspective is that, as a venture capitalist once told me, venture investors are investing two things: time and money. The concern with the financial investment is obvious. Less obvious, however, is the opportunity cost in terms of time. Because the cost of continuing to invest time in the entrepreneur's venture is the inability to take on another, potentially much more lucrative venture, the venture capitalist often has an incentive to shut down the venture and move on before the entrepreneur is willing to do so.

Success in the venture does not necessarily eliminate this tension between entrepreneur and investor, either. They may also differ in their patience when it comes to the timing and form of an exit for a successful venture. Venture capitalists are more likely to favor IPOs and to favor them sooner than entrepreneurs will. An IPO provides liquidity for the venture firm's limited partners and provides a concrete measure to bolster the return on the current fund. Such concrete data can be useful to have in the bag as they raise subsequent funds.

The entrepreneur may prefer a longer time horizon, both because it may be possible to demonstrate more progress and also because the IPO itself and the public scrutiny that comes with it may be unwelcome distractions from continuing to grow the business. Of course, in the longer run an IPO is a welcome liquidity event for the founders and team as well. As other forms of exit become more common, it is possible that entrepreneurs will more readily welcome those that do not involve greater public scrutiny, as long as the financial returns are commensurate with what had been expected when IPOs were more readily done.

Yet another frequent difference of opinion centers on the ability of the founder to "scale" the firm as it grows. Although many venture capitalists eschew the claim that they often are unwilling to give the founder an opportunity to stay at the helm once the company is big, that is certainly the perception and fear among many venture-backed entrepreneurs. It is interesting to note that many young entrepreneurs who managed to build their companies with little or no reliance on venture funding have indeed managed to scale very well with their companies. Bill Gates, Steve Jobs, Michael Dell, and Larry Ellison are notable examples. Critics wonder whether these successful individuals—among the wealthiest and most successful captains of industry today—would have been given the opportunity with venture capitalists in control of the board room, where a bias for introducing "professional management" is sometimes in evidence.

Conflict may also arise over issues as prosaic as compensation, demands on time, and commitment to the enterprise. Compensation for the founders and the management team, whether in the form of cash, stock, or options, comes out of the investors' hide. And the company wants the full attention of its venture capitalist—admittedly on its own terms—whereas the latter has more to gain by spreading the time and attention across a portfolio of investments.

A Successful, If Uneasy, Marriage

The venture capitalists' business model allows the venture investor to commit capital to only a few of the entrepreneurs who seek backing each year. Moreover, the small number of entrepreneurs who do secure venture funding must navigate a number of inherent misalignments of incentives, even as the venture investors who have provided capital to the enterprise manage the same issues from a sometimes opposite perspective. Nonetheless, the existence of venture capital has proven essential to the formation of numerous companies that are household names and which have contributed products, technologies, and jobs to millions.

In Silicon Valley, we now take for granted the ability of an entrepreneur with nothing more than a germ of an idea to gather together the human capital, financial capital, legal advice, and governance talent to test the proposition that the idea can become a company. Often those ventures amount to nothing, and it is a testament to the resilience of the system that entrepreneurs who fail on their first venture often are as capable, if not more so, of obtaining funding for their next one. This ability for ventures with significant capital requirements to form, dissolve, and arise again, in ever-changing configurations—to fuel economic growth and technological innovation—would be much diminished without the contributions of venture capitalists and the risk-minded entrepreneurs whose backing they receive.

8

PIONEER INVESTING: TAKING VENTURE CAPITAL FROM SILICON VALLEY TO BANGALORE AND BEYOND

William H. Draper III
General Partner
Draper Richards L.P.

AUM: $1 billion

Location: San Francisco, CA

Grew up: Scarsdale, NY

Years in VC: 50

Year born: 1928

Location born: Scarsdale, NY

Best known deals: Apollo Computer, LSI Logic, Hybritech, Skype, AthenaHealth, OpenTable, Activision

Style: Intuitive

Education: B.A., Yale University, Class of 1950
M.B.A., Harvard Graduate School of Business, Class of 1954

Significant experience: Co-founder, Sutter Hill Ventures, President and Chairman of the Export-Import Bank of the United States, Under-Secretary-General, United Nations

Personal interests: Tennis, chess

The lesson: "A venture capitalist is only as good as his/her entrepreneurs."

William H. Draper III helped to pioneer a new age of technology-focused investing. From LSI Logic to Apollo Computer to Activision to Skype, he has invested in companies that became household names in the new Information Age. In doing so, Draper built on and expanded the legacy of his father, William H. Draper, Jr., who founded Draper, Gaither & Anderson, the first venture capital firm on the West Coast.

Late in his career, Draper took his work abroad and set up Draper International, the first U.S. venture fund focused on India. That country's largest Internet portal, Rediff.com, was among Draper's investments. Draper then dispatched an associate to Europe, leading Draper to become the first venture investor in Skype, the internet-based telephone service. Now, even in his 80s, Draper is exploring the latest trend in venture investing, social entrepreneurship, funding the micro-lending site Kiva.org, Room to Read, and dozens of others through the Draper Richards Foundation. His latest work keeps Draper where he likes to be, ahead of the crowd and leading the way.

⌇∞⌇

E very form of investment entails some risk. By definition, venture investors put their money into technologies that have not yet come to fruition, untested business ideas, undeveloped markets, and, often, entrepreneurs with virtually no track record.

While I'm still a strong proponent of higher education, there is a reason why it has become cliché to talk about the bright young person who drops out of Harvard to start what becomes a billion-dollar company. In point of fact, more than a few people from Harvard, Stanford, and a few other schools have done just that. They have succeeded in part because venture investors have been there, willing to put money behind the notion that these young people just might succeed.

Venture capital is by definition a pioneering form of investment. In most other forms of investment, it pays to follow what others have done. The returns are nearly as good, and the risks not nearly as great. In venture investing, it is beneficial to be first because that is where the highest returns are found. Of course, the cutting edge often turns out to be a bleeding edge, a place where success or failure can turn on the smallest of factors.

A Fiery Start

I learned about this knife's edge between success and failure right at the outset of my career in venture capital. In 1967, as the co-founder of the newly formed venture firm Sutter Hill Ventures, I was trying to raise $10 million in investment capital from a Canadian construction and cement company named Genstar Ltd. A friend of mine from college, a fellow Yale University alumnus, had told me that Genstar was looking for a way to get into technology.

We took the president of the company, Angus McNaughton, on a tour of a half dozen of our portfolio companies. One of the entrepreneurs whom we visited in Los Angeles had started a company called Duplicon, and he had developed a new technology that he believed could put Xerox out of business. He had built his first prototype and wanted to show it to us.

The guy was a showman. As if he were putting on some sort of start-up magic act, he asked McNaughton to take a bill out of his wallet. McNaughton took one out, a $100 bill, as he remembers it, and handed it over. With a flourish, our entrepreneur lifted the cover of his machine, slid the bill onto a sheet of glass, and closed the cover. So far, so good. Then he flipped the switch. A motor whirred—and the whole thing burst into flames!

The place went into a panic. Someone grabbed a fire extinguisher and sprayed down everything so the whole building wouldn't burn down.

I thought, "Oh my gosh, not only is his $100 bill burned up but there goes our $10 million."

Luckily, however, McNaughton liked our other innovative investments, and Genstar wound up investing with us anyway. We signed them up for a $10 million commitment, though we only ended up using $6 million. For years, the returns from our firm, Sutter Hill Ventures, filled in the gaps when Genstar's cement, construction, and housing businesses were not doing well. We were a counterweight to their otherwise very cyclical business. McNaughton told me recently that over the years Genstar made more than $700 million in profits on that $6 million. Sutter Hill had an internal rate of return of just about 40% a year for the 16 years that I worked there.

To me, the experience with Genstar and Duplicon is illustrative of what it means to be a venture investor. The work is not predictable.

Something that looks like a disaster is not necessarily so bad—although there are, from time to time, actual disasters that really do hurt your reputation or your earnings statement, and sometimes both. When we do our jobs well, when the entrepreneurs are right about the opportunity they see and we give them the capital and advice they need, we have the chance to be part of something big, part of helping, say, Skype or Activision or Measurex get started.

The work even gets the heart racing from time to time. After all, you don't get to spray a fire extinguisher on a flaming copy machine in just any line of work. The rewards, however, can come in at multiples far beyond what anyone had a right to expect.

The Family Business

My first experience in venture capital was at Draper, Gaither & Anderson, the first venture capital company in the West. The Draper in the group was my father, William H. Draper, Jr. His phase as a venture investor filled the middle chapter in what was a most remarkable career. As a young man, my father worked in Paris after World War II as an assistant to W. Averill Harriman, who was responsible for implementing the Marshall Plan. After that, he moved to California and started his firm.

Fifty years ago, in 1959, when my father founded the firm with Fred Anderson and Rowan Gaither, I joined as a young associate. By this time, I had studied economics at Yale, earned an M.B.A. from Harvard, and worked as an executive at Inland Steel in Chicago. We were helping to pioneer venture investing in the San Francisco area when the land around Palo Alto, Menlo Park, and other communities on the outskirts of Stanford University were still mainly fruit orchards and ranches.

There was no Silicon Valley at this point because, frankly, silicon-based computer chips were just becoming of interest, and the actual term would not be invented for more than a decade. It had only been three years, in fact, since William Shockley left Bell Labs in a dispute over credit for his invention of the transistor. He had shared the 1956 Nobel Prize along with two colleagues, but Shockley felt that he was not adequately compensated for his innovation. Shockley formed his own technology company, Shockley Semiconductor Laboratory, but soon after that watched in dismay as his own top engineers left him. In 1959, the Shockley refugees opened shop in Palo Alto as Fairchild Semiconductor, the company that built the first commercial integrated circuit. This simultaneous birth of venture capital and the semiconductor industry in the Bay Area has had a profound impact on the world in which we live today.

My first venture investment was in a company called Corbin-Farnsworth, the first company in the country to commercialize heart defibrillators. This was a brand-new healthcare device that required regulatory approval, but it was so useful that the approvals did not take long. We had a success on our hands, a big one, and eventually sold the company to Smith, Kline & French.

Of course, a big return by the standards of these early days has no relation to what people came to consider a big return in later years. We were not striving for a billion-dollar success at that time. We just wanted to get a reasonably good piece of a company that was brand new, take a risk by investing in it, and work to make certain that in the end the company earned a decent financial return and delivered a valuable service.

Off on My Own

After three years at my father's firm, I developed an urge to go out on my own. I had kept in touch with a friend from Inland Steel, another young executive named Pitch Johnson, whose father had been the track coach at Stanford. In 1962, when Johnson visited from Chicago for "The Big Game"—the annual gridiron clash between Stanford and U.C. Berkeley—we decided to form our own venture capital company. Semiconductors were really getting big by this point, and one of our first investments was in a firm called Electroglas, which made the first commercially viable gas furnace for manufacturing semiconductors.

When inventing new markets, timing is everything, and Electroglas had perfect timing. What it did not have, though, was a chief executive officer who could handle the company's phenomenal growth. Arthur Lash, the founder, had come out of Fairchild. He was a good engineer who knew how to make diffusion furnaces, but he was no manager. Therefore, we needed a manager.

When a man named Chuck Gravel first approached us during our search for a new CEO for Electroglas, he seemed like the last person who might run a company at the cutting edge of semiconductor manufacturing. He had just left a job as the advertising manager for a boat manufacturer in Minnesota because, odd as it may sound, he had made too much money.

The boat company had been suffering from dismal sales, so here is what Gravel did to remedy the situation: He took the company's entire $25,000 annual marketing budget and invested it in a single full-page ad in *Life* magazine. The ad invited people to sign up as distributors for the company's boats. It was a huge gamble. It also was a huge success. Prospective distributors from all over the country sent in money to buy one or more boats, and sales went through the roof. Now Gravel was rich, so wealthy in fact that he felt uncomfortable living in a small town in Minnesota. He came out west and introduced himself to me.

Gravel didn't know anything about technology, but he was good at selling, and sales were what Electroglas desperately needed. Building a company means a lot more than just having a group of Ph.D.s developing world-class technology and pushing the limits of science. Someone needs to budget. Someone needs to sell. The role of a venture capitalist is to try to put those pieces in place and help build a team that works well together. At the start, the companies are small and people have to wear many hats. Then, as they grow, there is more differentiation. As venture capitalists, we have witnessed this growth curve numerous times, so we can offer some good advice about how to handle the challenges. As it turned out, Chuck Gravel was an executive who could learn from our experience and turn even a technologically complex company such as Electroglas into a success.

The sort of informal approach we used in hiring Chuck Gravel and top managers at some of our other early companies has served us well over the years. One of the best breaks for me was my introduction to Wilf Corrigan, the founder of LSI Logic. I found Corrigan and helped him start LSI in 1981, only because I was in Los Angeles spreading the word about the venture capital business down there. After a speech I made to a business group, Corrigan approached me and said he was getting ready to start a company that would create customized designs for large-scale integration computer chips.

Corrigan had served as vice president at Fairchild, but he left after Schlumberger, the big conglomerate, took over the company. He had considered going into venture capital but decided he was more suited to starting his own company than for finding others in which to invest. Corrigan figured that it was "better to catch the money than to pitch it."

Seeing into the Future

I go through a short mental checklist when I am interviewing someone for a leadership position in a company or considering investing in someone's novel idea. Technological capability and other traditional measures play a small role relative to other considerations. I first want to feel as if I would like to be in business with this person. It's more than just a warm personality. At some level, I look for some marvelous flair, a charisma of some sort, and I look for energy, commitment, and intelligence. I want them to have done the necessary homework so that if I ask a question they have the answer or know quickly how to get it.

This may all seem easy enough, but there is also another dimension in venture investing: seeing into the future. After all, a business in which we invest is going to change dramatically from day one to maturity. Ideally, we select someone who can take it all that way. When his or her ideas either succeed or fail, I want to have an idea of how that entrepreneur might react. It is all about the future, of course, because we are trying to build something. We are trying to build a company that wasn't there before, often with technology that has not come into wide use.

Even if this sounds like a simple formula, it is not. It is the sort of sense a person develops over many years. It took me that long, anyway. Experiences become lessons, lessons become practices, and practices help us succeed or fail. Of course, I had figured out very little of this by the time Pitch Johnson and I set out on our own in 1962. We had no idea then that four decades later we would still be looking for the next new thing. We were not just pioneering technology, we were pioneering an industry, and we were trying to develop the experiences, lessons, and practices that would make us successful.

Searching the Orchards

At the start, Pitch and I were just a couple of guys trying to make our way. We needed to actively pursue potential deals, so we rented a pair of matching Pontiacs and drove through the orchards around Palo Alto, looking for signs that indicated someone was tinkering with silicon or electronics instead of raising flowers or fruit. We would introduce ourselves and explain that we were involved in venture capital. With little prompting, they would take half a day to tell us all about their business.

We participated in what became standard practices as we went along. For example, it became common for venture capital firms to collaborate on deals in pairs or groups of three. It was a way to share risk, and at the outset it was also a way to spread our relatively small pools of money into a larger number of deals.

It wasn't long before Pitch and I were talking to Sutter Hill, a real estate firm that was interested in getting involved in venture capital. They had money. We knew the venture capital business. Together, we had the makings of a good fit. We joked that we could really benefit from a fax machine and a receptionist, which they had. We had a deal.

For some time, Pitch had been talking about leaving the venture business so that he could learn what it was like to actually operate a start-up company. When Sutter Hill came along, their investment marked the right time for us to part ways. Pitch went off on his own, did some consulting work, and then fairly quickly wound up back in venture investing, putting his own money to work and making some great investments.

From Inventor to Manager

By that point I was quite familiar with what sort of person made a good venture capitalist. I also had developed a sense of how entrepreneurs were able to grow into new roles as they matured as executives and the markets developed around them. William Poduska was one of those people whom I saw grow into an impressive executive. When we funded Prime Computer at its outset in 1972, it was impossible not to be impressed by Poduska, the technology brains behind the minicomputer company. Prime was a big success. It came to dominate the markets for minicomputers and computer-aided design. Nearly a decade after our first investment in Prime Computer, I was visiting the company's headquarters outside Boston when Poduska sat beside me in the lobby and seemed to have something he wanted to say. We went to the parking lot, and I asked Poduska what was on his mind.

"You know, as a matter of fact, I've been thinking of starting a company," he said.

"Well, you know, I am in the VC business," I said with a chuckle.

Poduska was vice president of engineering at Prime, a position he had held since the company's founding, but he felt ready to jump to the next level. Within a week of our conversation in the Boston parking lot, Poduska was on an airplane with a proposal for a new company called Apollo Computer. He wanted to build graphics-intensive workstations. We agreed to fund Poduska—a $5 million start-up investment—over lunch at the Palo Alto Club, which Bill Hewlett and David Packard had started. I called Peter Crisp at the Rockefeller Brothers Venture Fund and told him I needed someone on the East Coast, closer to our new computer company, to invest with me. It took little more than that phone call to bring the Rockefeller money in and, in short order, close the deal.

The company flourished. From 1980 to 1987, it was the leading manufacturer of network workstations, and we ultimately sold it to Hewlett-Packard.

The Ones That Got Away

It was a period of big ideas and momentous change. I learned from experience that it was essential to be quick footed, connected, and on top of the latest technological changes in order to succeed. In 1981, we were invited to take a look at an early funding round for Microsoft, for example. Bill Gates wanted a $2 million investment in the company. I was ready to back Gates. He was brilliant. He was young. He was cocky. Steve Ballmer, who had dropped out of Stanford Business School to help Gates start Microsoft, was already with Gates.

There was only one hurdle in our way. At Stanford, Ballmer had roomed with a man named David Marquardt, who had become a venture capitalist and who is still very successful today. We had the feeling that Marquardt would have the inside track to fund Microsoft, and we were right. He became the sole venture investor in Microsoft.

Another big one—Apple Computer—simply got away. I had hired Len Baker, a brilliant math major out of Yale, and I wanted to give him a little experience. That's when Peter Crisp, of the Rockefeller firm, called in early 1978 to inform me about a company called Apple Computer down in Cupertino. Peter was in for $2 million. The well-known venture investor Arthur Rock was in for $1 million, and there was $1 million open for Sutter Hill.

I sent Baker down to take a look. Baker came back, and he said, "Well, the guys kept me waiting for 30 minutes, they wrote code during the whole meeting, and they had an arrogant attitude. The valuation is high, too—around $18 million for the whole company. I think we ought to turn it down."

I agreed. That decision ended up being my mistake, not Baker's. First, I should not have sent someone brand new in the business by himself for such a potentially important investment. Second, I knew the Rockefellers well. Peter Crisp never would have suggested something that was not of the highest quality.

Recognizing Genius

The face of genius changes all the time. The next great innovator or the next great venture opportunity can be virtually unrecognizable, particularly in new industries or with new technologies for which nobody has yet set a pattern for success. Activision became one of our better deals, but when the founders first came to me with their idea of breaking out of Atari and starting the first independent computer game design shop,· I was skeptical.

After hearing their proposal I said, "Fine, but what do you see yourselves doing in ten years?"

David Crane, Larry Kaplan, Alan Miller, and Bob Whitehead had only one thing on their minds. One by one, they essentially said the same thing. All they wanted to do was design computer games—not just right then, but for years and years. I couldn't help but admire their passion, but it was immediately obvious that if we were to back this group of men they would need a president who could actually run the business. Eventually we found the right guy: Jim Levy, who had a background in the music industry.

It was difficult for me to visualize how computer-game design could become a business. Up until that time, the most successful games were built for arcades, and they were pretty basic. Pong, designed by Atari, was the best seller. It was simple and black and white, and it had the most basic graphics imaginable. A small ping-pong-like ball bounced back and forth across the screen as the players batted at it by manipulating Atari joysticks. I told them I wasn't yet certain if this company would be a good investment, and I asked them for some reassurance.

"Do you play bridge?" Kaplan asked.

"Yes, I do," I responded.

Kaplan then handed me a cassette tape and told me to take it home and give it a try. At home I put that tape into a Radio Shack computer my wife had bought me, and the screen lit up. It had black clubs and spades and red diamonds and hearts, arranged into fan-shaped display, almost as if I were holding them in my hand. It played a decent game of bridge, too. I thought, "This is neat." I went back to the office and made the deal the next day.

An Expensive Missed Exit

Levy and his team envisioned a time in which successful game designers could become well known for their talents. Just as people might choose to see a movie by a certain director, they might buy a game because of its designer. They wanted to give credit and promote their designers. They began introducing the designers to game players with a one-page profile in the instruction manuals. One of their first big games, Pitfall, became the first game that was big enough to have a platform designed around it, and a few of their games became popular enough that stand-alone arcade games were built for them.

Activision went public in 1983. By this point, I was in Washington, D.C., working as chairman of the Export-Import Bank, yet I was still on the advisory board at the Stanford Business School. At one of the Stanford meetings, I was approached by the president of General Mills. They owned Parker Brothers, which had Monopoly and other board games, and they were interested in Activision. Soon after, I had lunch with Jim Levy and told him General Mills was interested in a deal.

Activision had a market value of about $500 million at the time, but it was still growing, and Jim thought it would be worth more. "I want to sell it when we can get $1 billion," he said.

As it turned out, the stock didn't stay at the levels it was at when General Mills made its approach. We should have done that deal. Something about Jim's response prompted me to sell my stock, though, and when the prices started going down, I was glad I did. This was an important lesson in one of the basic tenets of venture capital: Knowing when to exit an investment.

From Venture Capital to the Nation's Capital

The job at the Export-Import Bank marked the beginning of more than a decade of public service and also the end of my most active period of venture investing. Given my background, Washington made sense for me. I was profoundly affected by the important work that my father had done for the U.S. Government. In the diplomatic and military roles that he played, the consequences of his work were often bigger than the impact of venture capital might have been. For example, when President Harry Truman's Secretary of the Treasury, Henry Morgenthau, Jr., wanted to convert Germany to an agrarian state after World War II, his stand was politically popular because of memories of German industrial might during the war. My father, however, led the fight to resist the idea. It was the right thing to do, and the push to rebuild German industry helped create one of the world's most stable and successful democracies and one of our country's best allies.

I learned a lot from my father. He always associated himself with good people, and he believed strongly in the value of integrity and good ethics. After a family vacation to Canada, we were on our way home and had driven about 150 miles away from our hotel when my mother happened to mention that she had taken an ashtray that she and my father had admired in their room.

"What do you mean you took it?" he asked.

She explained that it had the hotel's name on it. "This is good advertising. I am sure they wouldn't mind," she said.

My dad turned the car around and drove the 150 miles back to the hotel. My mother was embarrassed, of course, and also angrier than

I had ever seen her before. It was a great ethical message for me though and because the hotel ultimately sold us that ashtray, it was one I remembered every time I saw the ashtray sitting in the living room of our home.

Dad believed in public service. After his years in Europe and in venture capital, he went on to dedicate himself to population control and established the Population Crisis Committee. I have always appreciated the value of public service, too. After graduating from Yale in 1950, I went to Korea as an infantryman. I was in the 25th Division and fought in the Iron Triangle. Living in a foxhole that winter was the coldest I have ever been in my life.

Years later, I was honored when I received word that President Reagan wanted me to move from San Francisco to Washington in 1981 to take charge at the Export-Import Bank. When Reagan took office, he wanted to close down everything that could be handled by private industry and eliminate subsidies as much as possible. They put me in charge of the Export-Import Bank because they knew that I would have a business point of view and would do all that I could to make it cost effective. There were rumors that I was sent in to shut it down, but that was never the case.

As I got to know the people and the institution at the Export-Import Bank, I learned that the place was running pretty well. I could do the most good, I thought, by focusing on problems that would benefit from my business background. For example, prior to my taking office, British entrepreneur Freddie Laker had borrowed many millions from the Export-Import Bank to buy five airplanes to set up Skytrain, the first low-cost trans-Atlantic airline service. I was skeptical about whether he would be able to pay us back. Laker was buying his airplanes in dollars, but he was earning half of his revenue in British pounds.

"If the pound drops in value, you are going to go bankrupt," I told him on one occasion when he visited my office.

"Bill, you just don't understand the airline business," Laker said. "The important thing is just to fill those seats with more bloody arses!"

When the dollar appreciated, he did get squeezed. He also faced increased competition from British Airways, and the combination of these two factors forced him into bankruptcy. We wound up seizing and selling the airplanes, but Laker still owed us interest on his loan.

At the time, the British government was in the process of privatizing British Airways, and British Airways was planning to pay Freddie Laker $8 million so he would not sue for unfair competition. About this time, Colin Marshall, the CEO of British Airways, came to my office and asked me to sign a statement that released British Airways and Laker's airline from any claim that the Export-Import Bank might have.

"Wait a minute, Laker has common stock and you are planning to pay him $8 million?" I said. "Our loan has priority, and so we should be paid our full interest before he receives any payment."

Marshall refused. Then, about two weeks later, he was back in my office, offering to split the difference. I refused. Margaret Thatcher, Britain's Prime Minister, came to Washington and everywhere she went she complained that the Export-Import Bank was preventing British Airways from going public.

I began to hear the same thing from people at every department that she visited: "God, Draper, get that damn thing signed."

Eventually, Marshall did agree to pay the interest in full, and my holdout seemed to impress the Reagan team.

"You know, I really laughed today," said one of Reagan's aides during a visit to my office. "One of the bureaucrats said that Draper treats the Export-Import money like it is his own." He thought that was the greatest compliment that I could receive, and I did, too.

Big Money Comes to the Valley

After spending five years in Washington at the Export-Import Bank, I transitioned to a new role as head of the United Nations Development Program in New York. That work, organizing projects for developing countries with money contributed by wealthy member countries of the United Nations, gave me fresh perspective on conditions—and opportunities—in the developing world. For me, personally, the UNDP set a stage for the next important chapter in my venture life: my effort to start a new investment fund focused exclusively on opportunities in India.

As I started to look beyond the UNDP, I realized that the world of venture capital had changed considerably in the 12 years that I had been gone. The funds were much larger, the risks were more treacherous, and, because of that, business practices were considerably different. In 1979, a couple of years before I had left for Washington, I had gotten a glimpse of the changes ahead when John Weinberg, eventual co-chair of Goldman Sachs, visited my office.

There I was, sitting in my little office at Sutter Hill, entertaining a Wall Street big shot. I said to myself, "Something is happening around here." I certainly had heard of Goldman Sachs. The mystery was how they had ever heard of us.

The Goldman guys came to visit because they were prospecting, and they wanted to get acquainted with us venture capitalists so they could get the lead position for the next big initial public stock offering. We had taken Apollo Computer public and another firm, Measurex, which made control equipment for the paper industry. Until the IPOs started, we did not give much thought to our exit strategy. Our mindset at the time was to build great companies. Going public was not an exit; it was just another step along the way to building a great company.

There were just a handful of top notch venture firms back then. Kleiner Perkins was good. Mayfield and NEA were good. IVP was good, too. We shared deals with all of them. We were in a small familiar group and cooperated with one another, and life was great back then.

More than a decade later, in 1994, as I looked into leaving the UN and returning to San Francisco, I realized the money that had come into the business had changed the nature of the work and the rewards it created. Many firms kept their eye on the ball, but there were some that bid up the prices on deals, which inevitably brought returns down for everybody. Instead of worrying about their carry—in other words, their share of profits—and fretting about the increase in value of their portfolio, some venture capitalists were more concerned about their fees, or the amount of money that they charged based on the funds under management. The rise of the megafunds and the Wall Street transaction mentality inevitably increased the competitive pressure on everyone.

The advent of the big money era even changed the way venture capitalists dealt with each other. In his autobiography, Tom Perkins credited me with bringing Kleiner Perkins its first big success, Qume. I introduced him to Qume, one of Sutter Hill's investments, which created a replacement for the IBM "golf-ball" typewriter. It was a daisy-wheel printer, and it was a big hit. Perkins also brought Sutter Hill a number of good investments after that. This relationship is an example of the cooperation between firms that strengthened Silicon Valley in those days.

Today, some three decades later, the pressures are completely different. The big firms are raising giant funds, $1 billion and more, and with that much to deploy the last thing they want to do is share deals. I think that is unfortunate because cooperation brings more talent to the table and often better decisions are made.

Venturing Abroad

During my time at the UN, I traveled to 101 developing countries, an experience that made me wonder if it might be possible to export some of our techniques to countries where new investments could result in astounding change. This would be a new kind of pioneering, this time with an international dimension and an economic development purpose.

While I was mulling this idea, a friend named Bill McGlashan introduced me to Robin Richards, then a graduate student at Stanford. Richards had lived abroad and had worked with a vice president of Coca Cola on some venture capital projects. We decided to try venture capital abroad. Richards and I looked at China, Indonesia, Vietnam, and Hong Kong, but ultimately we decided that India made the most sense. Indian business people spoke English, which was helpful, and the rule of law was well established, a democracy was in place. Besides, we liked the food.

To start Draper International, in 1995 Robin and I put together an India fund, and we knew that we needed local expertise in order to succeed. The legal work alone that was necessary to found Draper International told us that. The partnership agreement was inches thick, and we had to initial every page. I had met Manmohan Singh, then the Finance Minister and now Prime Minister, through my work at the UN, so we had good connections right from the start. Through referrals, we heard about a young man named Kiran Nadkarni, who had run the venture fund of a quasi-government bank, ICICI, and he seemed like the local talent we might need.

Hiring from the Hospital

We flew Nadkarni to New York, but while attempting to catch a cab at Kennedy Airport he stepped off of a curb and broke his ankle. The bone literally was sticking through his skin, but he came to the Yale Club anyway to meet me. I called an ambulance and rode to Bellevue Hospital with him. After we arrived, Nadkarni was shuffled off to one side, and he was lying on his back on a gurney, waiting for treatment. Keeping Nadkarni company in the hall, I began speaking about our idea for an Indian venture fund, and we agreed on the details of his partnership compensation right there, before he was wheeled into surgery. The poor fellow probably would have agreed to anything at that point.

Odd as that hiring experience was, it worked out very well. Nadkarni had all the connections that we needed. After setting up shop in Bangalore, he quickly began generating deals. He introduced us to Rediff.com, an Internet portal similar to Yahoo; Geometric Software, a computer-aided design firm; Neta, a firm that manages Internet commerce; and Yantra, which markets software for value chain management. We hired another partner, a marketing professional by the name of Abhay Havaldar, who had worked at HCL HP, a joint venture of Hewlett-Packard and the Indian technology company HCL. Once Draper International got started, Robin and I flew to India four times a year for several weeks at a time. We probably made about 25 trips in total over six years.

Draper International worked out well over all. We invested in 20 companies and exited most of them through acquisitions by U.S.-based companies. By the time the Indian technology market collapsed in 2000, we had exited from most of our investments and returned 16 times our partners' money. It was a fabulous experience.

The Skype Encounter

At this point, the India adventure was behind me, but the world of venture investing was not. I saw a new opportunity coming when I met a young man named Howard Hartenbaum. His proposed company was not of particular interest to me, but Howard definitely was. He was an MIT graduate and had run a company for his brother. He listened carefully and followed up diligently. I felt that he would make a natural venture capital investor. He wanted to travel around Europe looking for deals, and that sounded good to me. India had worked well for me, so I thought why not Europe?

Soon after Hartenbaum had moved to Luxembourg, my son Tim, who has followed me into the venture business, told him to look up a company called Kazaa. Similar to Napster, Kazaa had developed file sharing software used to swap music files. Also like Napster, Kazaa was being hounded and sued by music companies and other copyright holders.

By the time Hartenbaum caught up with Kazaa, its founders—a 39-year-old Swede named Niklas Zennström and a 29-year-old Dane named Janus Friis—had moved onto something new: Internet telephony. Their new company, Skype, was still in the idea phase, but it promised to be an amazing breakthrough. It would use voice-over-Internet technology to enable people to talk over the Web for free. Zennström had an almost messianic belief that big monopolies, such as telephone companies, need to be attacked because they are inefficient, take their customers for granted, and have little incentive to bring new technology to market. Zennström and Friis epitomize what it means to be a disruptive innovator.

It was 2002, I was 74 years old, and I have to admit that it was a thrill to be pioneering a new kind of telephony with technology in Estonia driven by a Dane overseen by a Swede in a company based in London—and discovering it before my son or any other venture investor, to boot. Zennström and Friis had no business plan for Skype, so Howard offered to give them a hand. They knew the name Draper, from our reputation in Silicon Valley, I guess, and wanted us to invest. I put $100,000 of seed money into the company. Later, Tim's firm, Draper Fisher Jurvetson, invested several million.

Within 18 months, Skype had 40 million users. They started charging for calls that went to or from standard telephones. By 2005, with 53 million users and still growing, they were acquired by eBay for $2.6 billion. This made Skype the biggest hit I ever had, a return of 1,000 times my initial investment. The last time I checked, Skype had about 450 million users.

For-Profit to Nonprofit

This could have been a good time to pack it in and call it a career. I have to say there was some temptation to do that. Then, again, my father was into his 70s when he started up the Population Crisis Committee. The fact that, after a long and successful career, he devoted his time to a nonprofit organization was something that I strongly admired and wanted to emulate.

Inspired by my dad's example, I decided to diverge slightly from the path he had set by taking up one of the newest forms of venture investing: social entrepreneurship. Robin Richards and I formed the Draper Richards Foundation, which provides early-stage grants of $300,000 over three years to entrepreneurs with original ideas that might help make the world a better place.

Some people say social entrepreneurship is not actually that new. After all, John D. Rockefeller III coined the term "venture philanthropy" in the 1960s. But what we are doing is not philanthropy in the traditional sense. We don't just hand money over to people and hope that they spend it wisely. We refer to our grantees as "fellows" and treat them as we do any entrepreneur whom we back.

One grantee, Little Kids Rock, teaches city kids to play instruments and write music after school. Room to Read builds school libraries and schools in Africa and Southeast Asia, and Girls for a Change helps young girls take on problems in their communities. They all have common traits: an entrepreneurial-minded founder, a concept that can grow to a large scale, and a need for our money.

We have our own objectives; for example, we do not want to become just another source of funding for any of these ventures. We want to be the initial source that helps these entrepreneurs set their ideas into motion. We want to help them get started with coaching and contacts just as we do in the venture capital world. After three years, they are on their own, and they know that from the start.

One of the rewards of this work is the way we can make a difference in society while still drawing on the years of experience Robin and I have accumulated. One of my favorites is a nonprofit named Kiva, a micro-lender that uses the Internet to let individuals make contributions as small as $25 to tiny businesses anywhere in the world. Users can go on the site, literally shop for a business that appeals to them in Kenya or Ecuador or Tajikistan, and click to make a micro-loan.

With Kiva, Matt Flannery; his wife, Jessica; and Premal Shaw were quite consciously copying the ideas of Nobel Peace Prize winner Muhammad Yunus, the founder of Grameen Bank. Grameen was the first in the world to bring micro lending to huge scale, through its lending in its home country of Bangladesh. By taking this lending system to the Internet, though, Kiva has eliminated geography as a barrier to participation, both for the lenders and for the borrowers. It's an inspiring story, and one that benefited, I think, from our approach to social entrepreneurship.

We have treated Kiva, and all our grantees, just as if they were start-up businesses. For the three years that they are grantees we help them organize the board, secure new funding, find business partners, fine-tune their business strategy, and do whatever else is needed. I hired Jenny Shilling Stein and Anne Marie Burgoyne to run the foundation, and they have worked tirelessly to help the founders of Kiva and Room to Read and our other fellows achieve success. They have selected those fellows very well.

Looking back, I am thankful to have had such a rich and diverse set of experiences, especially those in venture capital. Society would not be as advanced, interconnected, and civilized as it is today were it not for the scores of talented venture capitalists who provided the platform for brilliant and passionate entrepreneurs to develop and nurture their world-changing ideas and innovative technologies. At a time when the world needs an inventive new form of investment, social entrepreneurship has come along. There is no end to invention, and I am fortunate to have seen so much of it in a lengthy and rewarding career.

LESSONS FROM BILL DRAPER

◈ **Be first.** The first to market is where the biggest returns are found. The view from the front is always the best.

◈ **Spread the risk.** Unfortunately, the majority of investments are often not successful, but if one spreads risk over a score of promising companies then the returns from the one winner can pay for all the rest. It's almost impossible to pick the big winner right from the start.

◈ **Team over technology.** The selection of a stellar team trumps the novelty of the technology, market conditions, and timing. Although technology is important, the hard work, optimism, vision, and luck of the entrepreneur—and the team—are the heart and soul of success.

◈ **Feed the winners.** Too often, promising companies get starved for attention and capital because venture investors spend too much time, money, and energy on futile attempts to save weak ones.

◈ **Think 10 years out.** A start-up will transform as it matures. Pick people and ideas that can survive through changes in markets, technology, and economic conditions. Envision the future.

9

CHANGE FOR THE BETTER: MANAGING FOR PROFIT AS MARKETS AND TECHNOLOGY CHANGE

C. Richard Kramlich
Co-Founder
New Enterprise Associates

AUM: $11 billion   **Years in PE:** 35+

Location: Menlo Park, CA   **Year born:** 1935

Grew up: Oshkosh, Appleton, and Milwaukee, Wisconsin

Location born: Green Bay, Wisconsin

Best known deals: 3Com, Juniper Networks, Silicon Graphics International, Healtheon/WebMD, Semiconductor Manufacturing International, Immunex (Amgen), Macromedia (Adobe), Dallas Semiconductor (Maxim), Ascend Communications (Alcatel-Lucent)

Style: Open, constructive

Education: B.S., Northwestern University, Class of 1957
M.B.A., Harvard Graduate School of Business, Class of 1960

Significant experience: General partner of Arthur Rock & Associates, the firm that funded Intel in 1968

Personal interests: Collector of media art, travel, tennis

The lesson: "There is an 80% chance you can solve a problem."

When C. Richard Kramlich co-founded New Enterprise Associates in 1978, he left a firm that was founded by Arthur Rock, the person credited with inventing the term "venture capital." A strong, consistent track record has enabled Kramlich to build a megafund that takes advantage of its size to bring outsized returns to investors.

Market conditions and technologies have gone through wrenching changes, but Kramlich's approach has remained consistent. He identifies top talent, systematically dissects entire market sectors in a search for opportunity, and remains open minded about adjusting his approach as market conditions change. Now spending half his time in China, on the other side of the planet from his Menlo Park, California home base, Kramlich is exploring new markets and bringing NEA's methods to one of the world's most dynamic economies.

⟨✖⟩

In June of 2006, we had invested $13 million in a Chinese company named Availink that had the opportunity to dominate the Chinese market for satellite-based, wireless communication. All they needed was a successful satellite launch.

On the vital day, I learned that satellite launches have three phases. There was the launch itself, which went great. Getting into orbit went great. Finally, solar panels have to open: did not go great.

One moment, we had a satellite in low-Earth orbit. The next, it was space junk.

It was immediately clear that our company's plan to put a Chinese-made satellite at the heart of a system to run WiFi, broadband, and other computer communications systems would not work out. Nobody panicked, though. Immediately, the company shifted gears. Chip making and software, two businesses that were much discussed but not really activated yet, suddenly became the future of Availink.

The longest lasting impact of the satellite mishap was that management immediately shifted gears, made chip making and software services the center of the business, and showed a resolve that even more seasoned professionals might not have mustered. Even as management refocused strategy, the company continued to push ahead with satellites, too, locating an international satellite to receive and transmit signals. The quick strategic switch, and cool handling of the crisis, earned the technologist who was serving as interim chief executive a permanent appointment to that job. Today, Availink dominates the market for communications chip sets in China, is moving into developing markets, and is even penetrating Europe.

Change is a constant, but just because we must deal with change all the time does not make it any easier to handle. Some changes can be anticipated and planned for. Others are as surprising as a satellite that becomes space junk. How one manages change can mean the difference between success and failure. For NEA, our ability to anticipate, manage, respond to, and capitalize on change has been an essential ingredient of our ability to grow into a firm that over our 32-year life span has helped 165 companies make initial stock sales, invested in 250 that were acquired, and currently has $11 billion in aggregate cash and commitments. I personally have taken eight companies from start-up to $1 billion or more in value.

Just as my own life and career have never stopped changing, the same goes for the type of companies we have invested in. At NEA, we spend considerable time managing change. For example, we draw up complex diagrams of industries to map where breakthroughs are needed and how new investment might pay off. This helps us create a key competitive advantage by seeing, before others do, where high-impact innovation might take place. This ability to quickly and aggressively deploy our investors' capital has become particularly essential as our firm has grown into what some people call a "mega" venture firm. The last investment fund we raised topped $2.5 billion—a difficult amount to invest if you don't start with a clear-cut plan.

Similarly, over the years, I have learned that some people are just naturally agents of change, as if they are born with a special talent that makes them that way. They see the opportunities change creates and embrace the need to shoulder risk. They can infect those around them with an appetite for invention. Jim Clark comes to mind. A man with a brilliant and restless mind, Clark is a serial entrepreneur of staggering success. He has helped form several iconic Silicon Valley companies: Silicon Graphics International, then Netscape, then Healtheon. Our experience in working with people such as Jim has shown us that there are certain unique individuals who create opportunity wherever they go, in part because they learn to make the most of change. Back a person like that, and change can become a good friend, indeed.

A Fortuitous Family Meeting

From the very founding of our firm, the willingness of people to embrace and even exploit change has been central to our success. We never suspected at the start, back in 1978, that NEA would become one of Silicon Valley's most successful firms and wind up funding more than 650 start-up companies. After all, our origins were as humble as can be. The first major fundraising breakthrough came in the most unlikely and bucolic of places: at the Muncie, Ind. offices of Ball Corporation, the company that makes the iconic glass jars. At a Sunday morning meeting there, on the day after Magic Johnson's Michigan State team beat Larry Bird's Indiana State squad in one of the great championship games in college basketball history, a man named John Fisher, who was then chief executive officer of the company, gave up an hour of time before Sunday church to listen to our investment pitch.

It would have been a memorable trip even if our fundraising efforts had not immediately paid off. The weather was –15 degrees. There was a coal strike in Muncie, and the power plant was operating at low capacity. To save power, the Holiday Inn I stayed at allowed only one light bulb per room. The television in the bar was the only one that worked.

My two co-founders and I visited Fisher, his lawyers, accountants, and members of the Ball family early that Sunday morning. We told him that the three descendants of founders Frank and Edmund Ball had expressed an interest in this new investment idea called venture capital, but Fisher was trustee for some of the family money so they needed his permission to proceed. He said he was skeptical about the risks involved in venture investing, but he met with us and heard us out. He warned us, though, that nothing would make him late for the 11 A.M. church service.

Fisher opened the meeting by addressing the Ball heirs, accountants, and lawyers gathered in the room: "You all want to give a million dollars to these guys, right?"

I spoke up and told him that was the idea.

He said to the room, "If you have that kind of money to throw around, you ought to buy some more company stock."

Ball was indeed a good investment, I told Fisher, but so was our proposal. I began explaining venture capital to him.

"I read the material. You don't have to tell me anything," Fisher said. "You are going to form a blind pool, is that right?"

"Yes."

"That means you don't know what you are going to invest in, is that correct?"

"Yes," again.

"You are telling me that this may be illiquid for as long as 12 years, and you are not going to promise any rates of return. Is that correct?"

"Yes, sir. That is correct."

"Well what are you going to do?" he asked.

We didn't have many specifics. "I have had some experience in this, and my colleagues have some experience," I stammered. "And we are going to do the best job we can."

Fisher spoke to the room again: "Well, I still don't think you ought to do this," he told the Ball heirs and advisors. "But if you want to, it's okay with me. We've got to get going because church starts in 10 minutes."

That was our first limited-partner investment. And now, 30 years and 13 investment funds later, the Ball family is still with us. Barbara Goodbody, a Ball heir I had met while ushering at the wedding of a mutual friend, was at that first meeting, and she remains an investor today.

The Venture Capital Mindset

Fisher's skepticism and, despite that, his willingness to take the risk represented the essence of the venture capital mindset. Venture investors must be savvy risk takers, able to adapt to changing markets while helping to nurture creative ideas that might become huge successes. They know that sometimes they will fail completely. Fortunately for me, I was coming into my own in the business world at just the time when economics and tax codes were changing in ways that encouraged people such as me to take investment risks.

During the Carter administration, tax rates had risen to the point that taxation was a disincentive to investment. But, beginning in the late 1970s, a series of favorable changes occurred. The capital gains tax was cut from 50% to 35%. In early 1979, venture capitalists in Silicon Valley such as Bill Draper and Pitch Johnson helped persuade the U.S. Labor Department to change policies that had prevented pension funds from investing in alternative assets such as venture capital. Then, during the early 1980s, the chairman of the Federal Reserve, Paul Volcker, would go to war against interest rates, which had risen to nearly 20% at one point. The attendant reduction in the cost of capital encouraged investment throughout the economy.

My partners and I formed NEA just as all these changes were taking place. Frank Bonsal, Chuck Newhall, and I launched NEA soon after I had ended a seven-year association with Arthur Rock & Associates, a firm formed by the man credited with inventing the term "venture capital." In 1957, Rock had funded Fairchild Semiconductor, a breakthrough success that really was the cornerstone of the Silicon Valley tech revolution. Rock made a visionary investment in Scientific Data Systems, and I had just joined Rock in 1969 when he further burnished his legend by making a mere 15 phone calls in one afternoon to raise the $2.5 million needed to get Intel started.

I had graduated from Harvard Graduate School of Business and worked for a few years in finance at the Kroger grocery chain headquarters in Cincinnati before moving to Boston to work with some fine people in investment counseling and to learn the rudiments of venture capital. From there I moved to San Francisco to join Arthur Rock as a partner. I was with Rock during some dark days for investments. The capital markets were not quite as seized up as they got after the collapse of Lehman Brothers in late 2008, but they were as bad as anyone at that time could remember. I learned how to survive when there are no capital markets at work. You use a great deal of energy and imagination. Even then, we had to move slowly. Though we raised a $10 million fund, we never invested more than $6.25 million of it over the fund's seven-year life span.

On the Move

One time, out of nowhere, during these early years, Rock asked me, "Dick, have you ever been to Japan?"

I said no.

He said, "Why don't you go over there and raise some money for us?"

We had 13 companies in our portfolio then, and six were running out of money at the same time. So I went to Japan and did seven deals for six companies. One of them was Xynetics, a company that made precision cutting equipment that could be used both in cutting textiles and in positioning systems for electronics. It went from a start-up to a $50 million company over time. We eventually made money for ourselves and our Japanese partner on every one of those six investments.

Rock and I were talking about raising a second fund when Chuck Newhall swung out to the west coast and looked me up. He was with T. Rowe Price on the East Coast. Along with Frank Bonsal, who was a partner at Alex Brown & Sons in Baltimore at the time, Newhall had decided to start a venture firm. Over a series of dinners the three of us decided to form our own partnership.

The other two assumed, of course, that I would go back east, but I wanted to stay in California. Newhall and Bonsal eventually agreed to this arrangement, so right from the outset we were the first of a kind: A venture capital firm with offices on both coasts. T. Rowe Price had committed $1 million, and a firm that was running money for the John Deere family had committed, too. There was that money from the Ball family. Eventually, the commitments topped $16 million, which seemed like good money given the dire circumstances in the markets.

Thanks to the changes in taxes and the change in rules for pension investing that occurred just as we were opening shop, we went from having a very bleak outlook to having a rosy one. Even so, we had plenty of challenges at hand. We had to figure out how to make decisions within a small firm when the principals were working in offices on either coast of the United States. We had no e-mail or teleconferencing in those days, so the 3,000-mile distance felt greater than it would today. Communication and decision making were both huge hurdles that we had to overcome.

We decided that, rather than jumping into a batch of start-ups and other companies we did not know, we would start by investing in second- and third-round fundings for companies already familiar to us. We just wanted a mix of companies, not all of which were strangers. Because some were concentrated heavily in the San Francisco Bay area, I joined the boards of many of them. Newhall and Bonsal did their share in the East, also. The strategy worked. We were able to return our investors' capital within about three years at a substantial profit.

We have come a long way since then. Today, we are investing our 13th fund. We have raised, in aggregate, more than $11 billion. In addition to our offices on the east and west coasts, we also have offices in China and India. We are trying to elevate best practices wherever we go. Change is something we embrace, but we have tried to make sure that certain principles of our business do not change even as we have grown. In other words, we have tried to scale the business while keeping the art form in it. We have always maintained a democracy among the partners, wherein we all have the same draw from the firm's fees and the same participation in the carried interest, or investment profits, from our funds.

The 100-Year Firm

At the outset, Newhall said he wanted our firm to last 100 years. This felt at the time like a terrible burden for us to bear, but now we are more than 30 years into it, and the burden doesn't feel quite as heavy any more. We have a budget at the firm, from which we pay all our general partners the same amount. All over Silicon Valley, you hear about venture capital partners earning extravagant salaries. That does not happen at NEA. We don't let that happen, because it misaligns our objectives from those of our investors.

When a firm pays its partners too much, it might take 12 years to pay back the limited partners, rather than the eight years it takes when we keep our compensation in line. At NEA, we make money only after our limited partners make money. We don't spend much, either. Our firm's expenses each year run at about 1% of funds under management, and we keep our partners on board by vesting over 12 years, a longer time period than most other venture capital firms.

The secret to lasting one year, not to mention 100, is to be exceptionally adept at handling change. We have built this capability by splitting our partners into industry teams, according to different matrices of expertise. We operate the firm in many different vectors—electronics, life sciences, energy technology, and so on—and in each of those areas we try to have at least one "venture partner" to bring subject-matter knowledge to our work. The venture partners are our secret weapon: veteran professionals with deep expertise in their chosen fields.

We have a Nobel laureate and the former dean of the Duke University Medical School who used to run research at Genentech. They can really make a difference both in making investment decisions and in helping our portfolio companies through the tough technical challenges that always arise with new technology.

The 10 P.M. Phone Call

We might not have made it this far without a big hit early on, one in which our ability to capitalize on technological change was key to our success. That deal was our investment in 3Com, the computer networking company. In the end, we learned from 3Com that change can be good or bad, threatening or promising, depending on how you respond to it. In the face of change, it is important to speak up—to make certain everyone sees the change coming and has a chance to respond to it. I am a go-along person. I don't like confrontation. But, despite that, as I learned at 3Com, there are times when we have to step in and address changing conditions no matter how much of a personal struggle it might be.

We got involved in 3Com from the time the company started. It was 1981. I had been an investor in Apple, a company that claimed it gave individuals "a bicycle for the mind." Apple had become a big hit and seen positive cash flow almost from day one. Bob Metcalfe, who in 1973 was one of two co-inventors of the Ethernet, a predecessor to the Internet, was a founder of 3Com. Metcalfe approached me in late 1981 with an idea for a local area network—a group of computers, printers, and disc drives in close proximity that could be programmed and connected to work together.

I had a difficult time telling if this was genius or folly: It did strike me, however, that this could be another "bicycle." After all, I majored in history at Northwestern University, a background that gave me some sense of when historic changes might be happening. Metcalfe and I talked for a while, even discussing what my investment terms would be, but I told him to go pitch his idea to other venture capitalists and return to me if he still wanted me in.

It took about a month before my home telephone rang, about 10 P.M. one night, with Metcalfe on the line. He had seen about 40 other venture capitalists, but he was coming back to me.

"I have learned that a deal is not a deal," Metcalfe told me. "I really want to work with you."

With two other venture capital firms, we invested $1.1 million in 3Com, and I went on the board. Metcalfe set up offices at 3000 Sand Hill Road—an address that has become famous as the location of the well-known venture capital firm Sequoia Capital. 3Com, I believe, is one of only two companies that actually started operations at 3000 Sand Hill. Inside the low-slung office park, we assembled Ethernet boxes, pouring glue in the back so people could not get their hands on the circuit boards and reverse engineer them. Once we started selling, the business just grew straight up—$1 million in sales the first year, $5 million the second, then $17 million, then $47 million. People called 1981 the "year of the LAN." It was before the Internet came, and it seemed there was nowhere to go but up. Even so, Metcalfe was a scientist, not a manager, so we brought in a Hewlett-Packard executive, Bill Krause, as chief executive.

We had embraced Metcalfe's idea of technological change and, with Krause managing strategy, helped him build the company. By 1987, though, the market had changed dramatically. IBM had captured a larger market share than 3Com by adding LAN hardware and software to its computers. Krause had expanded the business into network software and servers, but this was not enough. With competition intensifying, Convergent Technologies approached Krause with a merger offer, and he and Metcalfe both wanted to do the deal.

The Perils and Promise of Change

Although change can be good, it also can be disastrous, and this offer seemed the wrong way to address the changes that were coming to the marketplace. By this point, our firm had distributed nearly 70% of its stock in the company. While this was a life's work for Metcalfe and Krause, it was an investment for me. Yet, I could not get over a nagging feeling that this deal would do nothing but damage the company. I thought 3Com should go more in the direction that Cisco Systems was taking—network equipment—and not toward where Convergent would take them, into UNIX-based workstations.

Paul Ely, the chief executive of Convergent, came in to make a presentation to the board. Ely, a former Marine and a very confident guy, drew a picture of the merger as a truly powerful idea. He talked about the number of customers they had and how 3Com's products would line up with Convergent's. I felt skeptical, but just did not have the technical capability to judge whether Ely was right.

"Paul, you know I am sort of a simple guy," I told him during the board meeting. "I would appreciate it if you could work up a matrix for me and just put in each of these boxes who the customer is and what the product is. I'd like to get some kind of idea of what the growth and margins are on the products."

When Ely came in a month later, for another presentation, I asked him about the matrix again, but he brushed me off.

"You know, I am really busy, and I don't have time to do that," he said.

I told Ely he needn't worry. I would do the research myself.

When I began calling Convergent's customers, I found the company had negative gross margins on virtually every product it sold. One customer of both 3Com and Convergent was AT&T. When I called the AT&T person in charge of those two vendors, I got a clear look into what a merger might mean for our company.

"Look, we believe in honoring our contracts," this person said. "But I want to tell you that I am never going to sign another contract with Convergent. They are gouging us. We are going to pay our bills, but this is it."

And you know what? AT&T was the only customer on which Convergent was making a profit.

Word got out that I opposed the deal. Even though we held only 3% of the shares, two big holders gave me their proxies. I now held 15% of the vote, which because of pooling-of-interests accounting was enough to block the deal.

As I drove to the board meeting that day, I was working out in my mind how I would explain my vote. Early on, I had promised my support to Krause and Metcalfe, but now I felt a duty to change course. Even so, because I do not like confrontation, I did not look forward to explaining views that conflicted with those of other board members whose opinions I respected.

I never had to make that speech. When the board meeting opened, a clean-cut, very educated guy began giving the fairness opinion on behalf of the board's investment banking firm. He went on for quite a while, and I was barely paying attention because in my mind I was rehearsing my own remarks.

Then, as he got to the end of his presentation, the banker said, "Therefore, for the following reasons, we are withdrawing our fairness opinion."

All hell broke loose. Krause called Ely, who brought his attorney, Larry Sonsini. They asked if this was a negotiation over price, and Krause said no. It was more than that. The deal fell apart, but by this time Krause would not change course. He thought he needed a merger to keep 3Com growing. Within a year, he had merged with Bridge Communications, but by that point we had distributed our shares so the Bridge deal was not my concern.

We didn't give up on the Ethernet business, though. We backed Grand Junction Networks, which eventually was acquired by Cisco Systems in a significant acquisition. In fact, we're still involved in gigabit Ethernet today. Our current Ethernet company, Force10 Networks, shows how much technological demands have changed and how we have adjusted to the changes, too. The 3Com systems had less than a gigabyte of processing power, and Grand Junction Networks at the time had up to one gigabyte. Force10 systems, in contrast, start at 10 gigs. At the time of our investment, the company was on its way to introducing some really significant technology to bring the systems to 100 gigs.

This is a big leap in what we call computer "exascale," and with that growth in processing power Force10 has grown well. In 2008, Force10 sold $57 million in servers to Google alone. One irony of this success is that one of our other companies that I was a director of, Juniper Networks, in the late 1990s had a shot at developing this market. They had systems built specifically to run alongside Cisco Systems' servers, but with purpose-built technology. Despite that, the founder and chief technology officer and I could not persuade the rest of the board to approve the move. The lesson: embrace change, or lose opportunity, although Juniper continues to do well in its own areas of expertise.

The Genius Quotient

Now, there are plenty of companies in which the executive team thinks they see a big opportunity and wind up running down a blind alley. At NEA, a partner named Peter Morris and I have developed some fairly sophisticated tools to avoid the dead ends. When we know an industry sector well, we will lay out a large ecosystem of all the relevant technologies. We jumped into Force 10, in fact, after looking at all the relevant metrics in Ethernet technologies. We got into a company called UUNet on the east coast that became the backbone of the Internet. Our managing partner, Peter Barris, went on the board of that company.

Our tools help us address such questions as what are the holes where the incumbents are not playing? As everyone in the world looks for ways to speed the movement of information, where should we position ourselves? We have applied this sort of thinking in a variety of industries, such as solar power, a sector where we now have about 15 companies thanks to others in our firm who have a deep understanding of the technology.

Most venture capitalists and company managers study reams of data, analysis, consultants' reports, and the like before committing to a decision. With upfront work such as that, they can adjust as market conditions change. A select few have the genius, the forward vision, to see the future so clearly, so conclusively, that they are ready to act with seemingly little forethought. In venture capital, we are lucky to run across such people from time to time. We are luckier still if we recognize these unique and powerful traits before others catch on and invest with them first.

Jim Clark is one of the rarest examples of the visionary who operates almost exclusively—and with remarkable consistency—on instinct. Clark's role as a serial founding genius has been well chronicled. From pioneering the computer graphics revolution with Silicon Graphics Inc., he jumped into Netscape to popularize the Internet. Then he had another flash of inspiration and formed Healtheon, a company that was designed to bring new efficiencies to the $1 trillion healthcare system. Healtheon fell short of Jim's view that it could completely rebuild the forms of compensation and communication in the national healthcare system, but with Healtheon Clark made at least as much progress toward a rational healthcare system as anyone else who has tried.

Board Wars

Most people spend a great deal of energy adjusting to change. Clark makes change and lets everyone else adjust to it. In that sense, Clark is a constant force of change. He has a knack for brilliant innovation that seems remarkably constant. It has persisted, seemingly unaltered, since before he left Stanford University's faculty to establish Silicon Graphics, alongside computer scientist Abbey Silverstone, in 1982. The founders envisioned Silicon Graphics as a company that could build powerful workstations and servers capable of creating three-dimensional computer graphics popular with everyone from Hollywood film studios to those working with complex scientific applications and computer-aided design.

We got involved at Silicon Graphics during a $15 million second-round financing. I was invited into the investment and went on the SGI board in 1983. Mayfield had incubated the company from the time Clark left Stanford University. At my first board meeting, I realized this company had serious troubles, bubbling into open hostility, in its boardroom. Entrenched, bickering tribes coalesced around one or another of the leading personalities in management and were struggling to create a vision for the company. Soon after that first meeting, a Mayfield partner, Glenn Mueller, called to say the firm had recruited Ed McCracken, one of the highest ranking executives at Hewlett-Packard, to take charge as CEO. What a relief.

McCracken in the early going was the very essence of the sort of top-flight management talent that can transform a company. He got the people issues ironed out, he rationalized the technology research strategy, he helped structure the company to face each of its markets appropriately, and he teamed up with the right strategic partners. Clark, meanwhile, seemed bent on causing disruption because he is both very intuitive and because he is never really satisfied. He is on to the next challenge. I know Jim well and like him enormously. His genius, drive, and engaging personality are a more than acceptable tradeoff for the troubles he sometimes makes.

The Fast-Change Artist

Clark developed a reputation for causing discord at Silicon Graphics. He had a habit of setting the company's engineers off in odd directions, diverting attention from tasks that were central to McCracken's strategy.

Clark was absolutely obsessed with the idea of the "telecomputer," a kind of hybrid computer and television that he was convinced would be the next big technology breakthrough. McCracken did not immediately buy into it—which nearly drove Clark mad—and the board moved to limit Clark's influence at the same time we rewarded McCracken for his excellent work by boosting his compensation above Clark's. This sent Clark into intense rages with some justification. Clark left soon afterward to launch into his next Silicon Valley breakthrough: Netscape, the search-engine company.

Here's the irony of Clark's departure: McCracken ultimately could not lead Silicon Graphics through the sharp, fast-paced changes that were reshaping the business of complex graphics work stations. At the worst possible time, he took his eye off the job following his decision to serve on a technology advisory board for President Bill Clinton. A partnership with Time Warner to experiment with Clark's telecomputer idea failed. Silicon Graphics, which had a big headstart on Sun Microsystems—so big, in fact, that the venture capitalist John Doerr once tried to arrange a merger of the two—quickly lost ground. Once you lose the magic, you never get it back, and that was the case with McCracken. We wound up having to replace him, but by then it was too late. Silicon Graphics ultimately filed for bankruptcy.

By the time Clark left Silicon Graphics in early 1992, he was angry with me due to his perception that I had favored McCracken over him. NEA was invited to back the Netscape launch, but we were outbid by John Doerr of Kleiner Perkins. The very next year, we backed Healtheon, Clark's next big venture. That decision came about because by that point Clark's relationship with Doerr had soured. Although Doerr and Kleiner were very involved at Healtheon, Clark's ever-shifting feelings toward Doerr and me is testament to the curious mix of friend and foe, partner and competitor, that typifies life in Silicon Valley. Either that, or it is just an indication of how mercurial Jim Clark can be. In point of fact, I believe it may be a combination of both.

Fixing HealthCare

The idea for Healtheon had occurred to Clark when he was in the hospital in 1995 receiving treatment for a rare blood condition he has, hemachromatosis, which requires a hospital visit every few weeks.

Once he got so intimately involved in the U.S. healthcare system, Clark quickly saw how much waste is created, how little actual communication occurs regarding patient health, and how the payment system is horribly outdated. With the use of computer technology, Clark explained when he came to our offices on Sand Hill Road and sketched out his plans, a company could squeeze billions in waste out of the system and improve care for patients along the way. Clark ultimately decided to split the difference in his like/dislike relationship with Doerr and me by inviting both our firms to invest in the launch of Healtheon.

I would say my interest in the Healtheon investment, and in several of our other biological sciences companies, was perhaps spurred in part by my own deeply personal experience. My first wife, Lynne, died in 1981 from a heart problem that might have been addressed by what is now a relatively simple procedure, balloon angioplasty. NEA later funded a company, Advanced Cardiovascular Systems, which helped lead the development and proliferation of angioplasty methods. Our firm also developed a relationship with a Stanford professor, Josh Makower, who has established a number of small companies that make devices that help fight heart disease, including his current company, Acclarent, which uses catheter technology to treat sinusitis.

Healtheon had an ambitious agenda: literally to squeeze inefficiency out of the U.S. healthcare system. Clark developed a decent relationship with the company's chief executive, but in serving a seeming need to be at war with someone he wound up fighting with the NEA partner who at first was in charge of our investment in Healtheon, Dr. Hugh Rienhoff. Both men are highly intelligent and both as mercurial as can be.

Within months of start-up, the relationship between Clark and Rienhoff was threatening to blow apart, so Clark called to ask me to step in, which I quickly did. We recruited a capable chief executive, Mike Long, who led the company through its signature acquisition, the purchase of WebMD. That Web-based healthcare company brought Healtheon into the market for online consumer health information. Clark, meanwhile, remained the beacon—as he always is—coming up with insights and visions and leaving it to others to figure out how to execute them.

The Search for Solar

Healtheon was a company built on an expertise in process innovation, backed up by technology. Our firm, though, has its technological strengths, and we have been big investors in semiconductors over the years. We have a general partner, Forest Baskett, who, in Jim Clark's words, is the "deepest and broadest" technologist around. Baskett was the Stanford electrical engineering professor who brought Clark to Stanford. His specialty is semiconductors. Drawing on all the expertise in our firm around the turn of the century as we searched for places where we could take advantage of the changes in demand for energy, it made sense that we should invest in solar energy.

Semiconductors are linked to solar. The key material is silicon, processing power is essential, efficiency is paramount, and manufacturing is key. In 2003, we conducted our classic matrix analysis, looking at all the opportunities, the gaps in the solar marketplace, and the need for investment. As we looked at the solar value chain, we looked at feedstock, sand silicon, and the fabrication of wafers into cells. We considered modules for collecting energy, power systems, and system installation. All that study led us to decide that the cell level, individual power cells, is the core value proposition. Just as in computing devices the semiconductor chip is the core value proposition, the cell would be the key in solar. So, we focused on silicon-based cells because that is where we could get the most differentiation, the most innovation, and the most value. In turn, our companies could get compensated for that value.

We built our portfolio on the basis of multiple technologies. For generation one, silicon, we have a portfolio company called Suniva, in Georgia, that is doing really well. We have multiple generations— organic is one of them—and multiple paths to market. As technology evolves, companies must take different routes in order to find their markets. So as to cover all our options, we have seven or eight investments in this area. In essence, we are filling the solar ecosystem with our companies, flooding the zone, as it were.

As we progress, we are building technology expertise and getting manufacturing operations to scale. We were one of the very few firms that invested in silicon from the fundamental materials on up the value chain, and we are doing the same with solar. This appeals to our portfolio companies, too, because they know they can benefit from their relationship to other companies in our portfolio. A cell maker might sell products to an installer, for example. One more point: Differentiation makes for better investment returns, too. The market assigns a multiplier of two- to three-times cash flow to, say, a Tier 2 solar provider, but differentiated technology providers fetch 8 to 15 times cash flow. We saw the same thing happen as silicon technology matured, and the cycle is repeating itself with solar. Technologies may change, but winning strategies persist.

An Evolving Strategy: Venture Growth Equity

Although certain strategies are worth repeating as technologies change, we must also be open to changing strategies as conditions evolve. For example, we never would have developed one of our most successful investment strategies—something we call venture growth equity—had we not reevaluated our approach as market conditions changed. The collapse of the dot-com bubble in 2000 had an effect on our firm that many people probably would not have expected. When we went to raise our next fund that September, we actually wound up with more money than we had planned for. The dot-com bust had created a flight to quality, and instead of our $1.5 billion target we wound up with $2.3 billion in commitments.

I'll never forget the day we realized we were going to go that big. I was in a board meeting in our building when Scott Kriens, the chief executive of Juniper Networks, caught me in the hall and said, "Dick, $2.3 billion? This is ridiculous. You can't possibly invest that much profitably."

"Scott," I told him, "we have a plan."

The idea actually had come from one of our newest partners, James Barrett, a Ph.D. who had at one point headed up clinical trials at Smith-Kline Beecham, the big drug company now called GlaxoSmithKline. Barrett left SmithKline to take over one of our companies that was struggling. He turned it around. He worked miracles and then went to another company and then started up one. After that, we brought Barrett into our partnership.

This was about the time we were closing on the $2.3 billion fund and trying to decide how we were going to manage that much money.

Jim offered up a simple observation. "Let's do fewer and more important things," he said. "The truth of the matter is, we are doing a lot of small stuff. Sometimes it's because of the experiment. Sometimes it's a lack of conviction. We should really commit to where we put our money."

Investing at Scale

Barrett's idea changed our whole way of doing things. To deploy so much money, we needed to up the size of our investments. Instead of an average investment of $6 million, we would put $40 million into the typical deal. We would go as high as $100 million, and we would invest in established companies instead of start-ups. If we could get, say, seven times cash flow on exits, this would have a multiplier effect on our performance. We also would not use debt. Most of these companies could not support debt anyway, so we decided to move in with total equity investments.

We added one final twist: On the last $250 million of the fund, we took no management fees. That way, if we never did find somewhere to put that money, there would not be pressure to invest it for the sole purpose of earning back our fees.

Tele Atlas is an example of how this worked. The company started as a division of Bosch, in Germany, doing location-based software for the automobile industry. In 2003, we jumped at the chance to put $70 million into a $200 million refinancing, along with Oak Investment Partners, which spun Tele Atlas out of Bosch and transformed the company. There were only two companies in the world doing this work: NAVTEQ, in Chicago, and Tele Atlas.

Alongside our investment in Tele Atlas, we brought management expertise to the second largest U.S. company in the business and let the Europeans continue running Europe. We got penetration into Japan, sold stock on the Amsterdam exchange, and at the end of the day sold the company for $4.3 billon. That made us about seven times our money. Get results like that from big investments such as we put into Tele Atlas, and it's possible to really move the needle, even with an investment fund of $2.3 billion.

Changing from China

In the last few years, probably the latter years of my career, I have embraced change in what some might consider a surprisingly personal way. I had developed an opinion, over a number of years, that any venture capital firm serious about its business needed to be active in China and India. Then, a few years back, when we were deciding who from our headquarters office should staff our China operation, I volunteered to go, thanks to my wife, Pam.

In 2007, when our China business was getting big enough that we needed to make this move, it seemed obvious that the partner in charge of our China efforts would be the logical person to go, but Scott Sandell had two young daughters and could not move until the end of 2008. I volunteered to go, in part because Pam told me it was time to put some action behind all the talking I had done, and the firm took me up on my offer. I had expected it to be a short assignment, but 2008 turned into 2009, and even as 2010 is imminent I still am commuting to China. One reason is that our firm has raised a new $2.5 billion fund, and with that much money to invest we need Sandell in Silicon Valley.

China is, of course, the Wild East. I've gotten back into the life sciences, which has always been one of my great areas of interest. I've begun developing a view that intellectual property in China—which is seen as one of the big drawbacks of investment in that country—will change over time. The Chinese are doing more research, more costly and complicated research, and with investment such as that I expect them to be as aggressive as any country at protecting intellectual property sometime in the next 20 years.

In the pharmaceutical industry, the Chinese are taking their research capability beyond the relatively simple task of just creating generic drugs. One of our companies, Novast Pharmaceuticals, is part of an industry that has begun taking blockbuster drugs that are about to come off patent, modifying them, and then obtaining patents on the new drug. Such drugs are called biosimilars, and the new patents will last for seven years.

There is plenty of room to make money in biosimilars. After all, blockbuster drugs worth $110 billion in sales are set to come off patent over the next five years. That's a big, profitable target for biosimilar research, and we have invested in companies capable of taking advantage of that opportunity. We believe this development will lead to better outcomes at lower cost for the healthcare industry.

China is energizing, really, because so much is happening at once, and investment firms such as ours likely will have an ability to exit through initial stock offerings in China long before the U.S. market bounces back. The initial public offering market has been all but dead in the United States since early 2008. Initial offerings in China are still trickling out, and the market there is likely to rebound more quickly than just about any in the world. The money and opportunities are both there. Before long, too, I expect to see more Chinese companies start registering stock offerings on the U.S. NASDAQ market. This is part national pride, part profit motive.

I am on the advisory board of a Chinese company called BioVeda, a venture capital firm in which we hold an investment interest. The chairman, Dr. Zhi Yang, is anxious to see the IPO market get going. "We want to go public with these companies as soon as it is feasible," he said. "I think we can see strong earnings multiplied." He looked at me with a smile and said, "That shouldn't be too big an issue."

Like the CEO of the communications company who performed so well when the satellite broke down, Dr. Yang is ready to go, regardless of how big the challenges. He expects to be compensated for his leadership and vision—and he will be.

It may be China. It may be 30 years since NEA went into business. Time passes, technologies and geographies change. But, no matter where you are in the world, and no matter how old you are or what technology is hot, 30 times earnings is an attractive return. That much is a constant because some things, after all, do not change.

LESSONS FROM RICHARD KRAMLICH

 Consult the market matrix. Assess the players and gaps between players when looking for opportunities. Particularly in markets where new technologies are king, consider which vectors will lead to success.

 Trust your gut, and speak your piece. Do not go along on an investment idea just because everyone else believes you should. Be willing to bust up a deal, or a strategy, if necessary.

✥ **Maintain the magic.** It is tougher to build momentum than it is to sustain it. If a strategy, a CEO, or a company is losing its magic, diagnose the problem and respond.

✥ **Technologies change, but strategies persist.** Reassess long-term strategies in light of technological change. Some changes merely reinforce existing strategy, others may force a change.

✥ **Do fewer and larger things.** When investment resources reach a certain size, smaller deals just cannot move the needle. To earn strong returns, take bigger positions in a handful of important deals. You don't have to risk too much at the outset, but build upon milestones.

10

BEYOND THE IVORY TOWER: TAKING LABORATORY RESEARCH TO MARKET

Steven Lazarus
Managing Director Emeritus
ARCH Venture Partners

AUM: $1.5 billion   **Years in VC:** 23

Location: Chicago, IL   **Year born:** 1931

Grew up: Long Beach, NY   **Location born:** Brooklyn, NY

Best known deals: Illumina, NEON/Sybase, Alnylam/Aviron/MedImmune/AstraZeneca

Style: Curious, imaginative

Education: B.S., Dartmouth College, Class of 1952
M.B.A., Harvard Graduate School of Business, a Baker Scholar in the Class of 1965

Significant experience: First director of the U.S. Department of Commerce Bureau of East-West Trade, director of Amgen for 17 years

Personal interests: Skiing, writing. Author of the book *Mind into Matter*, 2006

The lesson: "Know when to change course."

University politics, the uncertainties of basic science, and fundraising hurdles: Steve Lazarus had to overcome them all in order to make ARCH Venture Partners a success. After career stops in the U.S. Navy, the Pentagon, and healthcare giant Baxter Laboratories, Lazarus went to the University of Chicago to conduct an experiment in venture capital and discovered it indeed is possible to systematically commercialize the research from university laboratories.

Overcoming early skepticism from the scientific community, ARCH gives university scientists a share in the results of their discoveries, an arrangement that helps create new incentives and rewards for basic science. ARCH's start-ups have ranged from education company Everyday Learning Corp. to biotechnology firm Adolor, known for its pain-management drugs. ARCH manages technology, market, and financing risks with an eye toward bringing breakthrough new discoveries into widespread use.

⁂

I was too old to qualify as one of Robert McNamara's "whiz kids" at the Pentagon during the height of the Vietnam War, but I did work there for him. My job included the task of delivering to him the "Red Books" that tallied the Vietnam build-up. In the four years I was at the Pentagon, from 1965 to 1969, the United States sent its first full fighting forces into Vietnam, suffered the public relations setback of the Tet offensive, and saw McNamara depart amid escalating protests against the war. To this day, there are limits to what I can say about my Pentagon work.

If someone had told me then that I would, late in my career, move on to something as compelling as the McNamara years, I suspect I might have been skeptical. But that is exactly what happened with a venture that began when the University of Chicago asked me to run an experiment designed to help commercialize laboratory research. We would not be the first to do so. Stanley Cohen and Herbert Boyer would earn that honor with their patent for splicing DNA, but we led the way in systematically rummaging through university laboratories and academic treatises in search of breakthroughs that could become the kernel of great new businesses. Then we funded them, helped provide management expertise, and launched them into the marketplace.

This approach led to the creation of Everyday Math, a new style of mathematics education. We helped advance the ability to shop online with a company called NetBot. We also took a computer processing technology that was initially designed to help hospitals manage their data, tweaked it, and helped a company we called NEON create one of the fastest, most precise trading tools on Wall Street. Through a technique we developed—technology roll-ups—we helped create a family of pain-relief medicine that is not addictive and founded Adolor, one of the most novel biotechnology success stories. Finally, we founded Illumina, the leading company in genetic diagnosis and analysis, which today has a market capitalization in the billions. And there were many others.

We made plenty of mistakes, too, but along the way we learned a lot about how to work within the university environment. We started by overcoming the legitimate concerns of some professors and researchers who at first saw commercialization as a potential threat to the notion of pure academic research. We brought some of the disciplines of business to the research setting. We learned to identify potentially powerful science and to secure the rights to that intellectual property so as to protect its commercial potential. Above all, we learned the importance of the intangible human factor: how a uniquely talented handful of star researchers can become repeat performers, turning out great science again and again, as reliably and bankably as those serial dot-com entrepreneurs in Silicon Valley.

We did this all through a firm called ARCH Venture Partners, and I have to admit to taking some satisfaction from the fact that ARCH began as an offshoot of the University of Chicago, that great bastion of theoretical, not practical, knowledge. Though renowned as a proving ground for winners of the Nobel Prize in Economics, the U. of C. would hardly come to mind as an incubator for the commercialization of scientific research. With regard to the ever-present tension between practical and theoretical knowledge, the university when I arrived on the scene in 1986 had changed little since the legendary chancellor Robert Maynard Hutchins in the 1930s introduced the Great Books curriculum and installed the Socratic method as a primary means of instruction.

As ARCH developed, there were lessons for me to learn personally, too, about managing and encouraging the process of technology transfer. At ARCH, I would draw on all the work I had done previously in my career, as a Navy officer, as a Commerce Department trade negotiator, and as executive vice president of the international division for the pharmaceutical company Baxter International.

At ARCH, I would learn how to influence and guide uniquely talented scientists, probing and challenging without squelching their creativity. I also would come to admire how big a difference it makes when we create an investment incentive for a cadre of talented and creative individuals, thereby amplifying the chances of success and the opportunity for a return on investment. The techniques that have been so helpful to me might be useful to anyone trying to manage an enterprise that embraces risk in order to grow companies and turn a profit.

Profit vs. Research: A False Choice

The ARCH story begins with an energetic debate that was occurring on the board of trustees at the U. of C. in the early 1980s. In 1970, Stanford University and the University of California–San Francisco had patented their technique for gene splicing and were on their way toward earning $250 million in royalties from licenses on that patent by the time it expired in 1997. A similar story at the U. of C. was ending very differently. Around the time Stanford was converting science into endowment dollars, the U. of C. was letting a promising technology literally walk out the door. The university failed to legally protect its rights to a process, first discovered in the U. of C. laboratories, that eventually became the key to a synthetic hormone produced by Amgen that helps reduce anemia among people with kidney disease. Business-minded trustees at Chicago were determined not to let the financial return that can arise from technology get away from them again.

Pioneers Need Support

The U. of C. may not have the same reputation for innovation as Stanford, Massachusetts Institute of Technology, and other research-based universities that have built their names on science breakthroughs, but it does have a rich, if understated, legacy for advanced scientific experimentation with profound real-world results. Manhattan Project scientists during World War II conducted the world's first controlled nuclear reaction in a squash court under the grandstand of Stagg Field. The football stadium, incidentally, had been rendered obsolete by Hutchins himself, who in 1939 abolished the school's football program en route to withdrawing the university from the Big Ten athletic conference altogether.

Chicago, however, had a unique asset: It is the manager of the federal government's Argonne National Laboratory. Although Argonne is best known for its research into high-energy physics, the laboratory also is a leader in biotechnology research. As the University of Chicago began looking for ways to match Stanford's success in finding profitable patents in its laboratories, advanced materials seemed a sensible place to start. With the growth of Hewlett-Packard, Cisco, and others, the new science of superconductivity seemed to offer the most immediate promise for the transfer of Argonne's technological know-how into commercial use.

Conditions were ripe for such a move. Even as science was on the brink of a new wave of discovery, the nation's legal framework was changing in important ways, too. In 1980, Congress passed amendments to the Bayh–Dole Act, which gives universities the economic rights to the results of research conducted with government money. The same year, the U.S. Supreme Court ruled that it is legal to patent a live, human-made microorganism. The ruling, which granted patents to General Electric scientist Ananda Mohan Chakrabarty on a petroleum-eating bacteria he had invented, provided a powerful economic incentive for other biotech researchers.

The stage was set for Chicago to bring its research out of the labs and into the real world. Stanford was making millions by streamlining the licensing process through its Office of Technology Licensing, but the U. of C. trustees who were looking for a way to commercialize the university's research saw limits to the licensing approach. Once a technology was licensed, they felt, the university would lose control over its ability to ensure that the license holder would maximize the commercial potential of the research. A company might buy the license, locking up the right to use the technology, and simply put it on a shelf. Perhaps that company might consider the science as potentially competitive with its own business. Perhaps the science involved might not be a priority for the company. The licensing model offered too many unknowns and too little control.

We Needed a Champion

U. of C. wanted to take the Stanford and M.I.T. model to a new level, an innovation in university-funded research. The idea—spearheaded by Walter Massey, a physicist who had headed Argonne and then was vice president of research at the U. of C. —was to actually fund the start-up of businesses that would focus their efforts almost entirely on the commercial potential of the university's scientific breakthroughs. That approach faced a hurdle of its own: U. of C. had neither the know-how nor the people to do the job.

Massey and the U. of C. trustees needed someone to focus full time on the commercialization effort. With Massey heading up recruitment, the university approached John Robson, a protégé of Donald Rumsfeld who had succeeded Rumsfeld as chief executive of G.D. Searle & Company. Robson declined to be a candidate for the U. of C. job, because at this point he was weighing a job offer he eventually accepted, to become dean of Emory University's business school. Robson did suggest an alternative candidate for the job: me.

The timing was just as good for me as it was wrong for Robson. I had retired from Baxter immediately in the wake of its purchase of American Hospital Supply. As a middle-aged executive during a time of consolidation—at 55, I was the second oldest executive after Baxter chairman Bill Graham at the time—it seemed best for me to take retirement and consider the next phase in my career. I was about to begin commuting to Cambridge, MA, to co-teach a business-school course on health management, when Robson in the summer of 1986 invited me to breakfast.

"I've been asked to look at a job at the University of Chicago, which would be associate dean of the business school," Robson said. "They also want whoever takes the job to design some kind of mechanism to transfer technology. The interesting thing is they want to use business start-ups as one of their techniques."

A Creative Breakthrough

As I thought about and discussed the idea with Massey and others at the university, it emerged that Chicago's approach was one of those creative breakthroughs that change the way business is conducted.

Instead of accepting 4% or 5% of net revenue in a conventional licensing arrangement, the university would have an equity holding. That way, U. of C. could have a direct effect on how aggressively the technology was developed, and the arrangement would give the university some input in selecting the researchers, investors, and business executives who would help maximize the potential of their science. Beyond that, the university had astutely designated the new position as an academic appointment, a decision that would prove invaluable as the idea met with the inevitable resistance from the guardians of Robert Hutchins' legacy of academic abstraction.

I had no doubt that Chicago had potential as a seed bed for invention. Two years earlier, in an early stab at commercializing its research, the university had invited me to its Hyde Park campus for a review of university-sponsored research projects deemed to have commercial potential. As Baxter's head of research, I was definitely interested, but the process seemed off kilter—a parade of half-hour presentations, as if the science was entered in a beauty contest where the talent portion involved a remarkably high quotient of scientific expertise. If anything had worked for Baxter, it would have been the result of an almost incalculably random match of the University's scientific output and Baxter's commercial needs. In the real world, such coincidences rarely happen, and none did for us. There had to be a better way.

The university seemed to realize it needed a more expedient approach. That would not happen, though, until after the dons of Chicago—faculty members, as well as trustees—could settle an intramural debate about whether a commercial venture was appropriate on Chicago's famed academic midway. As the germ of a quasi-independent commercialization effort began to take shape, it attracted supporters and opponents in almost equal measure.

Standing Our Ground

What we really needed was an insider, someone who would have credibility with the faculty but enough savvy about the outside world to see the potential of the idea we were trying to pursue. Fortunately for our so-far fragile efforts, we had such a person in Walter Massey. It was Massey who masterfully brought peace to Chicago's squabbling fiefdoms, persuaded opinion leaders from the faculties of physical and biological sciences to speak out, and applauded the university president, Hannah Gray, in her vocal and unwavering commitment to the experiment. Among the trustees, Richard Morrow, then chief executive of the Chicago-based oil company Amoco Corp., and James Crown, scion of Chicago's wealthy Crown family, steadfastly rallied support on the board.

As I learned later about how the debate developed, this event became an important lesson for me—an extremely useful lesson—about the intricacies and dangers of university politics. At universities, fiefdoms and jealousies, tradition and inertia can threaten even the most positive ideas. Great ideas at other universities had foundered over just such obstructions, but Massey was determined not to let that happen at U. of C.

Whatever resistance arose among the faculty or even trustees, Massey had a masterful ability to focus debate on what he saw as the ultimate objectives of the program: To benefit society, to advance science, to create jobs, and so forth. Massey artfully avoided bringing any discussion to a premature conclusion, particularly if the discussion at hand was one that might put our venture at risk. Ultimately, though, trustee Robert Halperin, a Silicon Valley pioneer, found a way to crystallize the consensus that had developed among trustees.

"The purpose is to make money, and the only way you are ever going to be able to measure whether this thing is successful or not is whether you make money," Halperin said. "Then the other things that you talk about will occur as derivative consequences." Halperin was dead on, and after he put his argument that way any of the other possible benefits of the project were subordinated to the chief purpose: the ability to add funds to the operation of the university.

We named the new venture ARCH in recognition of the contributions expected both from Argonne—the AR in the name—and Chicago—the CH. Although words such as Halperin's mattered in getting us off the ground, so did a physical sign I received soon after arriving on campus in mid-1986. Evidence that the university had committed itself irrevocably to the project was actual office space, a rare and valuable university asset for what until then had been only a theoretical venture.

Jack Gould, dean of the business school, saw the project as a chance to give business students practical experience in entrepreneurship.

By allocating office space, Gould was giving us room to operate and sending an important signal of affirmation to the university's faculty and students. Making certain the message would be lost on no one, Gould also put out word among the business school's talented and ambitious students that ARCH would need volunteers in order to succeed.

Rewinding the Tape

As I settled into my work, I began to realize that I was embarking on a venture that would draw on my many experiences over the years. The experiences that unfolded in the months and years ahead were a reminder of something I first had heard in 1963, while a student at the Harvard Graduate School of Business. The Navy had sent me to business school as part of my mid-career development, and it was at Harvard that I gathered some particularly useful wisdom from Professor Georges Doriot. A former military man himself, a successful entrepreneur in his own right, and one of the fathers of venture capital, Doriot had a penchant for memorable and compelling metaphors that helped him teach lessons that lasted a lifetime.

"The chain of your activities just keeps getting longer and longer, and it never goes away," Doriot told us. "Our lives form a tape, over the years, and we carry this tape with us endlessly and become a product of what we have done over time.

"Your accomplishments, your failures, the way in which you interact with people, they all become part of your own, personal tape," Doriot concluded.

Doriot's lesson was clear: Build a strong tape, and know that both your accomplishments and failures will become part of your record. Treat people fairly and honestly, and you have a chance at success. It was common-sense advice, but the metaphor of the tape brought home the notion that life is an accumulated experience. What we do each day, for good or ill, builds toward the next, all connected, and always moving.

Lessons from Father

The emphasis Doriot placed on our need to treat people well was important, yet it was hardly news to me. It was something I had learned as a boy watching my father, an attorney and accountant, build his accounting business during the Depression. Jesse Lazarus would drive from our home on Long Island to visit gas stations, car dealerships, and tire companies and offer to do their books and, ultimately, their tax work.

In a business like that, character is important. The way you deal with people, the standards you set—it's a small world, and you can't hide anything. At one point during World War II, he got several offers to get involved in the black-market trade of automotive parts. He turned that down flat. He was the essence of honesty, and his clients and friends knew that.

From Dad, I also learned not to underestimate a person merely because of appearances. I had known growing up that my father fought during World War I in the Argonne as a medic—a traumatic experience, no doubt, but one he never talked about. So far as I knew most of my life, my dad had led a quiet, competent life, successful but nothing overly exciting. It was not until years after he was gone that I learned from a distant relative that my dad as a teenager had sneaked out of the house at night, ran to an Army recruiting station, and tried to enlist to fight Pancho Villa on the Mexican border. You just never know what is written on that tape of a person's life.

Navy Life

As for me, I had not intended to have a military career, but the Korean War persuaded me to start one. I had graduated with an English major from Dartmouth College in 1952 and was working as an advertising copywriter when the military draft started setting its sights on people like me. Rather than get drafted into the Army, I joined the Navy. A fast moving ship seemed more attractive than trying to fight my way up Pork Chop Hill in Korea.

The Navy showed me the world. My wife and I had two memorable years in Naples. I served on ships, but much of my work was in logistics and supply—useful training for a later business career. After Harvard, sent there by the Navy to round out my management background, came the Pentagon job and, eventually, a stint as trade negotiator in the Commerce Department.

At the Pentagon, I had learned to be a good listener and, importantly, how to avoid political pot holes that might destroy a career.

To the military staff, I was identified as one of McNamara's people, but my Navy background made me one of them, too. I learned to blend in with whatever group I worked with and focused on helping the sometimes conflicting factions to resolve conflicts, set aside differences, and focus on common aims.

Along the way, I met some interesting, even historic figures and learned a good bit from my dealings with them. I met Don Kendall, the legendary chief executive of PepsiCo, while negotiating a trade deal that helped Pepsi's efforts to forge partnerships in the Soviet Union—one of the few parts of the world where they did better than Coca-Cola. I worked with David Packard, a co-founder of Hewlett-Packard. People such as that gave me a view into how business is done at the highest levels of global commerce and, in Packard's case, the farthest reaches of innovation. (I also worked with Bill Hewitt, the chief executive of John Deere, and David Rockefeller.)

The Nixon Crowd and Other Acquaintances

In its odd way, the Watergate scandal was good for me. People at Commerce kept dropping from sight, almost like victims in an Agatha Christie novel. Pete Peterson left, an old Washington hand who eventually went on to form Blackstone Group, a major private-equity firm. As others departed, my responsibilities grew. I set up the Commerce Department's Bureau of East-West Trade, negotiated deals with the Soviet Union, and even helped start the Chinese liaison office. At one point, I was riding in a limousine with Armand Hammer, the California industrialist with strong ties to the Soviet Union, when he told me I would be named Commerce Secretary if John Connolly could win the presidency. He said it with such confidence, it seemed like something he could do. Since I was regulating a major deal Hammer was interested in, I excused myself and fled the limo.

At one point, the Nixon White House offered me a job as one of four associate directors in the Office of Management and Budget. With Watergate getting hotter and hotter, it sounded like a risky move. I had gotten to know Jeb McGruder and Charles Colson while working at Commerce, and called on Colson for advice. His carefully phrased response suggested that this probably was not the right time to be signing on with President Nixon, and I turned down the job. Sometimes, it's just as important to avoid a potentially devastating "opportunity" as to jump on a good one.

No one turned down President Nixon and just went about their business. You were a supporter or you were an enemy, and I feared that by turning down the budget job I had joined the ranks of potential enemies. Just as I started to look outside government, I got a call about a job at Baxter Laboratories. Bill Graham, the long-time chief executive liked to collect people like me. I had been written about in *Business Week*, I had a modest public profile, and Graham was somewhat starstruck by such things.

At a dinner meeting on my first visit to Baxter's headquarters in Chicago's northern suburbs, Graham told me he wanted to expand Baxter's international business, and with my profile I would be a good fit for executive vice president of the company's international division. I had no background in health care, which made this just the sort of opportunity I was looking for: a break with the past, something outside of government, heading up a line of business on day one, a chance to grow existing operations but also to start a lot of things from scratch, all in an industry that allowed you to do good while doing well. I took the job.

This was the tape of my career, and life, that I brought with me to U. of C. when, at age 55, I signed on as associate dean of the business school, the person in charge of ARCH. The place had incredible potential. The science coming out of Argonne was on the far reaches of physics and biotechnology. The head of the department of medicine was Arthur Rubenstein, who now heads the entire healthcare program at the University of Pennsylvania. There were lesser known but incredibly talented star performers at the bench level in almost any laboratory one could find.

Storming the Ivory Tower

The debate over the formation of ARCH had been settled. The university was committed to moving ahead, but in many respects the larger challenge of winning over the faculty was still ahead of me. I developed the view that there were two key points we needed to address. First, we needed to alleviate any fears that our venture was a threat to the purely academic and theoretical pursuits. And, second, we needed to let the scientists know—let everyone know—that they might gain personally from this venture. They might do breakthrough work, for starters, and they just might get rich.

We addressed the first concern by letting faculty and researchers know that there would be no limits on publication of scientific research. Deep down, many star scientists at the nation's universities go to the lab every day hoping that their work will one day win them the Nobel Prize. We knew not to trifle with that incentive, and we made it clear that once the university protected the intellectual property that their work produced, they would be free to publish, just as they ever were.

In my view, this whole debate about pure academia vs. the commercial marketplace had been overblown. The Robert Hutchins legacy was still very much alive at the university, but there was a flip side to that independent and inquisitive spirit. Dig a couple of layers down and there was an independent-mindedness that played to our advantage. There's a saying on campus, as old as some of the buildings themselves, that embodies the independent spirit: "You can do anything here, as long as you don't do it in the street and frighten the horses." That's the spirit we tried to appeal to while recruiting the faculty and scientists to work with us.

Times were changing in academia, in any event. At Argonne, before ARCH came about, the leadership used to celebrate whenever investigators successfully filed a patent. They would call the scientists together and present a $100 check to the investigator whose work had earned the patent, but those little ceremonies were becoming increasingly outdated. By the time I arrived at Hyde Park, everyone knew that Stanley Cohen and Herbert Boyer at Stanford personally had earned a share in the proceeds from their work that led to the patent for splicing DNA. Compared to the millions that Cohen and Boyer personally made, those $100 gratuities for university research were not just outdated; to some at the university, they were almost insulting.

We seized on this change in perspective from the start with the first big success arising from science developed out of Argonne. At the time we had our first public offering of stock based on research there, we printed up some of those big, oversized checks—filled out in figures ranging up toward $20,000—and presented them to the investigators whose work had helped create the company. That made an impression. Ultimately, we decided to offer 25% of either the equity or the royalty stream to the principal investigator whose research was the core of a business opportunity. Incentives are powerful tools, and financial incentives may be the most powerful tools of all.

ARCH in Operation

With the philosophical debates largely behind us, the focus now was on getting ARCH into operation. I had the office space I needed from Dean Gould, and the university and Argonne labs clearly were turning out intellectual property that would have commercial value. What I needed now was legwork—enough people who could scour the labs and who were smart enough to understand the science and savvy enough to sense the business prospects of what they saw.

These scouts also needed to be good judges of talent. In any profession, scientific research included, there are a handful of superstars. Such people have the talent and creativity to make breakthroughs, not just once in their careers but as a matter of course. Their colleagues and competitors know who they are, especially in a collaborative pursuit such as science where people on different campuses, or even far-flung continents, might be attacking a particular problem. It may sound elitist to say it, but it's still true: We needed to identify the super scientists, the ones capable of serial successes in the laboratories, people we could do business with as they pushed the frontiers of discovery.

Fortunately, there are few better places on Earth to find people with the kind of smarts and savvy I needed than the U. of C. business school. Many of these business-school students have returned to school after a few years out in the working world, so they have a seasoned eye. They are uniformly intelligent. Many are entrepreneurs in their own right. As I would soon learn, besides offering office space, Dean Gould headed an institution that would also provide me with a qualified labor force, and a volunteer one at that.

Raising Funds—and Volunteers

One day I was sitting in my office, lonely as usual, when a head appeared from behind the threshold of the open doorway.

"Are you the ARCH guy?" the person asked. He was a second-year MBA student named Bob Nelsen, and, although I did not know it when I first laid eyes on him, this was the beginning of what would become a partnership that has lasted nearly a quarter century. Some of the other earliest recruits are still my partners today: Keith Crandell and Clint Bybee. Bob was from Seattle and had done some venture investing earlier in his career. Keith had an entrepreneurial background, too.

Once these first recruits signed on, volunteering with me in addition to their class work, we split up the territory. Bob took the U. of C. labs, and Keith took on Argonne. Clint spent time in both places. As word spread about our work, in subsequent years we eventually had to sort through maybe 100 applications to fill 20 internship opportunities. Those who were chosen we dubbed the "57th Street Irregulars," an homage to our street address and to the mindset of the people who came there to work. It was also an homage to the troup of brilliant ragamuffins who assisted Sherlock Holmes, The Baker Street Irregulars. The name has stuck in my mind, I guess, because venture capitalists have to be a bit irregular, too, or else they would never take the risks or recognize the opportunities that most people avoid.

Now all we needed was the money necessary to make the whole enterprise succeed. In essence, the university was providing the raw material—the scientific knowledge—and my team was supposed to provide or hire the know-how to facilitate commercialization. Without seed capital, though, the science would never come to market, and it was my job to raise the money.

The Money Hunt

I figured we would need to raise an initial fund of $10 million to get off the ground. I talked to university trustees, and received strong support from the late Kingman Douglas who was chairman of the finance and investment committee. Arthur Kelley, an old friend of mine who later became a Chicago trustee, was a risk taker and he led me to several potential investors. Nevertheless, I was offering little more than smoke, a lab notebook, and a big idea.

I began what added up to more than 100 fundraising trips. Progress came very slowly. At Madison Dearborn Partners, John Canning told me this was too small a venture. John Doerr at Kleiner Perkins Caufield & Byers, in Silicon Valley, told me he had a gyroscope in his brain that turned him back west as he approached the Nevada border. We did no better on the East Coast. To many, the idea of a university-centered fund was novel but totally unproven, a risk they did not need to take. "Your track record is all ahead of you," I heard, more than once, from people who refused to invest with us.

Gradually the effort started paying off. Through some business contacts, I got a meeting with Len Batterson at Allstate, and he said the insurance company would put in $1 million if I could raise the other nine. That was a start. I got an appointment with Jim Bates, the vice chairman of State Farm Insurance. One Saturday afternoon in Bloomington, Illinois, Bates took a break from a tennis game, listened to my pitch for about an hour, and committed $4 million. I had my nut, and from that point the money rolled in. The university, through Douglas, matched State Farm's $4 million, and before long I had my $9 million. By the time I got back to Allstate, though, Batterson had left the company, and I never did get that last $1 million.

It had taken a year to raise the money, and we had been incubating a few deals by borrowing money without much formal authority from the university or Argonne. We started a dozen companies and had—for a start-up investor anyway—a fairly remarkable record of success: four abject failures, four reasonably successful public offerings, and four firms sold outright, at a profit to our fund.

Everyday Lessons

That first fund helped teach us an important lesson about remaining open minded in the early days of a business venture. The originating idea may not ultimately become the germ of the business, but if it is powerful enough it will survive the adaptations one has to make to craft an inspiration into a business success. We quickly learned that, when seeking to launch businesses out of a university environment, an investor has to be flexible and respond to circumstances. We launched

ARCH as a technology incubator, but the most successful investment from that first fund turned out to be a company that had nothing to do with technology: Everyday Learning.

Today, the Everyday Math teaching approach is a core mathematics curriculum in school districts around the country. In 1988, when ARCH came across the idea, it was the nucleus of a new approach to mathematics education developed by a University of Chicago professor named Max Bell. Prof. Bell believed children would learn mathematics more easily if lessons were tied more directly to the sort of numbers problems they see in everyday life.

As a prospective investment, Everyday Learning was a reach. Only one year of the six-year curriculum was developed, no textbook publisher had committed to the program, and no school district had committed to launch it. We recruited an able chief executive, a businesswoman named Jo Anne Schiller. We also committed $250,000 up front, as lead of a syndicate that totaled $1.5 million in support, and ARCH offered an option for another $150,000.

Everyday Learning never needed that second round of money. In its first year, with 10 field sites testing the kindergarten curriculum, they had $100,000 in revenue. Year two, with first-grade curriculum added, revenues reached $500,000. The business broke even, and revenues began doubling every year. Eventually we sold Everyday Learning to Tribune Company, earning a 25% internal rate of return on our initial investment.

An Optic Adventure

In that first fund we also learned the important lesson that one must never fall in love with technology. In our early scouting for breakthrough technology, we ran across research by Roland Winston, a University of Chicago physicist who had developed a prismatic light concentrator that increased the sharpness of images on a computer screen. We called the company NiOptics and got 3M interested in its commercial potential. There was a catch, though. The technology cost triple what other, similar technologies cost to produce, and it never caught on with computer makers. 3M eventually took NiOptics off our hands, but only for about 85 cents for each dollar we invested.

We learned it was important to have a willing buyer, at the right price, at the right time, in order to turn a promising breakthrough technology into a successful business. We also learned that at big companies such as 3M it was important to move up the organization chart, to the highest point we could reach. Our counterpart at 3M was enthusiastic about the NiOptics technology, but he could not persuade the money people to invest what it would have taken to make the product succeed. After that experience, I never hesitated to use whatever contacts I had—on the U. of C. board or elsewhere—to give us a chance of success.

NiOptics also was an example of something Doriot had tried to teach me back at Harvard, and it is a lesson I have learned more than once. In venture capital investing, Doriot said, it is important to understand who will buy the technology you're trying to sell. It is easy to fall in love with technology and lose sight of the fact that someone at some point will have to pay for it. An investor can lose a lot of money that way, and we have not been immune to such temptations.

By 1992, we had come to the point that ARCH's first fund was fully invested. If we wanted to continue doing business, it was time to raise more money. It also was time to take stock of some of what we had learned along the way. That would help us decide how much money we should raise, how many companies we should plan to invest in, and what improvements we should make in the way we operated.

Facing the Three Risks

We had learned that we were, indeed, creating a new style of investment. This was not seed capital, when early-stage investors—angels and the like—help a company get off the ground. In our case, we were identifying science literally at the site of inception, assessing whether it had commercial potential, and then erecting a commercial entity around it. It wasn't seed capital; it was virtually from scratch.

Broadly speaking, we faced three kinds of risks: technology risk, market risk, and financing risk. With the new round of capital we expected to raise, we knew we would be able to finance investments as needed. We were becoming experienced enough to make sound judgments about market risk. Our understanding of the science was growing, as was our network of knowledgeable experts in the scientific community.

I found it helpful to keep in mind something Tom Perkins of Kleiner Perkins memorably described to me regarding the formation of Genentech, when I met him during the first round of fund raising. When Stanford and UC-SF presented Kleiner Perkins with the chance to buy a license on the gene-splitting technology developed by Cohen and Boyer, Kleiner Perkins knew it had enough money to buy the license. The firm also knew that, if the technology was good, the market would be vast, but the science risk was profound.

Kleiner Perkins' response was to take $250,000 and split it among three different laboratories, asking each to duplicate the work of Cohen and Boyer. After all three labs replicated the results, Genentech was born. At ARCH, we did not have quite the same financial resources as Kleiner Perkins, but we always aspired to be as diligent in our assessment of science.

Invest with a Teaspoon

We also found our own ways to minimize our exposure. We tried always to gather a syndicate of investors to come in with us and support a new technology. This helped spread our financial risk and, over time, as we gained understanding of the talents and insights of our co-investors, it helped us better understand the market and science risks we faced. Beyond that, we tried to move carefully into our investments. We talked about it as "investing with a teaspoon," particularly with the first-in money. We offered future funding, often granting options to our portfolio companies, but made the additional funding available only if certain milestones were met: the hiring of a chief executive officer, scientific work, proof of market, and the like.

We also were, in a way, talent scouts. We had learned that discovery is a serial function. If someone discovers something once, chances are that person will discover something a second time long before a person who has never done one. And we knew, almost without testing the hypothesis, that a stellar scientist does not a CEO make. In virtually every instance, we had moved as quickly as possible to move the founding scientist out of an administrative role and put an experienced business manager in place. We intended to repeat this practice in the second fund and any subsequent fund raisings.

In fact, as our experience grew, we even began moving successful managers from one successful portfolio company into another. This proved to be a valuable way to improve our likelihood of success. After all, we were taking on enough risks in trying to commercialize research. By sticking with people we knew, and people who knew us, we were able to minimize another major risk factor: the risk associated with putting the right management talent in place. Just as we found that certain scientists were serial successes at finding breakthroughs on the laboratory bench, we found that certain managers could be serial successes, almost without regard to the specific scientific development they were working with.

On Our Own

For U. of C., the landmark moment for ARCH—the point at which it was time for us to begin a new round of financing—brought the university to its own moment of reckoning. ARCH had succeeded, beyond expectations really, in its original intent. In fact, in some ways it had succeeded too well. The university is a not-for-profit institution, and university lawyers were concerned about its active sponsorship of activity that was delivering financial returns of 25% and better on invested capital. After all, I was an administrator of the university, working out of university space, and employing university students as volunteers in a profit-making enterprise. I was told that at one meeting a lawyer joked that the IRS "is after us about our bookstore, no less this."

The time had come for us to go our separate ways. We had accomplished the mission for U. of C.—creating a path toward commercialization. Now, for ARCH, the point of departure opened new doors for us. We could set our own fundraising goals. We could begin to expand operations to other campuses and national laboratories. We could set up our own offices, and working with Bob Nelsen, Keith Crandell, and Clint Bybee we could professionalize our staff and support operations.

We agreed to continue to work closely with the university. At the same time, though, we no longer promised U. of C. a first look at investment opportunities. We established ARCH Venture Partners, and I left the university to become general partner of ARCH.

After consulting with other venture capitalists and Richard Testa, a Boston-based lawyer who had done path-breaking work in this area, we decided to set a $30 million target for ARCH Fund II and renamed our firm ARCH Venture Partners. We set the limit based on our expectation that, among the four of us, we could form at the most between four and five companies each year. Because we planned to invest at such early stages, we expected to spend a considerable amount of time actually working in each of our portfolio companies, especially at the start when we would be constructing a business around a scientific invention.

Shifting Gears

Once the fundraising period was behind us, we took ARCH in new directions. Over time, we would expand to five major bases of operation: Chicago, where we started, but also New York City, to capitalize on the research coming out of Columbia University; California; Washington State; and Albuquerque, NM, where we could tap into developments from the Los Alamos National Laboratory and the Sandia National Laboratories. Our first investment out of Seattle—in a company called NetBot that provides software agents to help online shoppers—we sold within a year to Internet search company Excite, returning a $9.9 million profit on ARCH's $1.3 million investment.

In California, we eventually decided to hire a full-time person just to keep tabs on the technology coming out of the University of California system. Kristina Burow is a Ph.D. biologist familiar with the top researchers on all nine campuses, and she provides a sort of incubation function for bright ideas. The value of this on-the-scene presence is hard to overstate. After all, we were in business in Illinois when Marc Andreesen and others at the University of Illinois developed Mosaic, the search engine that ultimately became Netscape and helped launch the Internet age. Andreesen, Eric Bina, and others were working around the clock and in plain view at the National Center for Supercomputing Applications down there. That discovery, had we happened upon it, would have been worth billions to us. We just never knocked on the right door. By putting people such as Kristina Burow in place, we try to make certain we don't miss that door the next time.

Outside the Ivy Walls

The new fund also gave us an opportunity to broaden our focus and to refine some of our investment strategies. NEON, a company in the information technology sector, became the first example of ARCH moving outside the university or government laboratory pipeline for an investment opportunity. NEON also set up shop in a sector, information technology, in which, to put it mildly, we did not have a comparative advantage. After all, Silicon Valley and other technology hot spots are overflowing with IT expertise and entrepreneurial talent. Besides, the half-life of an IT investment can be very short. That alone can create an unacceptable risk for a firm such as ours, which typically has a longer term investment outlook.

With NEON, our partner Keith Crandell was approached by someone he had come to know well as a sort of informal brain trust for ARCH. Rick Adam was a former Goldman Sachs administrative executive who had once reported to me at Baxter, and Keith had consulted him about several of the technologies we had seen at Argonne and U. of C. As it turned out, Adam had begun developing a tool hospitals could use to organize and access data and increase transaction speeds. The target market never developed because hospitals' IT protocols had not reached the point where they could maximize the potential of NEON's technology.

At this point, NEON was one of our larger investments. Keith and I were spending considerable time serving on the NEON board, trying to salvage ARCH's at-risk capital, and trying to find a market for technology that had to have a market somewhere. We just hadn't found it yet.

Eventually NEON did find its market: on Wall Street, where Adam had had a solid career. Merrill Lynch signed NEON to create a highly efficient, real-time middleware provider with the capability to guarantee the delivery of vital messages. In just five years, beginning in 1997, NEON grew to $180 million in revenues before it was acquired by Sybase, a leader in business intelligence software.

Adam is an example of the sort of person this work brings one into contact with: driven, imaginative, disciplined, and successful. Unfortunately, it does not always work that way. A portfolio company, R-2 Technologies, brought home for us the lesson about the vital importance of management talent.

R-2 was based on promising technology out of U. of C. and Lockheed Martin for eliminating false negatives during the reading of breast scans. Clearly, this looked like it had the potential to become a big, lucrative business, but the CEO, who had been recommended by a board member and passed muster with an executive search firm, failed to provide leadership. He was a misfit for us in any event, with a background in the imaging industry when what we needed was more scientific. We registered for an initial public offering, but when the accountants got in there they could not verify the financial results. We had to cancel the IPO, bring in a new CEO, and sell the company. ARCH turned a profit, but lord knows what return we could have made with a successful IPO.

Rolling Up Success

As we have become more sophisticated about our work we have begun to focus on moving more aggressively into certain markets. It's a process we call, somewhat disparagingly, "technology roll-ups." The idea is to find a winning idea, then look everywhere we can find—in the university and government laboratories, in corporate research departments to the extent any are still doing basic science—and obtain the rights to any potential discoveries we can find. That way, if it's a winner, we own a part of it, no matter which strand of the research ultimately proves to be most successful.

We did this successfully with a company called Adolor. Bob Nelsen was skiing in Vail in 1993 when he received a phone call from Graeme Bell, a U. of C. biologist known for his work identifying genes involved in Type 2 diabetes. For almost 40 years since the discovery of morphine, scientists had searched in vain for as many as three opioid receptors that might also be useful in fighting pain, perhaps without the addictive effects of morphine. We saw great potential for this, and investigative work by one of our scientific staff, with direction from Bell, led us to a company in Germany and a scientist at Harvard who were also doing research that was potentially complementary, or possibly competitive with, Bell's work.

Immediately we rolled up the technology, shelling out $50,000 for around five different option licenses—a pittance to spend on science that had the potential to become a blockbuster drug. Syndication was not easy because again the scientific challenge was so widely known and skepticism easy to find. Despite that, we raised the money and founded Adolor. The company became one of the great biotech success stories, and even went public after the dot-com crash of 2000. Shortly thereafter we founded Illumina, a genetic testing diagnostics company, which today has a market capitalization of over $4 billion.

The Tape Rolls On

Over time, ARCH has grown along with its portfolio companies. Though we run a streamlined organization, we currently operate with around 25 professionals distributed among several different offices. My own responsibilities have changed, as I serve now in an emeritus capacity. The title is different, but my input frankly has not changed much. As ever, I chiefly offer advice and counsel. Challenging assumptions, raising questions, offering a fresh set of eyes—I seek to bring experience and, at times, even wisdom to my colleagues.

I take pride in some of the products our companies have brought to market. Aviron, one of our start-ups, now part of MedImmune/AstraZeneca, has taken weak, live viruses researched at the University of Michigan and developed the inhalable flu vaccine called Flumist. Another, Ahora, pioneered the design of a detector used by homeland security to detect alien agents. Because of that company, people are allowed to carry liquids—granted, in small amounts—through security at airports. One never knows where our technology will go and whom it will reach.

If Professor Doriot were to review the tape on ARCH's existence, he would find a firm that relies on strong, trust-based relationships with scientists, investors, and other partners. He would see a firm with a systematic approach to identifying the commercial potential of the scientific work done at key academic and government research centers. ARCH focuses on four major areas: specialty materials, biotechnology, medical devices, and software. We emphasize underserved geographies such as the Midwest, New Mexico, and even Canada. And, finally, ARCH is a firm that, through its experience and expertise, seeks to reduce risks for the enterprises it helps create.

This is the tape I have created in the quarter century since I left Baxter to start ARCH and build it into something important. At one point in my life, I had thought those heady days at the Pentagon might be the high point of my career. Clearly, those days are an important part of my tape, but ARCH helped me change gears and move the tape onto a different reel—one that drastically altered the ultimate story. I would like to think it is a tape that others might be able to view, and use, to build success stories all their own.

LESSONS FROM STEVE LAZARUS

⬦ **Manage the "three risks."** Technology risk, market risk, and financing risk all can threaten the success of a potentially lucrative scientific discovery. Manage each with great care, both at start-up and as a venture matures.

⬦ **Invest with a teaspoon.** When putting first money into a new discovery, start with small amounts. Bring co-investors in to spread the risk. Contribute additional funds only as benchmarks and objectives are met.

⬦ **Remember your tape.** A person's life and the life of an enterprise are the sum total of actions and decisions over a period of time—a tape that never stops rolling, according to legendary Harvard Graduate School of Business professor Georges Doriot. Pay attention to that tape.

⬦ **Control the technology.** Take an ownership interest, not a license, in new technology in order to ensure it is maximized in commercial application. Use a roll-up strategy, acquiring all available technologies related to a particularly vital discovery, to dominate a new market.

⬦ **Avoid potholes.** Associate only with quality people. Avoid unproductive, intramural bickering. Let science lead the way. Learn to recognize technological failure early, and respond to market signals—both positive and negative—as events unfold.

11

FOSTERING INNOVATION: PEOPLE, PRACTICES, AND PRODUCTS MAKE NEW MARKETS

Franklin "Pitch" Johnson, Jr.
Founding Partner
Asset Management Company

AUM: $200 million   **Years in VC:** 47

Location: Palo Alto, CA   **Year born:** 1928

Grew up: Des Moines, IA; Palo Alto, CA

Location born: Quincy, IL

Best known deals: Amgen, Boole & Babbage, Coherent Radiation, IDEC, Teradyne

Style: Open, persistent

Education: B.S., Stanford University, Class of 1950
M.B.A., Harvard Graduate School of Business, Class of 1952

Significant experience: U.S. Air Force, steel production

Personal interests: Track and field, flying, golf, fishing, opera, education

The lesson: "Stick with things you believe in even when the going is difficult."

The term "Silicon Valley" was not yet invented when Pitch Johnson moved from the steel mills of Indiana to the entrepreneurial breeding ground of northern California. In more than four decades since then, usually investing his own money rather than raising a fund from limited partners, Johnson has been involved in some of the venture industry's big successes in investing such as Boole & Babbage and Coherent Radiation in the 1960s, Tandem Computers and SBE in the 1970s, and Amgen and IDEC in the early 1980s. He stuck with such companies as both an investor and director, sometimes for decades.

Johnson's low-key style matches a patient, persistent approach to the business. Working from Assest Management Company's offices in Palo Alto, Johnson explores complex technologies and has adapted to the days of interactive software games with Her Interactive, a company with products for adolescent girls. An early skeptic about the excesses of the late 1990s, Johnson has pursued a stick-to-the-basics approach that never goes out of style.

A steel mill in the Midwest may sound like the last place where a person might learn how to manage the process of innovation. I worked in Inland Steel's mill on the south shore of Lake Michigan, and it was a hot, smoky place that was anything but high-tech by modern standards. But what I learned there—about both people and process—has stuck with me over the years.

After my time in the mill, I went on to start a venture capital business in 1962 with Bill Draper in the Santa Clara Valley south of San Francisco, long before anyone called it "Silicon Valley." I helped recruit the chief executive who made the biotech firm Amgen a success and funded a company, Boole & Babbage, that became the first to offer diagnostic programs for IBM mainframe computers. I also learned the hard way, through a company called VisiCorp, how a business can go bad when it doesn't control its key technology. I have helped start venture firms in many countries, especially in eastern Europe. I currently serve on the boards of three U.S. companies, and one eastern European buyout fund.

One makes and markets the Nancy Drew computer games, another is working to cure Type 1 diabetes using stem-cell technology, and the third is working on very sensitive radios using superconductivity.

I didn't understand it at the time, but I acquired many of the tools I need to help spur innovative companies as a venture capital investor during the years I spent working at the Inland Steel mill in East Chicago, Indiana. Melting steel in an open-hearth furnace was painstaking, hot work using the most elemental inputs in industry: scrap steel, iron ore, oxygen, and fuel oil and ferro-alloys. If the melter supervising the furnace operators knows his job, each "heat" produces enough molten metal to make finished sheets, plates, and beams. If not, he winds up with up to 300 tons of useless material that has to be cut into pieces and remelted. It requires teamwork and good, quick decisions on when to put the heat into the ladle.

Investing as a venture capitalist, trying to ignite innovation, is remarkably similar, even if the sunny, high-tech world of Silicon Valley is a world away from the smokestacks of northern Indiana. For starters—and here is the most striking similarity—the crucial decisions must be made on the basis of inadequate information. The melter simply cannot measure everything he needs to know. He dips thermocouples into the furnace to measure the temperature and sends sample ingots to the lab for chemistry tests, but in the end he has to make judgments based on those changing measurements and looking into the furnace. He learns, over time, to trust the process and the men running the furnaces. For example, he learns the right time to lower a lance into the furnace to blow in oxygen to oxidize the carbon and impurities at a faster rate. He determines when to tap the molten steel into the ladle and where alloys are added to give the steel the final composition necessary to meet the differing specifications of an auto manufacturer, an appliance manufacturer, or a construction company.

In venture capital, we constantly make decisions based on inadequate information. We must decide whether or not to back an entrepreneur without fully knowing if the idea is powerful enough, the market big enough, or the management strong enough to be a success. But, if we can't make that call—if we can't, in a sense, tap that heat of steel—we can't do our business. At some point, we have got to say we are going to do it or not going to do it. The judgmental quotient of making that decision is vital to success. Steel isn't made much in open-hearth furnaces any more because of technology changes, and I am technically obsolete there, but the decision-making lessons I learned 50 years ago as I learned to cope with uncertainty are still very much alive.

You have to trust a proven process. I have invested a lot in biotech companies, Amgen being the most successful, and have found that no biotech company can succeed if its processes are not sound. It must control variables, be able to replicate results, learn from mistakes, and incorporate new information. These are all techniques that were vital to me at Inland Steel.

Beyond that, there was the human factor. I had grown up in Palo Alto. My father, who was a former Olympic hurdler, was the track coach at Stanford. It was a great life, but one that was insulated from many aspects of the working world. In the mills I first met large groups of eastern European immigrants. I first saw how working people struggle and sweat to succeed. Almost all of the workers knew more about steel making than I did. After all, many had grown up as children of mill workers. It was my job to lead them and guide them and make sound decisions, despite my scant experience in their business. To them, my Stanford engineering degree and Harvard MBA would have meant little, and I never mentioned them to my co-workers. This, too, is part of the venture capital trade: the ability to read people, to inspire or manage them, and to help them succeed, even if they might know more about the specifics of success in their particular field.

The Process of Innovation

I have a rather small venture capital firm. My friend Bill Draper, with whom I started in the business in the 1960s, later helped build a big, well-known firm called Sutter Hill. There are other firms that have gotten even bigger, such that they are as much about money management as innovation. I chose more of a solo route. At my firm, Asset Management Company, I invest almost exclusively my own money and my family's money, along with that of a few friends. What I am, mainly, is a co-founder, along with many others, of the modern venture capital business, the one that was so important to the development of Silicon Valley. In fact, Draper and I had been at work in the valley for nearly a decade before the writer Don Hoefler of *Electronic News* coined the term "Silicon Valley" in 1971.

Over some four decades of work, I have learned a great deal about the process of innovation. I have learned some of the tools and techniques needed to turn powerful ideas into great companies. I have learned the importance of working with the best people, perhaps the single most vital ingredient of success. Along the way, I have learned, too, some of the pitfalls to avoid. A person picks up a lot of lessons over time, and the person who pays attention, even in places as seemingly dissimilar as steel mills and biotech labs, has a good chance of backing the right people, with the right ideas, in the right markets. When all of those come together, you've got a chance of helping to create a great new company.

No single decision is more important in this equation than the one we make about whom, among the people we meet, deserves our financial backing. Virtually all the people a venture capitalist considers investing in have some elements of merit. They are creative enough to have a big idea and ambitious enough to put together some kind of business plan. The art of our business, this part of it anyway, is to select only the very best people with the strongest ideas. The people with drive, the ones who can execute, and the ones who can work with people are the ones who deserve support. They must see the whole market, a path to success, and the troubles to avoid. Those are the people who get our backing.

Success at Amgen

For me, the one who best symbolizes the model person in all those respects is George Rathmann, whom fellow venture capitalist Bill Bowes and I recruited to run Amgen in its earliest days, when its promise was great but its success far from certain. Before we found Rathmann to run it, Amgen had emerged as our possible answer to Genentech, the first significant biotechnology company. The venture capitalist Tom Perkins had backed Genentech since its start in 1977. In fact, Perkins had provided space for Robert Swanson and his co-founder Herbert Boyer to do some of the preliminary research necessary to get Genentech off the ground. In 1980, I got my chance. Bowes had come up with the idea for Amgen and invited me to invest in a very early round. The company badly needed a chief executive, though, and we found that Rathmann was just the person we needed.

Rathmann was an executive at Abbott Laboratories at the time, but Abbott appeared to have tired of biotech. In the late 1970s, after Stanley Cohen and Herbert Boyer developed the ability to splice genes, Abbott began experimenting with biotechnology but segregated its scientists within highly secure labs. Abbott also believed that working with DNA would cost too much and take too long before any commercially viable product could be produced. Rathmann was an experimenter by nature, a natural leader who was impatient to get going, so he needed a more risk-tolerant and innovative atmosphere than Abbott would provide.

Bowes and I learned about Rathmann through Winston Salser, a University of California–Los Angeles professor who had set up a DNA research laboratory at UCLA and had become the founding scientist of the newly formed company, Applied Molecular Genetics, or Amgen. Rathmann was on a sabbatical from Abbott in Salser's UCLA lab. According to Rathmann, Abbott had declined to form such a research unit, so he was immediately interested when we approached him to talk about our ideas for Amgen. On the other hand, he was not going to be a push-over, as we learned during our effort to construct a scientific advisory board for the company.

We and Salser had built a good scientific advisory board. There was some talk that this board would report directly to the company's directors, not to any of the executives at Amgen. Rathmann would have none of it. He had some experience with science boards when he worked in product research at 3M up in Minneapolis. Rathmann succeeded in helping lead 3M into the market for x-ray film, but he also believed the science board had the effect of squelching innovation at 3M, as all sorts of political infighting came about over science. There was fingerpointing when products did not turn out well. In some instances, the corporate board would lobby the company's science board for products that researchers such as Rathmann might never have supported. Rathmann worried that if we gave Amgen's science board a direct pipeline to the directors, it would only undermine the chief executive officer.

"It's an interesting idea," he said of our proposal. "But, if the SAB is going to be around the company, then they will report to the CEO, or I'm not going to be the CEO." His main hang-up after that became whether his wife, Joy, would be willing to move to the west coast.

We eventually hired Rathmann. Abbott tried to tempt him by offering him a research operation of his own, but we worked that out by offering Abbott a minority stake in Amgen. Rathmann went straight to work. He recruited top corporate scientists and top university scientists to work in Amgen's research labs. He was able to attract them and offer incentives to them in ways that kept them with us even once the company started succeeding and, because of their reputations, other firms tried to recruit them away.

The Scientist as Industrial Leader

Rathmann was not a scientist in the sense that some university professors are. He was an industrial leader with a strong science pedigree. He understood business, and he saw how to make money by getting products to market. He had the rare combination of understanding where the science might lead and envisioning what market would be there once the science arrived. Rathmann also set policy that geared Amgen toward the Food and Drug Administration approval process, so we could get drugs through the FDA pipeline more quickly.

Rathmann also got very involved in selecting and suggesting board members, which was an important part of the company's success. Working with Rathmann and the board, we figured out a way to get our business done even though we had a representative on the board from Abbott, a company that had the potential to become a competitor on certain of our products. Bowes, Rathmann, and I started meeting informally. That way we could hammer things out and decide what was in Amgen's best interests without sharing all that we knew with Abbott. Abbott knew about this process and felt comfortable with it, because they realized it was necessary for Amgen to have the freedom it needed in order to succeed.

And Amgen did succeed. It took 10 years from its founding before Amgen could get FDA approval on any of its products, but those approvals ultimately did come. Epogen and Neupogen became the biotech industry's first blockbuster products—more than $1 billion in sales each—and they brought many thousands of patients relief from anemia due to kidney dialysis and the side effects from cancer treatments. By 1981, the company went public, and some of the founding investors who were running venture funds sold out and did very well. Because Bowes and I were investing on our own behalf we were able to stay invested and earned another large multiple as the company kept growing.

Character Lessons

In a way, the role I played at Amgen, as at many of the companies I have invested in, was to coach a CEO who was extremely capable in his own right but who also benefited from my judgment and experience. Coaching is something that I grew up with, because I am the son of a coach. My dad, Pitch Johnson, Sr., was a track coach. He ran the high hurdles in the 1924 Olympics—the "Chariots of Fire" team—and wound up coaching at Drake University in Des Moines, where he directed the Drake Relays, one of the great track meets in the United States. In 1940, he got the job at Stanford as track coach and left in 1945 to enter business. My dad fostered in me a desire to win, fairly, that I retain to this day, and he helped me relate to the competitive men and women who start companies. My own years of being a track athlete in high school and at Stanford also taught me a lot about working toward goals and winning and handling loss.

While my dad taught me a great deal about people and character, much of what I learned about business as a young man actually came from my father-in-law, Eugene Holman, who was the chief executive of Standard Oil of New Jersey, which today is called Exxon Mobil. I actually met his daughter through track and field. While preparing to attend business school at Harvard, I complained to a guy I knew on Stanford's track team that I didn't know any women back East, and he gave me the name of Cathie Holman, a Vassar student, whom I began dating and eventually persuaded to marry me.

Mr. Holman had worked his way up from the oil fields. He was a great prospector for oil. He knew that the best way to build a career was to pay dues and build from the ground up. He believed strongly that, as an executive at a big public company, he was the custodian of other peoples' money. And he felt strongly about the value of hard work. One time when I was working in the mills, some friends of his visited Cathie and me and saw me return home from work in grimy clothes, even though I had showered at the mill. I had a Harvard M.B.A., and this couple wondered why I didn't have a better job.

Mr. Holman had a simple response: "That is what he wants to do," he said. And for him, as long as the work was interesting and satisfying, that was good enough. He understood there were jobs from which a person comes home with dirt on their clothes, since he had held them himself.

The Lure of Capital

For a long time, the work in the mill was good enough. I enjoyed making steel, and I was learning a lot about how to manage people, but then one of those unexpected things happened that can change a person's life. As I rose in the ranks at Inland Steel, I became eligible for stock options as part of my compensation. One time, before the annual meeting, I was reading the prospectus for the meeting and noticed that the descendants of the company's founders each owned hundreds of thousands of shares. It was 1961, I was 33, and I had worked at the company for seven years. I had options for 42 shares—nothing wrong with that—but the grandchildren of the founders had more than 400,000 shares each. I decided then that I needed to do something else. I needed to stop working for a salary, and I needed to start something so that, one day, I might be the one who could form capital.

I had two things going for me. I had saved $25,000, and a person I had met, a former salesman for Inland, was Bill Draper III. We had been neighbors in East Chicago, Ind. and colleagues at the Inland plant, but Draper had left a few years earlier to return to California and work for his father, William Draper, Jr., at a venture capital firm called Draper, Gaither & Anderson. Bill's father was one of the pioneers of California venture capital.

Cathie and I went out that year for the "Big Game," the annual football clash between Stanford and the University of California–Berkeley. Draper mentioned he was thinking about leaving his father's firm, where he was an associate, to set out on his own. I was interested in forming a firm, too. Over his kitchen table that weekend we drew up our idea of what our firm might look like. Along with my $25,000, Mr. Holman agreed to lend me $50,000, and Draper was able to raise a similar amount. By the middle of the next year, we had formed our firm as a small business investment company licensed by the Small Business Administration, and we started looking for deals.

Government Help

The Small Business Investment Company program is one of those rare government initiatives that actually works almost better than anyone thought it would. Under the SBIC program, which started in 1958, investment funds that raise a minimum amount privately can raise additional money as needed by issuing debt securities guaranteed by the SBA. In those days, the SBA was the direct lender. There were some abuses after the program first started, when people invested with their brothers-in-law and the like, but there were many more successful examples, as in our case. At the time we were getting started, we needed to raise $150,000 in order to get our SBIC license. Once we got that much, and increased our capital to $300,000 using some government debentures, the government would lend us three times as much to do deals. It was a great way to leverage our money.

We weren't the only ones in northern California to see this as an opportunity to kick-start the innovation that would come out of Stanford and other universities and the general entrepreneurial climate in the area. In fact, several of us SBIC investors put together a group called the Western Association of Small Business Investment Companies. Only half of us were doing what today would be called venture capital. The rest were doing mainly real estate deals, but we shared investment ideas, talked about our investment techniques, and gradually developed a fairly coherent way of doing business. To this point, the SBIC program has helped provide more than $50 billion of financing to more than 100,000 small U.S. companies. Intel, Apple, and Palm Computing are among the technology companies that started with SBIC-backed financing.

In 1962, as Draper and I got our SBIC license, we and the other venture investors in the area all started doing our early deals. We were innovating out of necessity, and we were inventing the business as we went along. We developed some customs and terminology. We developed the nomenclature of pre-money and post-money valuations and the idea of organizing rounds of financing. All of these evolved over time. The names of them now are called, pretty uniformly, seed financing, rounds A, B, C, and D. We hadn't given them those names yet, but the practice was becoming pretty standard.

We developed the idea that you put enough money into a company to get it to a certain place, and then you agree to put in more if the management team reaches certain milestones. This is standard operating procedure today, but it was a fairly new approach back then. Another custom that evolved, because we were all small, was the idea that we would all do deals together. This, too, was out of necessity. Most of us did not have enough money to fund many deals on our own, so we shared the work and shared the future financing commitments, too. I thought that was an important innovation. The Latin root of innovation is *novo*, which means "to renew." We weren't renewing things. We were doing one better: We were inventing them and then repeating the ones that worked.

Before long, the form of doing business evolved from the small private venture firms using their own capital to the limited partnership format. Many venture firms had outside investors who were trying to make a return on their money by providing capital for start-ups. Eventually, we began creating preferred stock, so we paid a lot more than the founders did, but we got our money out first in case of trouble. If anybody got any money out of a deal at all, the preferred stockholders came out before the common stock owners did. In a successful deal, though, the stock all converted at some rate into common stock. That way, everyone could cash out and get their returns.

On My Own

After about three years in partnership with Bill Draper, I was getting antsy just advising companies, and I wanted to operate one. Sutter Hill, a real estate company, wanted to get into the venture business, so they bought out our portfolio, and Draper decided to go into business with them. I had some real capital for the first time in my life. Simply because we had some time and some money to do it, Cathie and I went on a five-week trip to South America. Before we left I bought some stock in a public company, Memorex, and by the time we got back I had more than doubled my money in that investment. It easily could have gone the opposite way, but it gave me a bit more capital than I had figured on. I then started to look for a business to buy, but instead of that, I kept finding deals to do.

I never did wind up managing a single business, but by going out and setting up my own firm, I was plowing a path that differed from the ones many of my colleagues from this early period followed. I decided to invest just my own money, and my family's money, and grow it as big as I could. While many of my colleagues got into building their firms, raising fund after fund with dozens of limited partners, I was growing, albeit more slowly, that one pool of money.

By definition, the approach I took tended to give us different investment time horizons. When you're investing a fund and that fund has a limited life of around 10 years, you have to get the investments mature and liquid in a very few years and get your investors rewarded. If you're running a family firm or an "evergreen" firm like Sutter Hill, you have the luxury of patience. That's good, though I have to admit that there's a downside to that, too. If I've made a consistent mistake over the years, it's the mistake of staying in investments longer than I should, exercising too much patience, I guess.

The Power of a "Pitching Change"

One of the deals in which patience did pay, one of my most important early deals, was the software company Boole & Babbage. With this investment, what I learned about the value of patience as an investor was only part of the payoff. I also learned how important it is, when trying to spur innovation, to change leadership, if necessary, when the management cannot keep pace with changes in the marketplace. You've got to have the right people in charge.

I first heard about Boole & Babbage in 1968, when a couple of venture capitalists named Bill Edwards and John Bryan brought the deal to me. Actually, the company wasn't called Boole & Babbage just yet. The founders—Dave Katch and Ken Kolence—had named it K&K Associates, a name that didn't have much appeal. I asked them to come up with a new name, and they delivered: Boole & Babbage, named after the inventors of the mainframe computer and computer software, respectively. It's hard to say if the company would not have been as successful with a different name, but this illustrates, I think, that there are many important details when a company is getting launched.

It was a time when IBM mainframe computers ruled the business world, and one of the most successful of all, the IBM 360 series, was coming into common use. Katch and Kolence had an idea to build a company that could provide software that helped companies run their IBM computers better. Until then, most companies just wrote their own computer code, so our company would simplify their use of IBM's mainframes.

Boole & Babbage's founders also had the idea of packaging software that enabled companies to measure the amount of time their computers were running on a program. The software the company developed helped its clients save the expense and uncertainty of writing the programming themselves. Another of their major products helped organize the way printers, disk drives, and other peripherals are organized to work with the mainframe.

I was alerted to what a good-sized company this could be when at a Harvard Graduate School of Business alumni event I ran into a former classmate and good friend named Spike Beitzel, who was by then an executive vice president of marketing at IBM.

"You're competing with us," Beitzel told me.

I told him that couldn't possibly be true. We were too small to make a dent in IBM.

"You're making it so people don't have to buy new computers until much later," he said. He had a smile on his face, but he wasn't kidding.

IBM was tough, and, unrelated to my meeting with Beitzel, their salesmen began telling the customers that they had plans to bundle some products like ours with their mainframes so they needn't buy our stuff. IBM had set up a West Coast vice president for industry relations, to whom we complained, and they stopped the practice.

Despite the hit Boole & Babbage took once IBM started recognizing us as a competitor, the company kept growing, and as it grew I learned that there were limits on how well some founders can adapt as their company grows. Kolence was the chief executive, but he didn't have the executive skills to keep up with the company's growth. As chairman, I decided, with the board's consent, to bring in an executive vice president with management experience, a person named Bruce Coleman. I guess it's not surprising that Kolence didn't like that. He fought it and made the arrangement so difficult that I had to invite him to my house and tell him I was going to make a "pitching change." He actually expressed relief after hearing the news.

Still, it's amazing how much difference new management can make at a company such as Boole & Babbage. Sales and profits took off immediately after the change. But nothing is forever, and we had to make another change in 1991, after one of Coleman's successors had run into trouble. He had built the company's sales force so big that sales costs alone were higher than the revenues on several products. He had put the company into unrelated businesses and had a compensation plan that paid out $1 million in bonuses even though the company was losing money on $101 million in sales.

In this troubled environment, we named Paul Newton, already a board member, as the new CEO, and Newton quickly turned around those problems. By 1998, after sales had risen to $170 million a year, he sold the company to BMC Software in an $887 million stock swap. I was in that company 30 years. I made a strong return. Because of the time involved, it might not have created the internal rate of return that would satisfy someone who was investing on behalf of limited partners, but it was enough for my family. I wish I could have done more to make that company a lasting leader in the software business, but by any measure, the investment was a success.

Cloudy Vision

Not every investment turns out as successfully as Boole & Babbage did. In fact, it helps to have a failure or two or else you're just not trying. The key question is what you learn from the investments that go wrong.

For me, the highest profile bust turned out to be VisiCorp. The company started as a sort of partnership, forged out of Harvard Graduate School of Business, between Daniel Bricklin, a programming genius, and Dan Fylstra, who had more executive skills and also knew more about marketing. The seeds of VisiCorp's demise, though, were laid at the outset, when Fylstra agreed to sign a marketing contract for the product but obtained no other rights improving it. The programming was retained by Bricklin, through his company called Software Arts.

VisiCorp had a great run at first. The company had one of the first computer spreadsheet products, VisiCalc, which helped make the Apple II a success, because it ran on that computer. It's fair to argue that without VisiCalc, Apple wouldn't have had the early success it did. By the same token, the decision by VisiCorp's founders to focus on Apple, when it was by no means clear that Apple would become for a time the dominant personal computer brand, was a good decision.

The key failure with VisiCorp, though, was the company's inability to control its future because it did not own the software program that was at the heart of its initial success. VisiCorp tried to compensate for this shortcoming but could never quite get over it. The lesson from all this is that, in a market where constant innovation is the lifeblood of success, it's almost impossible for a company to succeed if it cannot control the key technology that will determine its future.

In VisiCorp's early days, the lack of control over new software development was not an issue. Its big program was selling, and no new products were needed yet. By the time VisiCorp was two years old, in 1981, it was selling more than 30,000 copies of its software each month. Success like that wouldn't go unanswered, though, and a competitor soon popped up. Mitch Kapor, a former VisiCalc employee, developed an integrated spreadsheet, word processor, and graphing program that essentially ate up the VisiCalc market. Kapor's product, Lotus 1-2-3, became the standard almost overnight, and it also became a chief tool by which the IBM PC and other compatible computers worked their way into the workplace, thanks to their ability to accomplish calculation-intensive office work with ease. Lotus 1-2-3 left VisiCalc in the dust. Almost overnight, VisiCalc's sales dropped from 20,000 a month in early 1983 to about one-tenth that amount.

Striking Back

We did all we could to save VisiCalc. Fylstra sued Software Arts for its failure to update and improve VisiCalc. The company's developers moved ahead on a new product that we eventually called VisiOn. And the board, with my support, brought in a new chief executive, Terry Opendyk, a former Intel programmer who had a toughness that no one else in management could muster. Intel was famous for its confrontational culture. Andy Grove, the chief executive there, liked to pit people against each other. He thought it brought out the best in his executive team, and that's the sort of mindset Opendyk brought to VisiCorp. My view, too, was that we needed to just begin developing a program that could run on the IBM and its compatibles, and one that had to match Lotus.

We simply couldn't salvage the situation fast enough. The new product, VisiOn, pretty much failed. And, eventually, VisiCorp lost its place in the market. The lesson from all this is that I don't want again to be part of a company that does not control its own product development.

Bob Noyce of Intel, the primary developer of the integrated circuit, wisely declined to invest in VisiCorp as a startup for this reason.

Another basic revelation from the VisiCorp experience is the importance of matching the CEO, and the top management team, to the challenges facing the company. Though Terry Opendyk at times was probably rougher on people than he needed to be, he was the right sort of person to go into VisiCalc and do whatever it might take to get that situation under control. It wasn't his fault that the company just couldn't get it done. I've been fortunate, really, to work with CEOs over the years who were well suited to the tasks they faced, and Opendyk was one of them.

The Tandem Approach

Fortunately, there are different styles to CEO success, and there could not have been a bigger contrast in style than the one between Terry Opendyk of VisiCalc and Jim Treybig at Tandem. What's interesting to me as a venture investor and a student of management, is that both styles work. The art we try to deploy as venture investors, when we are called on to put a CEO in place, is in matching the right CEO to the particulars of the challenges facing the company.

Treybig was founder of Tandem and one of those bigger-than-life Texas characters. He pulled together a really strong team: a terrific marketing guy, a strong financial guy, and different sorts of people in hardware and software design. They worked like hell all week, and on Friday nights they would sit down for a few beers. It was a tradition Treybig maintained even when the company had thousands of employees and they needed special insurance in case there were any accidents as people made their way home after a pop or two after work.

The idea was to have a flat social structure, with openness to everyone in the organization, which Treybig probably brought with him from Hewlett-Packard, where he had started in the computer business. Bill Hewlett and David Packard were famous for sitting in the employee cafeteria and leaving seats open at their table. Those places were reserved for the rank-and-file workers who might want to sit down with the bosses for a lunch, the sort of workers who had no other casual opportunity to rub shoulders with the founders of the business.

Hitting the Plan

It would be a big mistake, though, to think Treybig ran a loose company just because he had this informal style with his employees. The business plan that he generated worked right from the outset. For five years he was as close to his plan as I have seen at any company before or since. He came close on profitability, on sales, on just about anything worth measuring. This was a guy who knew business and his business, very well.

Treybig also was decisive, which is absolutely essential in a leader. Not every CEO is as decisive as he or she needs to be. With one of our portfolio companies, I went to a board meeting one time, and the CEO said, "I've got three courses of action, which one does the board want?"

That is a turn-off right there. I want to hear him or her say, "Here is where I want to go. Here's why I want to go there, and here's how I want to go there."

The board can always reject the proposal because they think the company should do something else. Offering a choice of options to the board, without a management recommendation, is not leadership. Sometimes boards have to be led, too.

The Research Lifeline

A completely different sort of leader, though just as effective in his ability to spur innovation, was Alex d'Arbeloff at Teradyne. Along with Nick DeWolff, a classmate at the Massachusetts Institute of Technology, d'Arbeloff had started Teradyne in 1960 based on the theory that the computer industry would need high-precision testing equipment as it moved toward mass production. D'Arbeloff was a boss, an old-line, hierarchical type of leader. There was no doubt about that. And he showed remarkable cool even though Teradyne's sales were, by definition, highly cyclical. Semiconductor makers bought the products when they were launching a new product line, but very rarely bought when they were between product introductions or when sales slowed. Recessions hit the company particularly hard.

D'Arbeloff's big insight was that it was vital to keep investing in product development, regardless of downturns in the sales cycle.

That way, when the cycle turned up again, Teradyne would be there with the best products. It's hard to overstate how gutsy such decisions can be. As I worked with d'Arbeloff over the years, I developed a deep appreciation for the way he learned his lesson in the mid-1970s, when Teradyne lost its leadership position to Fairchild Semiconductor because it failed to anticipate the move to large-scale integrated circuits.

D'Arbeloff wasn't about to let that happen again. Beginning in 1976, as the industry emerged from a recession, d'Arbeloff more than tripled research investment, to $17 million. As a new recession set in beginning in 1980, he bumped investment further, to $20 million a year, even though earnings fell from $11 million in 1980 to $4 million in 1981. The company lived for years off of the breakthrough research that was launched during one of the darkest periods in Teradyne's history. It surprised nobody that d'Arbeloff had such a remarkably long-lived tenure. He retired as Teradyne's chairman in 2000—after 40 years of service to the company.

Staying Power

That sort of staying power is rare. It's a real anomaly. And, in a sense, the way I have approached the business is out of pattern, too. The venture capital business has changed over the years, but I haven't really changed with it.

After the dot-com crash of 2000, when the venture market came back, it came back in a different form than previously. It became a big money management business. All of a sudden, there were several multibillion-dollar funds. This has changed the mindset of entrepreneurs, too. They don't want to start a company unless they can get $10 million to $20 million in backing. The venture capitalists, because they're running so much money, have got to make big deals, too. For them, a bunch of smaller deals just cannot add up compared to the huge fund they've got. I'm not sure that's healthy.

My firm, Asset Management Company, manages just $60 million in its latest fund. With all our equity holdings, including companies such as Amgen that I have held for decades, we have about three to four times that under management. It might sound like a lot to most people, but it's not. In this business, in Silicon Valley, we are small, and our family capital is small, but I don't feel small because by any rational measure we are not. More importantly, though, it's because the nature of the business is so rewarding.

What I like about the business now is that it has gone back to the basics. If anything good has come out of the turbulent economic times that started around 2007, that return to the fundamentals is it. Instead of focusing on building larger and larger funds, venture investors are back to starting companies, finding people with breakthrough ideas, and helping them succeed.

Before the dot-com crash in 2000, something had just gone wrong. People got short-term greedy. They came into the business for the quick-hitting part of it. They had no intention of really innovating, of taking a big idea and building a company out of it. The entrepreneurs set out to make fast money, they got backers, and they succeeded. Everybody had a share in it: the entrepreneurs, the investment bankers, the venture capitalists. There were plenty of Porsches rolling around here that were the result of those deals, and guys built big houses and got out of the business.

I'm not talking about the Yahoo founders, or Google, or all these people who built real companies and made great money doing so. I believe in that. But I think that we paid a price when that bubble collapsed in 2000. It set the business back, and it had a lot to do with the quick-hit people. We are in tough times again, and it is difficult to get liquid even when we build successful companies. We and others are doing deals in this slow time because by the time these new companies grow, we think the market for their stock will come back.

Entering New Markets

What such people lose sight of, or what they might never get to know, is how the process of fostering innovation helps to create new economic opportunity. I'm a pilot, and I fly my plane four or five times a year to eastern Europe to help people start businesses. I helped start funds in Russia, Poland, Romania, and the Czech Republic, but you don't have to travel that far to get involved in start-ups that still mean a lot because the people involved are making products they believe in, building marketing plans, and adjusting to the signals the market sends.

The market moves fast, and you've got to be prepared to move with it. If you don't, you might miss the next big wave. I totally missed the social networking thing. Maybe age was a factor. I don't text people; I still send e-mails. I've got some younger people who work with me, and they missed it, too. Maybe we just weren't paying enough attention.

Innovation does not always have to be a world-changing new development the way Google was, or the way social networks such as Facebook or Twitter are becoming. Sometimes, it's as simple as just making changes to a product or listening to market signals, lining up your company with what the market demands. Sometimes it means backing a person who is just a really committed, creative chief executive. The reward from venture investing comes in watching that person, and the business, grow.

One of my favorite recent cases is a company we are invested in now called Her Interactive. I got involved in the company just as it was starting out, in Albuquerque in the 1980s, and it was called American Laser Games. They were making training films for cops. These films presented police with situations where they had to decide to shoot or not shoot. A cop is in a garage where he sees a guy trying to break into a trunk. The cop challenges the stranger. The guy reaches into the trunk, and the cop has to decide whether or not to shoot. In one ending, the guy is just changing a tire. In the other, he's got a gun.

What nobody expected was that a guy in the Middle East ordered one of these, just to play with at home. Based on that, the then-president of the company, Bob Grebe, thought we could make a product for the arcade-game market. Grebe got it right. This was at the height of the arcade boom, and we had many tens of millions in sales. Then the arcade business died. PC games came along and killed it—and almost killed the company, too. We had to file Chapter 11.

Somewhere along the line, Grebe had licensed the Nancy Drew name from Simon & Schuster, publisher of the books. While we were in Chapter 11, I ran into some people at Microsoft who had great programming skills that Microsoft had little interest in developing. We decided to move Her Interactive to Seattle, but we needed leadership. We met a turn-around guy named Jan Claesson, formerly of Microsoft. Just to check Jan out, I called Steve Ballmer, Microsoft's president, whom I knew from when he was a business-school student at Stanford.

Steve said that Claesson was a very strong leader, although "too tough for us." He said Claesson was just the guy for the job I had described, "as long as you don't mind how many Marines are left lying on the hill."

That was the most unusual positive recommendation I ever heard. It was particularly surprising coming from Ballmer, who's not exactly a soft touch. Claesson earned the recommendation, though. He turned the company around and used our Nancy Drew license to get us going into that market, mostly for girls. He also did it without leaving too many casualties from the company behind.

Embracing Uncertainty—and the Future

With innovation, you've always got to be prepared for change. Claesson completed his turn-around duties by suggesting we promote our creative director, Megan Gaiser, to the presidency, and this goes back to something I mentioned right at the outset about steelmaking— the need to, once in a while, make a decision based on incomplete information.

Gaiser had started her career as a documentary filmmaker. She had gone to Microsoft and worked on its first interactive-only product, a program called CarPoint. Claesson had brought Gaiser over from Microsoft, and she was the one who really understood the potential of the Nancy Drew license. Gaiser's idea was to keep Nancy Drew whole-some, as she is in the books created by the writer Millie Benson. The mothers would buy these games a lot, and they wanted their daughters to have a wholesome experience. Gaiser understood teenage girls better than most any adult. She knew that they like cooperative games and they like sitting in groups and working on puzzles. That cooperative effort is exciting for many girls.

As Claesson was putting that gender-sensitive stamp on the product, we all had to keep in mind that we were a company that had just been through bankruptcy. I was pretty much the only venture money behind it. We had to keep costs down—spend $100,000 to develop a game, not a couple million. The trick was having a few people, not a big organi-zation, and just those few dedicated people who love gaming working hard and efficiently to design these fairly simple games.

Innovation, in the end, really does go back to what I learned at the steel mill. Her Interactive was not some great beam that became part of the structure of the new economy. It is a game, a diversion—a decoration of sorts. It won't change the world, but it does make customers happy. It is a good business for a handful of dedicated people to run. It lets young girls use their brains to solve a mystery in a wholesome setting. Perhaps the greatest innovation was the hunch that it might make sense to use technology to introduce that great character, Nancy Drew, to a new generation of young women. That entrepreneur's hunch is now helping Her Interactive to become a growing, profitable leader in its field.

If innovation, even on that small a scale, can be plenty fulfilling, just imagine how rewarding the big breakthroughs can be.

LESSONS FROM PITCH JOHNSON

 Act on incomplete information. A person will never have all the information one would want when making investment decisions. Get the essential data, and then trust your gut and forge ahead.

 Match the people to the challenge. The brightest ideas are nothing without the right people working in the right ways to bring them to market.

Control your key technology. A company that does not control its core technology cannot control its future.

 Size is not everything. It does not require a billion-dollar fund for a person to make a big difference in promoting innovation. In fact, smaller can be better.

Be patient. Don't be driven by short-term exit strategies. Innovation can take time before it really pays off.

12

RISK, THEN REWARD: MANAGING VENTURE INVESTMENT IN RUSSIA

Patricia M. Cloherty
Chairman and CEO
Delta Private Equity Partners, LLC

AUM: $449 million   **Years in VC:** 37

Location: Moscow, Russia   **Year born:** 1942

Grew up: Pollock Pines, CA   **Location born:** San Francisco, CA

Best known deals: DeltaCredit Bank, INTH (Russia Channel 3), Lomonosov Porcelain, Tessera Technologies, Agouron Pharmaceuticals, Centocor, Biocompatibles International, PPL Therapeutics P.L.C., which cloned Dolly the sheep

Style: Intellectually curious and goal oriented

Education: B.A., San Francisco College for Women, Class of 1963 M.A., M.I.A., Columbia University, Class of 1968

Significant experience: Peace Corps, Patricof & Co. Ventures, which became Apax Partners, Deputy Administrator, U.S. Small Business Administration

Personal interests: Former competitive downhill skier, hiking, gardening, reading

The lesson: "Never micromanage."

In a career that made her one of the first female partners of a major venture firm, Pat Cloherty saved her most audacious first for last: moving to Russia, where she currently still resides, to run Delta Private Equity Partners' $449 million portfolio of investments. In Moscow, she has deciphered opaque balance sheets, jousted with unscrupulous or imperious negotiating partners, and once even hired bodyguards after a deal broke down.

The move to Moscow, initially necessary to turn around Delta's troubled first investment fund, now is turning in exemplary results. Delta's portfolio companies have introduced mortgages and credit cards to Russian consumers, brought better programming to Russian television, and helped modernize Russian retailing. Lessons from Cloherty's experience can equip investors and managers doing business in Russia or any developing market where the rules are not all written and the risks not quite known.

I n 1994, when the U.S. government first asked me to help launch a new venture capital business in Russia, I was at Apax Partners, doing a good business in mainly early-stage science and technology companies. I had not been to Russia and didn't speak the language. While I thought it was a good idea to lay the seeds of actual, free-market capitalism in Russia, it had never occurred to me that I would be the person to do it.

I got involved, tentatively at first, by joining the board of the U.S. Russia Investment Fund, which was formed pursuant to the Support for East European Democracy Act of 1989 as part of foreign development assistance to the former Soviet Union and its former satellites after the fall of the Berlin Wall. I joined the board as a *pro bono* director while still at Apax, from which I retired in 2000. Frankly, though, the group's first deal taught me that there was no way to be tentative about any aspect of doing business in Russia. The board and staff had committed to an $8.2 million investment in Dieselprom, a company that was licensed to make Daimler-Benz diesel engines in Russia. There was no system for transferring funds to Russia yet, so the staff sent the first payment, $850,000 in cash, by courier in a plain black suitcase.

The briefcase was never seen again. Nobody likes to lose an entire investment, but at least the money usually gets to its intended destination before it disappears.

I did not take this loss as an omen. Instead, I figured, with a start like that, there was no way to go but up. Certainly, the economy and business practices would both take shape.

I have done interesting work in my career. Together with Alan Patricof at Apax Partners, we initiated the East Coast branch of the venture capital industry. Though we eventually would build Apax to $10 billion in assets under management by the time of my retirement in 2000, at the outset in the early 1970s we were helping to invent the new investment discipline now known as venture capital. Nearly three decades of such work gave me the tools I would need to succeed in Russia or anywhere, but so would some of the odder experiences in my life. There was the time I got death threats while working at the Small Business Administration, of all places, because I was investigating alleged improprieties in an agency program. I have backed dozens of companies, ranging from dollar stores in the West to the Scottish company that cloned Dolly the sheep—proof, I like to think, that I am open to challenge and opportunity, no matter where it comes from.

All of the experiences of a 30-plus-year career in venture capital gave me the technical know-how, appetite for risk, and long-term perspective I would need to navigate as a venture capital investor in Russia. Yet, in some ways, none of my prior work fully prepared me, either. To succeed in one of the most unpredictable, laws-in-process, and capital-hungry countries on Earth, I would need to adapt and improvise or risk causing Delta Private Equity Partners' two funds to lose a lot more than a suitcase full of cash.

What I have learned so far—and particularly since I moved to Russia in 2003 to work full time in making Delta Private Equity Partners a success—offers lessons about the risks and potentials for investing in foreign markets. Attack the challenges aggressively, but with due care and thought, and the returns can consistently outperform those from less risky, more mature markets. But, misplay the risks of politics, economics, culture, and business, and you can run into serious trouble.

After all, the Russian private economy is young—less than 20 years old. It still is influenced by a small group of powerful oligarchs. Although mobsters and corruption still exist, they are less common problems than they were in the 1990s. There are signs, in fact, of a developing maturity.

I have been threatened only once, and after that particularly unpleasant meeting I hired bodyguards for a brief period. The rule of law is still a goal but it is starting to take shape. The Vladimir Putin–led government, more predictable and sensible than one might expect from reading the Western press, has been a positive influence in nearly every aspect of business.

Rules for Russian Investment

In Russia, one has to be flexible and yet disciplined, much as one has to be in the Peace Corps, for which I served in Brazil in the early 1960s. What works in more developed economies may not work in Russia, and *vice versa*. In many ways, I have consciously chosen to modify the rules that have led to success in the United States and other developed economies. For example, I have certain sectors I almost always avoid in mature economies: no food, no clothing, no shelter, no feature films.

So, where have we invested successfully in Russia? Food, clothing, and shelter, for starters. We like financial services, consumer products and services, and media and telecommunications, but not technology, as there is no enforceable intellectual property protection in Russia. We also steer clear of the 42 areas deemed "strategic" by the government, for obvious reasons. Only feature films are nonstarters, no matter where in the world I do business. Someone somewhere must be making money by making movies, but not me and not many investors, as far as I can tell. To me, films are frequently vanity projects, not investments for profit-driven people. And vanity projects are out, no matter where in the world our investors' money goes.

Russia has other obvious areas to avoid investing in. Early-stage science and technology is one such area. As in most developing economies, people tend not to understand intellectual property yet, and the important IP cannot be protected in the absence of an informed judiciary. Investments that are dependent on technological innovation are subject to piracy or other forms of theft in the absence of enforceable proprietary rights.

While some practices are unique to Russia, other approaches that are standard in the United States serve us remarkably well in Russia, too.

For example, micromanagement should always be avoided no matter what the geographic location of an investment. Micromanagement leads you to back weak people, because you think you can always control a situation. You can't. Get the strongest people possible, and let them perform or not, as the case may be.

As a rule, we avoid single-product companies, because they can be put out of business too easily by forces out of their control: a spike in commodities prices, a new competitor, any sort of major surprise. We also stay away from husband-and-wife management teams. Business is hard enough without the marital relationship adding complexity. Oh, and one more—never say "Oink." Remember the old adage that "Pigs get fat, hogs get slaughtered"? It's true. Be satisfied with a reasonable profit. There is more risk than reward in holding out for every last penny.

The Call to Moscow

Years of on-the-ground experience give one guidelines for any complicated market such as Russia. My own Russian experience started in 1994 with a call from the White House Personnel Office. They were forming a private board of directors to oversee an economic development assistance program initiated by congressional statute in 1989 as the Berlin Wall fell. In an effort to open private markets in formerly centrally planned economies, the U.S. government was experimenting with introducing a series of financial tools: equity investment, debt, insurance, guarantees, technical assistance, and training. This effort at jump-starting entrepreneurship had started in the former Soviet Block countries—Romania, Hungary, the Czech Republic, the Baltic States, and so on—with mixed success.

In 1994, Congress extended the program to include Russia, and the Clinton Administration needed a private, volunteer board of directors. The fit sounded farfetched, at best.

"Russia?" I said to the friendly sounding voice on the phone from the White House Personnel Office. "You have got to be kidding. I have never been there, and I don't even speak the language."

"They told us you would quibble," said the recruiter.

"Quibble?" I said. "This seems material."

But I accepted the seat as a form of unpaid public service while continuing to make my living at Apax. With other colleagues in business and finance, I would bring my expertise to bear on a project that sounded well intentioned, even if the other board members had no more experience in Russia than I did. There were no clear guidelines, but the general thrust was clear. An unpaid board of financiers and business people would start up some sort of development venture, get it staffed with locals, and, once the market talked back, form a private successor organization. There was no formal exit plan, other than the board's listening for the market to talk back, to tell them what might work, and when it was time for Uncle Sam to call it quits.

There was room for improvisation and, as experience showed, a fair chance of failure. In the Czech Republic, the program failed, and in Central Asia the money disappeared. Mainly, though, there were successes that gave testimony to the creative spark that a bit of capital can ignite. In several of the Baltic States, the program evolved into mortgage lending. In Romania and Albania, the program midwifed the creation of investment banks. In Hungary, it led to a fellowship program. In Poland, the U.S. investment had by far its biggest early success. Starting with $260 million in 1991, the fund made several successful investments and repaid the initial capital after about six years.

The U.S. Russia Investment Fund began later, in 1995, with an initial commitment of $440 million from the U.S. government of which $329 million was actually put up before the program was "zeroed out," in government language. From the start, the board decided that an important focus would be the financial services sector. Any economy needs that, of course, and we would work hard to make it happen. There was another aspect of our work that became a continuous theme throughout: the introduction of good governance practices and rational business structures into the Russian economy.

The fund ended up putting $329 million into 44 Russian companies, and by early 2009 it was almost 50% ahead of value at inception in 1995. The $120 million successor fund formed in 2004 has invested in 11 more companies, and by early 2009 it had a net internal rate of return of 209%.

The "Transparency Premium"

One of our first important deals, a television network, came to us through an American expatriate living in Moscow by the name of Peter Gerwe. His project illustrates the work we had to do on governance in most of our deals. In 2005, Peter came across an opportunity to buy television spectrum. He had a theory that commercial television was about to take off. The idea sounded promising, but it would take a real turnaround to make it work. The station had been managed by an old Soviet *apparatchik*. He would talk and talk and never take a breath to listen. He had done nothing to make the programming worth watching, and the studios were dingy—dirty old carpets hanging on the walls were their less-than-optimal way of improving the acoustics.

The management structure of the stations was just as decrepit as the physical space. The place was run by a sort of "workers' council" system that traced back to the Soviet era as surely as the rugs on the walls did. It had no board of directors and no financial discipline. We created a board that included seasoned Hollywood types and introduced the concept of working with other people's money. In other words, there must be accountability, controls, planning, and execution. Only after those structures and systems were put in place did Peter's network, or, really, any of our businesses, have a chance.

Once we got the governance structure in place and put our money in, Peter and his team went to work making Channel 3 a success. They began showing soap operas from Mexico and Brazil, pretty torrid stuff but popular right away. Before long, he was achieving $25 million a year in net cash flow.

By 2006, we prepared to exit the investment and hired investment bankers to list the company on the London Stock Exchange. Many companies in Russia do very little public disclosure, so it is difficult to determine value. In this case, though, we had very detailed financials— annual audited financials—of the parent company, INTH. We never got to market. One of the local pools of capital approached us and offered a price that was $100 million higher than the high end of the range our banker had estimated for the initial public offering, with no lock-up, no market risk, and virtual assurance of antimonopoly approval.

We had a board meeting, and one of the members, a Hollywood producer, asked, "What are his metrics?"

"Well," I said, "I don't think he's in the back room with his Hewlett-Packard calculator crunching the numbers, if that's what you mean."

It was clear to me that this pool of Russian investors wanted the television station, and price was not the issue. This is another revelation about how business works in Russia, not to mention an important consideration for venture capital investors doing business there. For purposes of exiting the investment, the public markets have been almost irrelevant in Russia, even through today. In recent years, multinational companies looking for strategic investments have competed with oligarchs, the wealthiest families in Russia, to purchase well-conceived and well-managed companies. Even when a company does register for an IPO, it often sells to a private investor first.

This liquidity phenomenon has been unique to the Russian market. Liquidity is the key consideration for venture capital investors anywhere—the ability to exit from an investment. Before we put money into a company, we plan how we may sell it. In the United States, the public markets are generally part of that planning. In Russia, there is plenty of capital, but the public markets are virtually irrelevant, with a dozen major players accounting for the bulk of trading. Thus, we place a premium on working with the local pools of capital and with the multinationals and even paying close attention to our own management teams, who sometimes have shown an ability to arrange their own exit events.

We sold INTH to ProfMedia, a local media group, for $400 million, or 14.3 times our cost. I believe a lot of that success was due to the transparency in the numbers of the company. Many Russian companies are opaque. Either they don't publish meaningful numbers or the numbers they do publish are not reliable. We have worked hard to develop a reputation for transparency, and I believe we get a premium, a transparency premium, of at least 10% on our deals, sometimes more. On the INTH deal, it was bigger than that.

Out of the Mattresses, Into the Banks

Even as we were learning through our experiences with Channel 3 to introduce corporate governance practices into our portfolio companies, we were hard at work on another other major charge from the U.S. government: expanding and deepening the Russian financial services sector.

To get our bearings, we hired a consultant from Barclays in the mid-1990s to assess the country's banking capabilities at that time. He looked at some 200 of what were called banks but in fact were mainly money-laundering operations or outfits set up for "tax-optimized" cross-border trading. These same issues showed up across industry sectors as tax schemes were the norm, not the exception.

As we dug deeper into the financial services sector, other questions arose. For starters, there was no history of consumer credit in Russia and little faith in banking at all. Russia was and still mainly is a cash economy. People kept their wealth—what wealth they had at this point, anyway—in their mattresses. In most economies, people need mortgages to buy homes, but Russia was different. After the Soviet system dissolved in 1991, the citizens of Moscow, 11 million people, were given the chance to buy their flats for anywhere from $25 to $50 each. People didn't need mortgages because they could just save and buy their apartments.

The challenge, then, was to demonstrate to Russians that banks could be safe and that credit, well-used, could make their lives better. At one point in 1995, I suggested to our staff on the ground in Moscow that perhaps we should consider a joint venture with the Russian Orthodox Church. They own property, they handle money, and, after all, they're a church.

One of the women there, a mortgage specialist, said to me, "Pat, I don't think the Russian people will trust the church."

"Let's form some focus groups," I said. "Let's go and find out who the Russian people will trust with their money."

After a few weeks, our mortgage specialist had her answers. She had been correct. Russians did not trust the church, but there were two groups they would trust with their money: intellectuals and foreign banks. Given that Russian history has produced the likes of Dosto-evsky, Tchaikovsky, Sakharov, and Sozhenitsyn, I felt we would have a difficult time persuading the populace that we were intellectuals. The other option immediately felt more obtainable.

"Well, we're a foreign bank," I said. If we could pilot a bank, we could measure and adjust to consumer response.

While we worked to start two banks, we also were investing in a diverse array of other companies. Although we had indeed lost that

$850,000 that disappeared en route to Moscow, we did not let that stop us. We backed a department store in Moscow, a newsprint company, and a company that sold bottled spring water, among others. We were beginning to collect a cohort of Russian entrepreneurs—some of them old timers from the Soviet era, but others younger and more entrepreneurial-minded businesspeople. We also found we had to turn down a fair number of Americans who thought the fund had been created to back Americans in Russia, irrespective of deal or business quality.

Peter Gerwe at Channel 3 was an exception among the Americans who applied for financial backing. After all, he had lived in Russia much of his career, and he had a very solid business idea. There were others. We invested chiefly in Russian entrepreneurs, but we felt the purpose of the fund was to encourage high-quality private entrepreneurship in Russia, whatever the nationality of the entrepreneur.

The Upside of Economic Crisis

As we were getting deal flow started in these years, the 1998 economic crisis occurred, triggered by Russia's defaulting on its sovereign debt. Alongside the dramatic downturn that hit the global economy in late 2008, the economic breakdown that came to a head in Russia in August of 1998 was the most serious crisis in the country's modern era. Seven years after the collapse of the Soviet empire, the country's balance of payments was in shambles. Oil prices, a chief engine of the economy, were near historic lows. The country was effectively bankrupt, and the ruble collapsed.

But, in the same way that a forest fire can bring new growth and, ultimately, a healthier ecosystem, the 1998 crisis had a cleansing effect on the Russian economy. For starters, as hard as the collapse was on individual citizens, it wiped out fewer than might have been expected. In this instance, Russia's cash-in-the-mattress economy protected some people from complete catastrophe. And, because some people stashed that cash in U.S. currency, not rubles, the ruble's collapse actually gave many people more buying power. In the business sector, the crash wiped out the speculators, carpetbaggers, money launderers, and others who really were not contributing to the economy. In the real economy, import substitution began on scale, yielding a crop of new companies that grew into the decade that began in the year 2000.

For the U.S. Russia Investment Fund, this palliative impact was not immediately evident as the 1998 economic crisis hit. By that point, we were invested in some 20 companies. Many were weak, and one bit the dust immediately: Frank's Siberian Ice Cream. The entrepreneur's main problem was that his inputs were denominated in dollars and his customers were paying rubles for their ice cream. A company set up like that cannot overcome the collapse of the revenue currency. It took about five minutes after the ruble collapsed for Frank's business to go into the deep freeze.

Dieselprom—the company where the U.S. Russia Investment Fund lost that initial $850,000—didn't make it, either, nor did a radio paging company in which we had invested. We learned much, though, from two pharmaceutical distribution companies that failed. When we did the postmortem on these pharmaceutical companies, we came across a pattern that had become all too familiar in Russia: an organization chart filled with subsidiary companies, offshore entities, and other tools Russian business people tend to favor when they are trying to avoid taxes or to take money out of a company. In fairness, sometimes those structures are built to protect against such financial maelstroms as that of 1998 and, indeed, 2008. More often than not, though, there are other reasons.

Baleful Boxes on the Organization Chart

In 2004, we hired Price Waterhouse and Russian customs and tax experts to develop templates of the illegal structures most commonly used by Russian businesses. They graphed six basic schemes, most of which involved corporate entities in obscure jurisdictions—Belize, the Seychelles Islands, places like that. The operators who run the Russian-based companies place all their corporate liabilities into these dummy companies, and then bankrupt them. Other offshore units may be fronts used to siphon off money or, worse, for businesspeople to launder their funds.

It would be easy to write this off as a sign of runaway corruption in Russia, but as I grew to understand Russia better, I also began to understand why the Russians sometimes set up their businesses this way. After the Soviet Union collapsed, the economy was in transition, and no one had a job. There were no banks or other sources of capital to finance companies. Equity markets were nonexistent. The most efficient way for a business to raise capital, even one that wanted to be legitimate, was to keep funds out of the tax system. Instead of reporting income and paying taxes, they set up boxes on their corporate organization chart to use the money that would have been paid to Mother Russia in taxes. The objective was to help their companies grow, instead. That's how relatively legitimate operators saw things. The bad ones? Who knows what they did with their money.

The boxes have another effect. In resource-intensive industries, they create a temptation for operators to strip off the best assets and leave just the shell of a company behind. Especially in the 1990s, Russia was rife with people making money by stripping assets rather than devising sustainable corporate strategies. We have tried to avoid such companies, mainly by staying away from resource-intensive industries.

This box system of corporate structure, much of it driven by tax gamesmanship, has an insidious effect on Russian industry. It makes it impossible for a Western company, certainly for a U.S. company, to finance a Russian company that has dozens of strange organizational units in exotic locations. It is a fiduciary risk, for starters, because there is no way to track cash. It would be an invitation for trouble under the Foreign Corrupt Practices Act and the Patriot Act, too.

This problem is serious enough that I wrote Dmitry Medvedev when he became president and suggested that he establish a tax amnesty for all companies with less than $100 million in sales. This would bring these companies in from the cold and ultimately lead to growth because they suddenly would be eligible for financing by institutions that would never touch them today.

The 1998 crisis reinforced something we already knew in trying to grow companies in Russia: the basic tools and understanding of business still are in utterly short supply. To address this, we created a Center for Entrepreneurship as a way to introduce best practices. We in-licensed intellectual property from the Ewing Marion Kauffman Foundation, which has developed extensive materials designed to teach novice businesspeople how to manage cash flow, value their companies, hire and keep key people, and the like. Along with Ernst & Young in Russia, we started an Entrepreneur of the Year Award program, which has become a major event in the Russian business community and a way to create positive role models in a place where so many less than positive ones exist. The program also serves as a key networking and talent-scouting tool for our fund.

While all these positive effects emerged from the 1998 crisis, one particular result impacted our fund concretely: J.P. Morgan, the U.S.-based banking giant, fled Russia after the 1998 crisis, along with many others. It surrendered a clean bank license to the Central Bank of Russia. We took over that license, and soon were in business with DeltaBank, our consumer credit bank, and DeltaCredit Bank, our mortgage bank.

Charging to the Future

Opening the banks involved introducing Russians to what, for them, was a new concept: consumer credit. Russia had not yet been exposed to the joys and sorrows of credit cards, but they certainly were ready to learn. With the economy rebounding slowly, showing fundamental growth for the first time in generations, consumer demand, something that was nonexistent for 80 years, became real.

The business challenge for DeltaBank was to introduce this concept and grow it quickly into a business, and the best way to do that was to partner with an established brand. Ikea, the Swedish retailer, became our partner for this strategy. Ikea for years had sourced product from Russia, and as part of its international expansion it chose to build stores in Moscow, among other venues. The stores were immediate hits. I say it somewhat jokingly, but it is actually pretty true that most Russian citizens would rather choose a sofa than choose a president. Until recent years, they never had been given much of a choice on either issue. They had never had consumer choice, much less seen affordable consumer goods such as those at Ikea, and they began trading up, including with their apartments.

DeltaBank worked a deal with Visa to offer Visa-branded cards inside of Ikea's megamall on the outskirts of Moscow. I'll never forget stopping in that store—a beautiful big-box—on my way to the Moscow airport in September 1999. Signs said: "What is a credit card?" Yellow lines on the floor led customers to DeltaBank clerks who explained the concept to them. Visa provided instant credit—$20 credit lines for first-time borrowers, a decent chunk of money in Russia at the time. The Russian consumer and the credit card began to take off, but on a very conservative basis, as appropriate.

A Career of Broken Barriers

For me, personally, the work in Russia—helping to create new markets, introducing new governance structures, identifying and nurturing management talent—was a challenging and rewarding chapter in my professional life, especially considering how late in life I happened across it. I came of age at a time before women were common at the top of business. I was part of a cohort of other women who sometimes found ourselves breaking ground with each forward step. I did not see this as a mission of mine. I was not a "women's libber" in that sense. But I did find that I would have to break old patterns and even be a bit pushy if I wanted success in business. And I always have supported other women in their professional development.

I was raised in Pollock Pines, California, a small logging town near Lake Tahoe. My Irish immigrant father had started his own career at age 11 as a messenger for the Southern Pacific Railroad in San Francisco. He later worked mainly as a logger and construction worker. My mother came to the United States from Canada. She sold some real estate and served on the local school board, all the while being a wheelchair-bound invalid with serious rheumatoid arthritis. Like many immigrants, my parents valued education, even though they had little of it themselves, and had an utter dedication to accomplishment.

Learning always came easily to me. I won scholarships and fellowships, skipped a grade, and went to San Francisco College for Women on a California state scholarship. I loved it. Scholarship holders who had interests in areas not taught at the college could have private tutors, so I had a private tutor in classical Greek.

I joined the Peace Corps soon after President Kennedy launched the program and quickly found myself hybridizing tomatoes and castrating pigs in Brazil. Before long, I won a Ford Foundation Fellowship in International Economic Development and attended Columbia

University's School of International Affairs. I completed two master's degrees and was heading for a doctorate in 1968 when student protests shut down the campus. Rather than deal with riots and disruptions on campus, I went to Cuernavaca, Mexico, and ran seminars for political exiles from Chile, Brazil, and other Latin American countries. When I ran out of money, I called home, got my mom to wire funds to me, and returned to New York.

Launching into Venture Capital

By chance in 1969, I met Alan Patricof, a well-established figure in finance, who was starting something called a venture capital fund.

"Do you want to learn the business from the bottom up?" Patricof asked me. The answer was "yes." Only later did I learn that particular turn of phrase was Patricof's code for not paying me much...until I understood the concept of "carry." My payoff would not come from salary, I learned; it would come from my share—my carry—of the net capital gains achieved from the sale of the companies we invested in. Once I learned that, I was on my way.

The start-up work at Patricof & Co. Ventures was excellent preparation for what I eventually would do in Russia. We started in 1970 with only $2.6 million under management and several clients on retainer and one office. When I left in 2000, the firm had $10 billion under management in five countries. By then, I had done dozens of deals. More than that, though, we were able to pioneer in the venture business, shaping the rules and regulations as we went, as I would be called to do in Russia years later. For example, in the 1970s institutions generally did not invest in venture capital as an asset class, so we raised $2.6 million from nine wealthy families: the Lehman family, the Motts from General Motors, people such as that. We would commit our small fund to a deal, and then each individual investor would decide on the investment, deal by deal. This forced me to truly understand the investment case for each deal before presenting it to this group of highly intelligent, sophisticated people.

It was during those early Patricof days, in 1977, that I got a call from the White House about the Deputy Administrator position at the SBA, a political appointment. I took the job out of political interest.

The SBA is one of the most political agencies in Washington. It represents all the small businesses on Main Street, not those on Wall Street, and every lawmaker on Capitol Hill wants that large constituency served. I had to focus much time on preferential loans to a range of legally defined disadvantaged groups—African Americans, Eskimos, Aleuts, women, Vietnam veterans, and so forth.

I will never forget one SBA experience. We were cleaning up one of the agency's portfolios, foreclosing on loans that were far past due, when we took a look at the foreclosure of a defunct pencil company run by the Blackfeet Indians in Montana. At about the time that the foreclosure notice on their $350,000 loan arrived, tribe members had simultaneously received per-capita payments pursuant to agreements related to subsoil mineral rights from the Bureau of Indian Affairs of the Interior Department. So, they hired a 747 airplane to fly everyone to Washington to discuss the matter with me. Everyone came!

The sole-source set-aside program frequently was a magnet for politically, not economically, based requests. The 95 field offices of the SBA bore the brunt of the burden. Only special cases arrived at my desk for handling. I left the SBA after two years with great fondness for the agency, its people, and its mission. At the time, though, the Administration wanted us to put out another $2 billion in sole-sourced contracts for a program about which I had serious misgivings, so it was the right time to leave.

Lessons to Invest By

After the SBA, my then-husband and I partnered to form a company with a scientist from AT&T's Bell Laboratories and his wife. We secured a license from Bell to the technology to make high-precision optical fiber connectors. The scientist, Jack Cook, was a waveguide guru. He initially wanted to invent a passive optical switch, but that research alone might have cost $100 million and the technology was not proven. Instead, we chose to make the connectors, which had immediate commercial potential.

An experience from this company has stuck with me. Jack had a research colleague from Bell Labs who joined us, but after a few months he was questioning his decision.

"Pat," he said, "do I understand this correctly? We are going into business to make something we already know how to make?"

I told him that's generally the way business is done: You know how to make something, and you do so. For him, though, his mission was different. A true scientist, he wanted to advance scientific knowledge, not refine fiberoptic connectors for commercial use. It was an important moment of self-knowledge for him and for me. He went back to the research bench, back to work he enjoyed. Jack, his wife, and I ultimately sold the company successfully to 3M. The Cooks went to New Hampshire to run a charity, and I had real money for the first time in my life.

I rejoined Patricof Ventures as a partner, a coming home of sorts, as Alan and his wife, Susan, have been family to me since the early 1970s. The timing of my decision to rejoin Patricof was fortuitous. A 1979 regulatory decision changed the "prudent man rule" under the Employee Retirement Income Security Act rules of the Labor Department to enable pension institutions to invest in venture capital for the first time, without personal liability for the trustee. Our firm had begun to expand overseas in 1974, partnering in the United Kingdom and France and later in Germany, Israel, and Japan. I resumed my pre-1977 activities, backing diverse companies. I have always been attracted to opportunities with heavy intellectual property content, such as life science and semiconductors. It was in these deals that I developed one of my favorite rules of thumb: Don't pay more than $40 million post money, and always sell for at least $1 billion.

Other rules I use today mostly came about as a result of experiences during this period. One key lesson was to always spread risk. We had one company fail because of the chaos created when President Nixon froze wages and prices during the early 1970s. That company provided low-cost feed supplements for poultry. Prices of finished products were capped, but input prices were not, creating an immediate negative margin. Three decades before we saw Frank's Ice Cream in Russia collapse, we saw the same phenomenon in the poultry feed business. Another company, a thriving steel mini-mill on the Louisiana Gulf Coast, depended on the Mississippi River to transport finished product. The Mississippi River ran low one summer, though, and the company couldn't make it through. Again, we had failed to account for such risks.

Taking Action in Russia

In Russia, the risks are multiple and can threaten the viability of a business almost overnight. The economy is vulnerable to volatile oil prices. Corruption is an issue, although in recent years substantial improvements are apparent. Russia still operates on personal connections, with a small network of powerful people having an inordinate ability to influence events. I have been around long enough to understand how this works in this young economy. Over time, we have developed an ability to do business with these leading financial groups.

Inasmuch as I am officially retired and, fortunately, well off, my motives in getting involved with the U.S. Russia Investment Fund in Russia have been largely altruistic. It's a bit like having another Peace Corps experience stapled onto the end of my career, as it was at the beginning, but with a wealth of equity investment experience to bring to the job

I started as *pro bono* director on the board from 1994 to 2003, since I only retired from Apax in 2000. Then, because the Fund was not getting the needed investment traction, at the board's request I moved to Russia in an executive capacity in 2003.

Within five months, we reduced the investment staff from 17 to seven people and began shaping the portfolio. We sold 30 companies in five years and made 29 new and follow-on investments. One of the first sales was of DeltaBank to GE Consumer Finance for 4.3 times its book value, a good way to start.

Part of the transition involved setting up the funds in a way that could sustain the investment effort. We formed Delta Private Equity Partners, a management company, to run the U.S. Russia Investment Fund and a private successor fund, Delta Russia Fund. We launched the Delta Russia Fund in June of 2004 and ultimately, between two funds, invested $450 million into 55 Russian companies. With $120 million in committed capital, the Delta Russia Fund is now 80% invested and has a net internal rate of return of about 209%.

The lesson from this initial flurry of activity was clear. To survive, we had to act swiftly and aggressively. To sustain progress, though, we found we would need to meet two key objectives. We needed a coherent investment strategy, and we needed professional management of our portfolio companies. This was the genesis of our list of excluded investment areas: no real estate, no oil and gas, no commodities, no greenfields, no pure technology risk, none of the Russian government's 42 strategic areas, and so on.

The governance side would prove in some ways the greater of our challenges. We discovered we would need a more hands-on approach than is typical in a U.S. venture fund, but without micromanagement. Portfolio company managements had to learn how to align their interest with those of investors and, most important, to see why it was in their own interest to do so. To that end, we introduced stock options as part of the compensation.

DeltaCredit Bank was our test case for stock options, and right from the start it was obvious the idea would take. In introducing the concept to DeltaCredit managers, I rattled off an explanation of stock options: how they work and how they become valuable if the company's value increases. When I asked for questions at the introductory session, the first questioner wanted to know about antidilution protection. The Russians got it, immediately.

DeltaCredit, the mortgage bank, gave us a window into different aspects of doing business in Russia: how to handle the power plays and the importance of top leadership. When I arrived in Moscow, I knew that the bank was in trouble. I asked Igor Kouzine, a Ukrainian-born former McKinsey consultant, to do a depth probe on the bank, and his analysis was superb: overstaffed, underleveraged, and poor processes in place.

None of that seemed to matter to the then-president of DeltaCredit. Soon after I arrived in Moscow, he invited me to breakfast and opened the discussion with a simple, declarative sentence: "I would like to buy the bank."

I asked him the price, and he offered one that was half of the book value. I asked where he was getting his capital, and he would not say. I told him that, as chairman of the bank's board, I had a fiduciary obligation to know how his bid would be funded. Then I asked if there was anything else for me to know.

"Yes," he said. "If you don't agree, my top ten people and I will leave."

"I wish you well then," I told him. "Let's go get security and you all are out today."

We promptly hired Kouzine, the consultant, as CEO, and the new management team quickly made a difference. Kouzine reduced staff from 185 to 95 and increased lending volume to four times previous levels, profitably. Before Kouzine came on, the bank was closing just 3% of loans. Within a few months, they were closing 85% of them. Before long, we secured a $120 million line of credit at a 6% interest rate over 15 years. Can't beat that.

We had taken a bank that was underperforming and transformed it into a winner. We wound up selling it for 2.8 times book value to Société Générale, but even then the potential was just barely tapped. We had a 40% market share, but with only 3,500 mortgages on the books in a nation of 143 million people, the potential was vast. And the Russians pay; delinquencies were less than 1%. There was plenty of room for DeltaCredit to grow.

Although it was important for us to bring in people like Kouzine to broaden business understanding, it was just as vital that we at Delta learn to navigate the state of the Russian business community as the economy privatized. A chief concern is the lack of understanding among Russian business people about the importance of good corporate governance. Prior to the wave of privatization that began in the 1990s, Russian business operated under a very patriarchal system. The rights of shareholders were little understood and barely respected.

Relationships with boards of directors proved to be particularly vexing. Russian business people are not accustomed to taking into account the views of people who are not part of the day-to-day operation of the business. Board meetings can become tempestuous, with battles for control between the management and nonmanagement directors. As a major investor in these companies, I deal firmly with this issue, but that does not make it any easier to manage. Many of these difficulties fit under the category of growing pains.

To get some perspective on where the Russians are coming from, keep in mind that in the early 1990s many young business people in Russia told me that they learned much of what they knew about business by watching films such as *Wall Street* with Michael Douglas. I found this terrifying. The trading culture and "greed is good" mentality have nothing to do with running a good business, which is all about putting capital to work for a reasonable return over time.

The notion that the understanding of business was so low in the early and mid-1990s that young Russians were using Gordon Gekko as a role model is one of the revelations that led us to start the Entrepreneur of the Year program with Ernst & Young.

A "Roof" for Protection

One of the key elements of success in Russia is the notion of having what Russians call "roofs" for protection. A roof is any form of safeguard against disaster. The most effective roof, though, is a well-placed, honest person on whom one can rely for straight information, on-the-ground knowledge, and other help that might advance or guard us against trouble.

I got a taste of a good roof in a deal involving the sublicense the fund had secured for the SPAR supermarket chain in Russia. It opened two SPAR operations in Russia, one of which, in Middle Volga, we sold the year I arrived in Moscow for an 86% internal rate of return. The SPAR Moscow effort was a different matter. The company couldn't get sufficient retail space in Moscow, a market that was heating up at the time.

Staff had been working for two years on a deal to sell the company, but the deal was unattractive. There was no cash, only paper in a highly leveraged company. I was pressured to sign the sale documents, but due to my doubts I hired a security service to do a background check on the proposed purchaser. In Russia, such checks can turn up surprising and unwelcome prior pursuits—money laundering, gun running, market manipulation, and the like. Fortunately, the capability of security services are quite impressive, in part because many in the business have prior KGB experience, so a thorough background check typically turns up just about anything we need to know. In this particular case, the result was not encouraging and would not have passed the test of the Foreign Corrupt Practices Act and the Patriot Act, so we called off the deal and set out to find a better buyer.

This is where my roof came in. A friend who had connections at high levels in the Russian government steered me toward a man I had not previously known. There was an air of secrecy about our first meeting. I was told to look for a man in a blue sweater on a Saturday morning in the downtown Marriott. He had not previously run a business, but he had led a fascinating life: a guard on the Chinese border as a young man, an analyst of the U.S. defense budget for the Russian government, and, of great interest to me, a recent stint allocating retail space in downtown Moscow for the city's mayor.

It took just that one conversation for me to realize I had found the right person for the SPAR license. I suggested that he buy it, and that we would back his investment. I rattled off all the numbers I could remember, he liked what he heard, and after some minor haggling we shook hands on a deal on the spot. The basic outlines of our deal have not changed since. For all one hears about the troubles of doing business in Russia, there also are people who are honorable, savvy, driven, and intelligent business people who are the best hope for better times in their country.

The story did not end with that handshake at the Marriott, though. When the other would-be buyer heard I had struck a different deal, he was furious. He sent some fairly gruff associates to ask about my decision.

"What do you want from me?" I asked. "I'm a fiduciary, and this is a better deal." After two hours of haggling, their offer still was no good, and the deal in hand was for cash, with our fund still retaining a 15% stake.

When the visitors left, my colleagues at Delta said they were worried about my decision. They said I might need bodyguards. The whole situation seemed silly to me, but I acquiesced. The result was that I spent a marvelous few days with a pair of fit, kind, and polite young men who carried my bags and opened car doors for me. If this was what it meant to have bodyguards, then I was all for it, but after a few days it felt like an extravagance and I resumed my normal program of traveling the streets of Moscow on my own.

My decision to sell to the new buyer was a winner from the start. He did everything he promised—came through with the cash, built up the chain, and expanded regionally. One of his stores, an hour outside Moscow, did $1 million in business on its opening day. We reinvested with him when we launched our second fund and ultimately sold that 15% stake for a 212% internal rate of return.

The Sieges of Moscow

One aspect of doing business in Russia that may change over time is the tendency Russians have to negotiate, *ad nauseum*, over the valuation of companies. Private property is a new concept, so negotiations focus exhaustively on price with a wholly inadequate emphasis on the strategic development of the company. The two-year squabbling over the initially proposed SPAR deal was not unusual. Part of this reflects the way many companies are structured to optimize taxes. Russians are not used to the concept of building enterprise value over time, so they are not familiar with figuring that into their negotiating strategy. Mix this with the Russian business person's inordinate fear of getting beaten in negotiations, and the fascination with various arcane tax dodges, and we find that Western concepts of profit motive do not always drive negotiations.

Because of the tenacious negotiating style, we have learned to shape the future of a company even while we are still negotiating to buy it. It's risky because there is no assurance that we ultimately will get a deal. On the other hand, it would make no sense to let one of our target companies languish, growing weaker during the months and sometimes years it takes to buy it.

Noviy Disk, a computer games company, is illustrative. An entrepreneur started the company in 1991, selling pirated DVDs to tourists in Red Square. By the time we came across it some 15 years later, the company had title to a number of popular computer games and had begun game development of its own. It also was moving into producing computerized training materials for schools. We started negotiations in June 2007 and proceeded on two tracks. On one track, we restructured the business. On another track, we pitched in to assist the company in securing a Nintendo license and a Disney library for localization into the Russian language. Meanwhile, in negotiations, price was a moving target—and it and other key issues in our negotiations kept changing, well beyond the point when both parties would have walked away in frustration from such talks in the United States.

We finally found a way to bring the discussions to a close. After we reached agreement on one aspect of the deal, we and the seller would sign a memorandum that memorialized the terms. "This is a blood pact," I would say, only half in jest. This methodical approach helped us winnow down our list of issues one by one and ultimately reach a comprehensive agreement.

In 2007, the company achieved $95 million in sales and generated $25 million in cash flow. We ultimately put $12 million into the company, and if the business keeps growing as it should we will do well on resale, although the financial crisis that began in late 2008, including especially the ruble devaluation, has provided some challenges for the company to get through.

Onward!

The learning curve has not flattened in Russia. We continue to adjust our approach as we move along and as our fund and the financial markets evolve. We have worked to develop a systematic way to share best practices among our various companies. We emphasize financial results and challenge the managements of our portfolio companies to become more transparent in the way they report results. We standardize reporting periods, require analytical information benchmarked to comparable companies, and occasionally conduct depth probes on specific issues. All of this emphasizes how important it is to measure results, while giving us as investors a very clear view into the condition of the business.

I have learned to value highly the Russian people I have done business with. These are the roofs who help protect us from mistakes or can connect us with key contacts. We also could not succeed without the entrepreneurs who inspire us with their success and character. Some of our work, I hope, has helped the aspiring young business people think less about the movie *Wall Street* and more about the way business is really done—through shrewd investment, tireless work, creative thinking, and honorable conduct. The challenges still exist in Russia, but so do the people and practices that give hope for the future.

Venture capital is challenging under any circumstances. Operating in a formerly centrally planned economy—the antithesis of capitalism—is a learning experience all around. The Russian people have embraced it. The capitalist genie is out of the bottle, and it promises to raise the standard of living for average Russian citizens. I am pleased to have been part of introducing the financial tools that, along with many positive changes on the Russian business scene, can help make that all possible.

LESSONS FROM PAT CLOHERTY

◈ **Go local.** Rely on local management for their knowledge of the market. Use your street smarts to handle powerful groups and tricky operators, just as you would elsewhere.

◈ **Seek the "transparency premium."** In a marketplace where financial reporting is opaque, transparency can be an advantage. In the author's experience, it accounts for a 10% price premium when a company is sold.

◈ **Do not micromanage.** Tempting as it may be in a market where business practices are not fully developed, micromanagement by outsiders only succeds in training local management to be weak. Export your knowledge, but let others do the work.

◈ **Spread risk.** Know which industries are potentially hazardous politically and which are safe for outside investment. Steer clear of any industry defined by the state as strategically important. Companies in basic products and services—foodstuffs, apparel, financial services, and so forth—are attractive.

◈ **Beware of "boxes."** Be wary of offshore entities, asset stripping, money laundering, and other devices used in Russia and other developing economies in an effort to minimize taxes and divert cash.

APPENDICES

TOOLS OF THE TRADE

In any skilled profession, there are masters, and there are all the rest. From apprentices to journeymen, to veteran practitioners, all are in some ways not quite at the same levels of the true masters, and one aspect that sets the masters apart is the effective use of specialized tools.

The masters of private equity and venture capital have evolved their own mission-critical set of tools. Spreadsheets and charts help them measure the risk and performance of their portfolios. Dashboard software on computers automatically command attention and create templates for a firm's internal communication. Some private-investment pioneers use specific criteria to select directors and chief executives, while others operate according to rules of practice expressed in colorful and memorable language.

Just as the management lessons in the preceding chapters lay out the techniques, strategic thinking, and tactics of these leading private-equity professionals, the tools are implements of the trade. Most have not previously been shared outside the firms represented here. All can contribute to a track record of success.

APPENDIX 1

CHECKLIST FOR EVALUATING INVESTMENT OPPORTUNITIES

Franklin "Pitch" Johnson, Jr.
Asset Management Company

The "old guard" who started in the 1960s had no specific templates or tools. They used their instincts to gauge what seemed important and learned by pain and reward. Along with other venture capitalists, Pitch Johnson of Asset Management Company, quickly decided that he could succeed only by closely following and helping his portfolio companies. Then, as now, Johnson and his contemporaries had to make decisions with inadequate information but enough to move ahead.

Had the earliest pioneers of venture capital drawn up a template for success, it might have looked like the following:

- People
  - Integrity
    - First impression:
      - From the moment you shake a hand: Is the person open and honest?
      - Guidable? Do they see the potential relationship the same way as you?
      - Is this group to be trusted?
      - Are they able to describe in two to three sentences the idea of the business?

- ■ Check them out with previous associates.
- ○ Experience
  - ■ Very important to have experience in an operating company, even in failed start-ups
  - ■ Understanding of the marketplace
  - ■ Needed and complementary skill sets in group
  - ■ Attributes of a clear leader
- ● Marketplace
  - ○ Is it big enough to accommodate the aims of the company?
  - ○ *Diligence note:* The Masters developed a coterie of friends who were in positions to assist in evaluating a given technology or market ... a trading of favors is the entry into such a group.
- ● Technology/product
  - ○ Vital uses in existing or proposed market
  - ○ Protectable/defendable
  - ○ Production or reproduction ability at workable cost
- ● Financial plan
  - ○ Plan for future financings as to workability and valuation.
  - ○ Make own plan and evaluate that of entrepreneurs.
  - ○ Ensure the plausibility of final numbers used for decisions.
- ● Negotiating the deal
  - ○ Estimate value of holding in five years, allowing for dilution of original percentage.
  - ○ Aim for a 10× multiple on investment in five years, or 58% internal rate of return (IRR) on the deal; compromise this standard when risk is less. This level is necessary to get limited partners returns for whole fund in the 20% range, after losses and expenses.
  - ○ Can start-up to success be achieved in a reasonable time frame?
  - ○ Are development costs, burn rate, and projected sales workable?
  - ○ Develop a one-year detailed plan and five-year projections.
  - ○ Project earnings as to timing and growth rate.
  - ○ Be sure price enables firm to become part of a portfolio of winners/ losers built to show 35% IRR and 18 to 20% net to the LPs.

APPENDIX 2

GUIDELINES FOR TRANSFORMING RESEARCH INTO COMMERCE

Steven Lazarus
ARCH Venture Partners

Converting basic science into commercial ventures is a challenging assignment that ARCH Venture Partners has chosen as the centerpiece of its business. As Steve Lazarus of ARCH explains, to be successful requires a mixture of political savvy, scientific acuity, and private investment know-how. Lazarus' call for a flexible and versatile approach has application in many walks of business far beyond the university labs.

Harmonize Cultures. Academicians see business people as narrowly fixated on profit, while executives see researchers as insulated and naïve. Focus on the potentially complementary nature of the two cultures, melding the academic's ideas with the businessman's capital and management skills.

Go Where the Science Is. We have moved investment professionals from Chicago to science-rich geographies such as Seattle and Austin. We devote personnel exclusively to major multi-campus educational systems. But be aware of the risk of a single-institution perspective. To avoid being blindsided by science from somewhere else, leverage the firm's geographically diverse partnership against the dispersed scientific opportunity.

Network Both Discovery and Investment. Compatible and complementary science simultaneously emerges from multiple university laboratories. Roll up all materially relevant science and defy conventional wisdom by making seed and early-stage investments in dispersed and decentralized organizations. Networking technology aids in communication.

Find the Stars of Discovery. Only a few investigators at any institution are true, often serial, discoverers. They are the scientific elite and can be identified by analysis of publications, citations, memberships in highly regarded societies, referrals by other elite scientists, and by personal interview. There are about two degrees of separation among any of them.

Avoid Building False Hopes. Too many university technology transfer offices are under pressure to spend time and money with every faculty member, regardless of the quality or promise of their inventions. This can lead to disappointment and recrimination that reduce the effectiveness of the transfer mechanism. Be direct and honest with researchers from the start.

Sidestep University Politics. Some are feudal in nature and have multiple points of approval in the technical transfer process. This raises transaction costs and delays progress. Deal flow in this space is too rich, and the speed too fast, to waste time in refractory organizations.

Avoid Specialization. ARCH does not specialize in life sciences, information technology, or any discipline. Just as universities are multidisciplinary, so are we. Venture investors need to follow the academic trend toward interdisciplinary centers involving multiple complementary scientific pursuits. These convergence opportunities represent an increasing proportion of our investments.

Avoid Exclusive Arrangements. Do not formally tie in with any particular institution. We do not need a contractual right of first refusal so long as we respect the academic culture, work with the technology transfer office and establish ties with local or regional investors. We encourage scientific publication, once the rights to a technology are safely locked up.

Find Good Company. Rely on track record to reduce variables in all areas. Work with experienced co-investors, serial discoverers, and experienced entrepreneurial management. Be ready to step in and manage directly. Design the business structure so each participant is treated equitably and fairly. Keep your word.

Seek Professional Management. Resist the temptation to permit the discoverer to manage the new enterprise. Few scientists, however brilliant, have the skill set, patience, or experience to manage a start-up. Keep the discovery team close to the start-up by naming them as scientific advisors or technology chiefs.

Eliminate Risk and Manage Cost. Determine where the deepest risk resides and devise programs to minimize it at earliest possible points. Replicate key findings, at multiple locations, to help mitigate science risks. Keep cost control by investing in carefully designed tranches aimed at specific endpoints. Begin with an investment syndicate capable of supporting three investment rounds without new investors

Protect the Intellectual Property. Understand the patent estate in which you are investing. This is the primary collateral for the earliest investment. If protection of the intellectual property is weak or incomplete, the level of risk increases geometrically.

APPENDIX 3

WHAT WE WANT IN A CEO

Joseph L. Rice III
Clayton, Dubilier & Rice

What could be more imperative to the health and success of a portfolio company than having the right chief executive officer? At Clayton, Dubilier & Rice, Joe Rice and the firm's other leaders believe the CEO sets the tone for all other employees and must therefore have the ability to instill a performance-driven culture from top to bottom. He or she must be able to seamlessly accomplish a wide range of responsibilities and tasks while overseeing day-to-day operations, supervising the security of employees, and ensuring the financial health of the company.

Clayton, Dubilier & Rice values proven leaders with successful track records who have demonstrated execution skills across a broad range of activities. The successful CEO of a portfolio company will be able to:

- Deliver attractive results while navigating the ups and downs of the business cycle.
- Identify where operational and financial improvements are needed and take accountability for follow-through on these initiatives.
- Utilize a disciplined process that ensures accurate and transparent financial reporting.
- Recognize employee strengths and weaknesses, promoting talented individuals who can handle increased responsibilities and parting with individuals who do not meet expectations.

- Effectively prioritize, knowing how, when, and to whom to delegate tasks without overloading employees and company resources.
- Pick up the slack or delegate to a person who can when someone is not able to complete a task or cannot ensure successful completion.
- Become a present and visible figure among employees, making oneself available for day-to-day interactions, advice, and problem solving.
- Lead by example, exhibit team-building skills, demonstrate a talent for implementing a variety of management skills, and, most importantly, spread enthusiasm.
- Distinguish the delicate balance between confidence and ego; knowing one's limitations, the CEO must ask for help when a task is simply too difficult.
- Seek new opportunities while still keeping the strategy focused and closely aligned to company goals.

The CEO is the nucleus of any company and bears primary responsibility for creating a clear strategic vision for the enterprise, translating the vision into an action-oriented business plan, and executing against the business plan.

APPENDIX 4

PORTFOLIO COMPANY VALUATION TEMPLATE

Patricia M. Cloherty
Delta Private Equity Partners, LLC

There are hundreds of details to track while building a successful business and measuring the performance of a portfolio of businesses. At Delta Private Equity Partners, Pat Cloherty and her colleagues have built a tool that tracks each investment literally from first dollar to anticipated exit. Budget information, capital investments, major business developments, and valuation: All material information is available at a glance.

Company Name ["Short company name"]
Contacts: Name of the person who is first on deal
(D – director board seat, if any)
Name of the person who is second on deal

Business: [Broad industry description]

Location: [City, country]

Current stage: [Early-stage, expansion, work-out, exit]

Date invested:

Status rating: [A, excellent; B, good; C, focus; D, work out problems]

Other major investors:

Total investment dollars raised to date: $____M

The fund's valuation of the company: $____M

Financial data (000s):

	Three Months		FY09	FY08
	12/31/09	12/31/08	12/31/09	12/31/08
Sales				
EBITDA				
Net income				
Net worth				
No. of employees				

Note: Fiscal year ends December 31. EBITDA, earnings before interest, taxes, depreciation, and amortization.

Business description: [Business description]

Recent developments: [Developments over the recent quarter, plus small coverage of future plans]

Purchase Dates	Type of Security	No. of Shares	Common Equivalent	Cost ($)	Last Quarter's Valuation	Current Quarter's Valuation
Current holdings:	Common stock loan					

Valuation method: Valued [at cost, write-up or down basing on the third party transaction or impairment in value].

APPENDIX 5

"WATERFALL ANALYSIS": THE STRESS TEST FOR POTENTIAL PORTFOLIO COMPANY

John A. Canning, Jr.
Madison Dearborn Partners

In assessing the potential risks and rewards of an investment, Madison Dearborn Partners seeks to assess all possible material events. Carefully listing each development—a major restructuring, securing or losing a major customer, a sharp decline in same-store sales, and so on—the firm then seeks to project the economic impact of each event. The tool helps the firm evaluate the financial prospects of each proposed deal. After the economic events of late 2008, MDP began substantially extending the life span of the negative-scenario stress tests.

Project Light
Waterfall Analysis
MDP Case Based on '06 Mgmt Est.
All Cases Assume $1,494 PP and 6.4x Total Leverage

	MDP Case	A — Slowdown in Wholesale Growth: Reduce Specialty Home Accounts to 5% and No New Accounts	B — 1% Reduction in Wholesale Margins	C — Reduction of First Year Sales of New Retail Stores to $500K	D — Reduction of SSS Growth and Labor Growth in 2007-2011 to 0%	E — Reduction in New Retail Store Openings to 10/yr	F — Reduction in Illuminations New Store Openings to 5/yr	A+B+C+D+E+F
					Downside Cases			
Sponsor IRR @								
7.00x EBITDA Exit Multiple	17.5%	15.2%	16.4%	16.8%	16.6%	16.5%	16.9%	10.7%
7.50x EBITDA Exit Multiple	20.5%	18.3%	19.4%	19.8%	19.6%	19.4%	19.9%	13.9%
8.00x EBITDA Exit Multiple	23.1%	21.0%	22.1%	22.5%	22.3%	22.1%	22.5%	16.8%
8.50x EBITDA Exit Multiple	25.6%	23.6%	24.6%	24.9%	24.8%	24.6%	25.0%	19.5%
9.00x EBITDA Exit Multiple	27.9%	25.9%	27.0%	27.2%	27.1%	26.9%	27.3%	21.9%
Capital Gain								
7.00x EBITDA Exit Multiple	$447.0	$371.7	$410.5	$422.2	$416.2	$411.0	$426.1	$237.9
7.50x EBITDA Exit Multiple	553.0	473.5	514.7	526.7	520.4	514.0	530.3	330.7
8.00x EBITDA Exit Multiple	659.0	575.2	618.9	631.3	624.7	617.0	634.5	423.6
8.50x EBITDA Exit Multiple	765.0	677.0	723.1	735.8	728.9	720.0	738.8	516.5
9.00x EBITDA Exit Multiple	871.0	778.8	827.4	840.4	833.1	823.0	843.0	609.3
Revenue								
2006	$684.7	$684.7	$684.7	$684.7	$684.7	$684.7	$684.7	$684.7
2007	743.5	736.3	743.5	743.2	740.7	740.8	741.4	728.7
2008	791.0	777.3	791.0	789.3	785.5	782.5	784.7	756.2
2009	835.3	817.2	835.3	832.1	827.0	820.9	824.9	782.4
2010	881.4	858.5	881.4	876.7	870.2	860.9	866.7	809.8
2011	931.3	902.1	931.3	925.4	917.3	904.7	912.4	839.6
5 Year CAGR	6.3%	5.7%	6.3%	6.2%	6.0%	5.7%	5.9%	4.2%

EBITDA								
2006	$185.0	$185.0	$185.0	$185.0	$185.0	$185.0	$185.0	$185.0
2007	199.0	196.6	195.7	198.9	198.2	198.4	198.6	191.6
2008	209.3	204.8	205.8	208.4	207.7	207.2	208.0	196.0
2009	218.4	212.5	214.8	216.7	216.1	214.8	216.3	200.0
2010	228.0	220.6	224.2	225.5	224.9	222.8	225.0	204.3
2011	238.7	229.2	234.7	235.4	234.7	231.9	234.7	209.1
5 Year CAGR	**5.2%**	**4.4%**	**4.9%**	**4.9%**	**4.9%**	**4.6%**	**4.9%**	**2.5%**
EBITDA Margins								
2006	27.0%	27.0%	27.0%	27.0%	27.0%	27.0%	27.0%	27.0%
2007	26.8%	26.7%	26.3%	26.8%	26.8%	26.8%	26.8%	26.3%
2008	26.5%	26.3%	26.0%	26.4%	26.4%	26.5%	26.5%	25.9%
2009	26.2%	26.0%	25.7%	26.0%	26.1%	26.2%	26.2%	25.6%
2010	25.9%	25.7%	25.4%	25.7%	25.8%	25.9%	26.0%	25.2%
2011	25.6%	25.4%	25.2%	25.4%	25.6%	25.6%	25.7%	24.9%
Total Debt / EBITDA								
2006	6.35x	6.35x	6.35x	6.35x	6.35x	6.35x	6.35x	6.35x
2007	5.67x	5.74x	5.78x	5.67x	5.69x	5.67x	5.67x	5.88x
2008	5.11x	5.25x	5.22x	5.14x	5.16x	5.14x	5.13x	5.47x
2009	4.58x	4.74x	4.69x	4.62x	4.64x	4.63x	4.61x	5.04x
2010	4.04x	4.23x	4.15x	4.10x	4.12x	4.11x	4.08x	4.59x
2011	3.47x	3.69x	3.59x	3.54x	3.56x	3.54x	3.51x	4.10x
(EBITDA-Capex)/Cash Interest								
2006	1.47x	1.47x	1.47x	1.47x	1.47x	1.47x	1.47x	1.47x
2007	1.55x	1.53x	1.52x	1.55x	1.55x	1.58x	1.57x	1.53x
2008	1.69x	1.65x	1.65x	1.68x	1.68x	1.71x	1.70x	1.62x
2009	1.90x	1.83x	1.85x	1.88x	1.87x	1.90x	1.90x	1.76x
2010	2.12x	2.03x	2.06x	2.09x	2.08x	2.11x	2.12x	1.91x
2011	2.47x	2.33x	2.40x	2.42x	2.41x	2.45x	2.46x	2.15x
Cum Debt Paydown (2011)	$346.8	$328.7	$333.7	$341.6	$339.9	$353.7	$350.9	318.0
Beginning Debt	1,175.0	1,175.0	1,175.0	1,175.0	1,175.0	1,175.0	1,175.0	1,175.0
% of Beginning Total Debt	29.5%	28.0%	28.4%	29.1%	28.9%	30.1%	29.9%	27.1%
% of IRR from Debt Paydown	49.2%	53.8%	50.5%	50.7%	51.0%	53.7%	51.8%	72.2%

Project Light

Waterfall Analysis

MDP Case Based on '06 Mgmt Est.
All Cases Assume $1,494 PP
and 6.4x Total Leverage

	MDP Case	Upside Cases					
		Dividend Recap (1)	Increase of SSS Growth to 3%	Increase in New Retail Store Openings to 30/yr	Increase in Illuminations New Store Openings to 15/yr	$15mm Increase in Indebtedness	
		G	H	I	J	K	H+I+J+K
Sponsor IRR @							
7.00x EBITDA Exit Multiple	17.5%	20.0%	21.4%	18.6%	18.1%	17.9%	23.4%
7.50x EBITDA Exit Multiple	20.5%	23.4%	24.2%	21.5%	21.1%	20.9%	26.2%
8.00x EBITDA Exit Multiple	23.1%	26.4%	26.8%	24.1%	23.7%	23.6%	28.8%
8.50x EBITDA Exit Multiple	25.6%	29.1%	29.1%	26.6%	26.2%	26.2%	31.2%
9.00x EBITDA Exit Multiple	27.9%	31.5%	31.3%	28.9%	28.5%	28.5%	33.4%
Capital Gain							
7.00x EBITDA Exit Multiple	$447.0	$380.1	$590.9	$483.0	$468.0	$440.6	$641.4
7.50x EBITDA Exit Multiple	553.0	486.1	705.1	592.0	575.7	546.5	760.2
8.00x EBITDA Exit Multiple	659.0	592.0	819.2	701.0	683.5	652.5	879.1
8.50x EBITDA Exit Multiple	765.0	698.0	933.3	810.0	791.2	758.4	997.9
9.00x EBITDA Exit Multiple	871.0	804.0	1,047.4	919.0	899.0	864.4	1,116.7
Revenue							
2006	$684.7	$684.7	$684.7	$684.7	$684.7	$684.7	$684.7
2007	743.5	743.5	749.0	746.1	745.5	743.5	753.7
2008	791.0	791.0	802.2	799.4	797.2	791.0	816.9
2009	835.3	835.3	852.5	849.8	845.7	835.3	877.3
2010	881.4	881.4	904.7	901.9	896.0	881.4	939.9
2011	931.3	931.3	961.0	958.0	950.2	931.3	1,006.6
5 Year CAGR	6.3%	6.3%	7.0%	6.9%	6.8%	6.3%	8.0%

	Col 1	Col 2	Col 3	Col 4	Col 5	Col 6	Col 7
EBITDA							
2006	$185.0	$185.0	$185.0	$185.0	$185.0	$185.0	$185.0
2007	199.0	199.0	202.4	199.5	199.4	199.0	203.3
2008	209.3	209.3	216.2	211.4	210.6	209.3	219.6
2009	218.4	218.4	229.0	222.1	220.6	218.4	234.8
2010	228.0	228.0	242.4	233.2	231.1	228.0	250.7
2011	238.7	238.7	257.0	245.5	242.6	238.7	267.7
5 Year CAGR	5.2%	5.2%	6.8%	5.8%	5.6%	5.2%	7.7%
EBITDA Margins							
2006	27.0%	27.0%	27.0%	27.0%	27.0%	27.0%	27.0%
2007	26.8%	26.8%	27.0%	26.7%	26.7%	26.8%	27.0%
2008	26.5%	26.5%	27.0%	26.4%	26.4%	26.5%	26.9%
2009	26.2%	26.2%	26.9%	26.1%	26.1%	26.2%	26.8%
2010	25.9%	25.9%	26.8%	25.9%	25.8%	25.9%	26.7%
2011	25.6%	25.6%	26.7%	25.6%	25.5%	25.6%	26.6%
Total Debt / EBITDA							
2006	6.35x	6.35x	6.35x	6.35x	6.35x	6.43x	6.43x
2007	5.67x	5.67x	5.56x	5.67x	5.67x	5.75x	5.64x
2008	5.11x	5.11x	4.92x	5.09x	5.10x	5.20x	4.96x
2009	4.58x	6.50x	4.31x	4.53x	4.55x	4.66x	4.33x
2010	4.04x	5.99x	3.71x	3.98x	4.01x	4.13x	3.71x
2011	3.47x	5.44x	3.09x	3.40x	3.43x	3.56x	3.08x
(EBITDA-Capex)/Cash Interest							
2006	1.47x	1.47x	1.47x	1.47x	1.47x	1.45x	1.45x
2007	1.55x	1.55x	1.58x	1.53x	1.54x	1.53x	1.52x
2008	1.69x	1.69x	1.76x	1.68x	1.68x	1.66x	1.71x
2009	1.90x	1.90x	2.02x	1.89x	1.90x	1.87x	1.97x
2010	2.12x	1.48x	2.31x	2.13x	2.12x	2.08x	2.27x
2011	2.47x	1.65x	2.76x	2.49x	2.48x	2.41x	2.73x
Cum Debt Paydown (2011)	$346.8	295.6	380.7	339.9	342.7	341.2	364.2
Beginning Debt	1,175.0	1,175.0	1,175.0	1,175.0	1,175.0	1,190.0	1,190.0
% of Beginning Total Debt	29.5%	25.2%	32.4%	28.9%	29.2%	28.7%	30.6%
% of IRR from Debt Paydown	49.2%	NA	43.0%	45.1%	46.7%	48.8%	38.2%

Note:
(1) Assumes dividend recap in 2009 with leverage at 6.5x

APPENDIX 6

MANAGING DIRECTOR SELECTION CRITERIA

John A. Canning, Jr.
Madison Dearborn Partners

There is no one characteristic that makes a perfect leader. At Madison Dearborn Partners, John Canning and his colleagues have codified a tool by which they can assess attributes of the firm's managing directors. A sliding scale, from weaker to stronger, measures the leadership skills and cultural contributions of these individuals.

Managing Director Selection Criteria

Culture	← Stronger		Weaker →
Culture	• Consistently places Firm success above individual interests. Embodies what it means to be a "team player." • Treats all individuals, whether senior, junior, Firm or non-Firm, with highest level of fairness and respect. • Always exhibits highest standards of reliability, honesty, integrity, and ethical conduct.	• Consistently behaves as a team player. • Guided by what is best for Firm. • Attitude respectful of others, reputation for fair dealing. • Viewed as honest and ethical, without exception.	• Often places personal interests above the Firm's. • Views issues through prism of "What is best for me?" • Conduct often influenced by hierarchy. • May treat subordinates or non-Firm contacts inconsistently or harshly. • May cut corners or shade the facts to achieve desired outcome. • <u>Any</u> question exists as to honesty or integrity.
Leadership	• Inspires Firm and colleagues to higher levels of achievement through dedication and personal commitment to excellence. • Consistently contributes with superior insight and originality to investment decision-making process. • Makes exceptional contribution to Firm beyond team/sector focus. • Known as outstanding coach and mentor to younger professionals. • Instills Firm culture in younger professionals, and maintains the confidentiality of matters of difference or disagreement among senior Firm leaders.	• Makes leadership contributions to firm and colleagues. • Constructive participant in investment decision-making process. Exhibits insight and sound judgment. • Contributes to Firm beyond team/sector focus. • Good mentoring skills.	• Modest leadership contribution to date. • Infrequently contributes substantively to Firm's investment decision-making process. • Uneven or infrequent engagement beyond team/sector. • Satisfactory, but not inspiring, development of younger professionals. • Unable to confine disagreement with Firm decisions to appropriate forums.
Sector Expertise	• Has developed recognized industry-leading expertise and presence in particular industry sector.	• Has strong industry sector expertise. Regarded by colleagues and third parties as being an "expert."	• Developing sector expertise, but not yet considered an "expert."

Managing Director Selection Criteria (Continued)

Culture	◄──────── Stronger		Weaker ────────►
Sector Expertise	• Reputation within sector consistently leads to high-quality differentiated deal-flow. Opportunities "find" him/her. • Uses sector expertise to proactively generate investment themes and ideas of a less competitive nature, or to differentiate and advantage Firm in competitive processes.	• Uses industry expertise to effectively triage opportunities, enhance diligence process, and distinguish Firm competitively. • Infrequently generates proprietary opportunities, but always on the "short list" within sector.	• Expertise not yet sufficient to confer a competitive advantage upon Firm. • Sector focus has led to modest deal-sourcing opportunities to date.
Transaction Execution/ Management	• Consistently generates unique, and often proprietary, investment opportunities. • Demonstrates exceptional creativity, insight, discipline, and judgment in forming and articulating an investment thesis, transaction development, negotiation, and execution. • Has demonstrated the ability to lead a transaction team, with distinction, through all phases of a complex transaction (development, diligence, negotiation, closing, investment thesis execution, and liquidation). • Excels at forming effective working partnerships with portfolio company management teams, and maintains and expands strong relationships with service providers and bankers.	• Has developed good sources of deal-flow. Further improvement expected over time. • Able to effectively lead a transaction team through all stages of a transaction. • Forms effective partnerships with portfolio managers and maintains productive relationships with service providers. Does not "burn bridges." • Enjoys complete confidence of investment staff for thorough and unfiltered presentation and discussion of transaction-related risks and opportunities. • Is fully conversant with key issues in transaction-related documentation and agreements. Capable of leading negotiations. Mastery expected to grow in time.	• Modest sources of deal-flow. • Possesses generally satisfactory judgment, but inconsistencies apparent. Requires "adult supervision." • Not yet ready to lead transactions. • Still developing skills to work with a management team as the senior Firm representative. • May treat service provider relationships roughly. Occasionally burns bridges for Firm. • Any question exists regarding objectivity of presentation of investment considerations. • Desire to do deal can color judgment and assessment of risks. • Needs further experience negotiating transaction documentation.

(Continued)

Managing Director Selection Criteria (Continued)

Culture	← Stronger		Weaker →
Transaction Execution/ Management	• Enjoys complete confidence of investment staff for thorough and unfiltered presentation and discussion of transaction-related risks and opportunities. • Has exceptional time management skills. Readily identifies highest impact/highest probability opportunities where Firm has an advantage or edge. • Highly effective at using Firm's professional and financial resources efficiently, productively, and in a manner proportionate to the opportunity. • Has exceptional command of, and has successfully led the negotiation of, all transaction-related documents and agreements.	• Generally prioritizes opportunities effectively. May occasionally pursue low probability transactions or transactions where Firm has little advantage. • Usually manages Firm's resources carefully and productively.	• Time management skills need further refinement. Is frequently inclined to pursue opportunities that may be marginal or where Firm enjoys little competitive advantage. • Frequently uses Firm's professional and financial resources ineffectively, unproductively, or in a manner disproportionate to the opportunity.

APPENDIX 7

PERFORMANCE METRICS FOR MILLENNIUM VILLAGES

Jeffrey Walker

JPMorgan Partners/Chase Capital Partners

Tracking and measuring performance are, of course, the essence of good management. This principle applies, too, in the operation of a not-for-profit enterprise. Jeff Walker and his colleagues at Millennium Promise use spreadsheet tools such as this to monitor performance across a wide variety of metrics.

Jeffrey Walker
JPMorgan Partners

Millennium
☐ Promise
Extreme Poverty Ends Here

Millennium Villages Select Q1 Tracking Indicators by Site

Performance Indicators:		Ethiopia Koraro	Ghana Bonsaaso	Kenya Sauri	Kenya Dertu	Malawi Gumulira	Malawi Mwandama
1. Outpatient visits		4,545	6,640	32,926	1,491	2,059	28,334
2. Individuals placed on ARV treatment		37	3	129	0	0	20
3. TB patients successfully treated		8	14	40	15	0	7
4. Number of babies delivered in a health facility		49	154	178	24	9	98
5. Pregnant women receiving antenatal care		431	361	1,838	101	36	623
6. Farmers growing high value agricultural commodities introduced		0	240	3,200	66	0	348
7. Students enrolled in primary schools	Girls	8,443	3,692	8,520	289	725	5,277
	Boys	7,403	4,053	9,078	633	813	5,671
8. Avg. pupil attendance rates in primary schools	Girls	68%	86%	93%	Not Available	91%	Not Available
	Boys	65%	88%	93%	Not Available	91%	Not Available
9. Avg. teacher attendance rates in primary schools		69%	87%	78%	Not Available	98%	Not Available
10. Farmers using ISFM practices		1,300	240	Not Available	NA	0	1,000
11. Health facilities connected with electricity (grid or off-grid) services		1	0	2	1	0	0

Mali	Mali	Nigeria	Nigeria	Rwanda	Senegal	Tanzania	Uganda
Tiby	Toya	Ikaram	Pampaida	Mayange	Potou	Mbola	Ruhiira
2,944	1,641	5,694	1,158	7,512	7,693	9,162	20,696
0	0	2	0	8	NA	13	29
6	2	0	0	8	NA	0	0
446	77	56	23	243	214	150	676
671	159	230	122	1,391	1,022	917	1,353
416	443	200	57	151	1,700	25	278
2,933	451	2,302	743	Not Available	2,182	3,906	79%
3,396	397	2,120	859	Not Available	2,353	4,201	85%
Not Available	86%	96%	94%	97%	NA	97%	85%
Not Available	86%	93%	93%	97%	NA	92%	87%
Not Available	100%	48%	96%	93%	99%	97%	91%
2,960	1	0	0	4,440	1,700	2,000	133
0	0	4	0	Not Available	0	0	5

APPENDIX 8

"CARLISMS": KEY PRACTICES FOR PRIVATE-EQUITY INVESTORS

Carl D. Thoma

Thoma Bravo, LLC and predecessor firms Golder Thoma & Co.;
Golder Thoma Cressey Rauner, LLC and Thoma Cressey Bravo, Inc.

Carl Thoma, of Thoma Bravo, is a person of few but memorable words—plain-spoken expressions that have become familiar to the partners, entrepreneurs, and advisors with whom he works. These phrases, heard frequently by anyone who works with Thoma, seem designed to focus attention and serve as a shorthand of success in a competitive, fast-moving private-equity marketplace. Listed here are some of the best Carlisms.

Buy and Build. Partner with great management teams to grow companies in consolidating industries. Grow cash flow over time via a three-pronged strategy of (A) operational improvements, often identified during due diligence and completed quickly post-close; (B) add-on acquisitions; and (C) organic growth.

How Can We Pay More? A private-equity firm should develop a special, unique angle it sees in the business and leverage the experience and other resources that only it has. Make sure our return is higher than the next investor's. That way, we can afford to pay more if necessary.

Can We Get It for Less? As a value investor, figuring out how to creatively pay a lower price is part of adding value. You get what you negotiate.

Learn More. Never be caught off guard by surprises. When interviewing management, management candidates, customers, or competitors, go off the list of typical questions and points of reference. Track specific performance at prior stops. Challenge answers. Quality of earnings at close is important. Send in your best accounting team; look under all stones.

Improve Multiples. Add-on acquisitions, operational improvements, organic growth, and/or expansion through merger and acquisition bring size, scale, a better company, and higher exit multiples.

The Game Plan Is Simple; Sticking to It Is the Tough Part. Making money and building value stem from a relatively simple set of tenets. The challenge comes in discerning when actions and strategies are beginning to divert from plan. Have the wisdom to know and the discipline to stay within the guard rails of strategy.

When You Can, Stretch It Out. Looking at companies over time and as long as possible through a cycle can be helpful. If a slower pace does not put the deal at risk, do not go too fast. Press hard on key items.

Don't Make Mistakes. This isn't venture investing, where a few highly successful investments will offset a large number of failures. Avoid the mistakes that create the losers, and aim for returns from every investment.

Inexperience Can Be Very Costly. Try to know what you—and your team—do not know. Use study and experience to focus on sectors you can know as well as any strategic investor. Keep in mind that younger personnel likely have not been through economic cycles and volatility. Acknowledge your limits. Recruit people who will do the same.

We Can Raise All the Money You Can Spend Responsibly. If a CEO or founder can develop a strategy that will create a return, an institutional investor can raise virtually unlimited resources to make that happen. Show me the returns, and I can show you the money. This comes as a revelation to CEOs or founders with no prior private-equity experience.

Doesn't Matter How, Just Get It Done. Process and organization are not goals unto themselves, just means to the end of making a good investment. As staffs get larger, the risk rises that people will focus on process and lose site of the real goal. Within the vital limits of law and ethics, it's getting the deal done that counts.

No Deal Is Done Until It Is Done. Have the discipline to divorce any emotion or sense of obligation from a decision to close, even if you have signed a letter of intent. If performance erodes or you find out that something is not as represented, be willing to walk. Work due diligence until pencils are down. Keep challenging the investment case until the deal is done.

When Are You Moving to Akron? If a deal is not performing, the deal professionals may well find themselves living with it—moving to the headquarters, if necessary. This is a form of internal threat or gentle reminder that if management is not fixing the problem then we need to.

Are You Building Personal Equity? I Can Help Dwarf What You Make Now. This is the basic case for why a CEO or founder should accept an infusion of private equity. If we can make them more money than they can make themselves, that should be the basis of a productive partnership.

The Only Person Above a CEO Is the Owner. While management's skill, experience, and dedication are critical, the controlling investor ultimately is responsible for the business. When necessary, step in as an owner to make the tough decisions.

INDEX

Rienhoff, Hugh, 188
RJR Nabisco, 26
Roberts, George, 120
Robin Hood Foundation, 98
Robson, John, 200
Rock, Arthur, 68, 160, 178
Rockefeller, David, 205
Rockefeller, John D., III, 169
Rogers, Kevin, 77
Romania, 248
Roof, 263–264
Room to Read, 169
Rubenstein, Arthur, 206
Rubin, Bob, 54
Running, 70, 71
Russia, 243–267
    boxes, 253–255
    call to Moscow, 247–248
    Center for Entrepreneurship, 254
    consumer credit, 255–256
    early years, 260–263
    economic crisis, 252–253
    Entrepreneur of the Year award, 255
    financial services sector, 250–252
    lessons learned, 267
    liquidity, 250
    negotiation, 265
    risks, 260
    roof, 263–264
    rules, 246–247
    transparency premium, 249–250
    valuation of companies, 265

Sachs, Jeffrey, 99, 101, 113
Saloner, Garth, 141
Salser, Winston, 226
Sandell, Scott, 192
Satellite launch, 174
SBA, 258
SBIC, 229–230
Scale the firm, 149
Schiller, Jo Anne, 211
Sector expertise, 290–291
Self-satisfaction, 70
Semiconductors, 189
Service businesses, 47–71
    American President Lines, 58–59
    basics, 49–50
    Greifeld effect, 67–69
    guilty until proven innocent, 59
    industrial leverage, 62
    learning from mistakes, 51–52
    Lehman Brothers, 54–56
    lessons learned, 71
    Levi Strauss, 56–58
    minority ownership, 50–51
    paging industry, 63–64

staying in the race, 70–71
transition period, 69
wireless sector, 63
working capital, 65–66
Service Employees International Union, 23
Shared effort, 102
Shared risk, 102
Shaw, Premal, 170
Sher, F. Patrick, 108
Shipley, Walter, 106
Shoar, Antoinette, 27
Shockley, William, 154
Siegel, Don, 23
Silicon Graphics, 186, 187
Silverstone, Abbey, 186
Simon, William, 99
Singh, Manmohan, 166
Single-product companies, 247
Size, 242
Skype, 168
Skytrain, 163
Small Business Investment Company
    (SBIC), 229–230
Smith, Frederick, 79, 120
Social entrepreneurship, 169. *See also*
    Not-for-profit work
Social impact of private capital, 13–14
Solar energy, 189
Sole-source set-aside program, 258
Sonsini, Larry, 184
Soros, George, 111
SPAR supermarket chain, 263
Specialization, 274
Spread the risk, 170, 259, 267
Stanton, John, 63
Staying power, 238–239
Steelmaking, 223
Stein, Jenny Shilling, 170
Steinbrenner, George, 76
Stereotype of private-equity investor, 18
Stress testing, 134, 135
Stretch it out, 298
Stromberg, Per, 20
Style drift, 132, 133
Suniva, 189
Sutter Hill Ventures, 153, 158
Swanson, Robert, 225

Tamke, George, 35, 42
Tandem, 236–237
Tangible cash flow calculation, 50, 62
Target industries, 80
Team, 82–83, 171
Technology risk, 212, 219
Technology roll-ups, 197, 217
Tele Atlas, 191
Telecom boom and bust, 130, 131

About the Authors

For the past twenty years, Robert Finkel has been investing as part of the Chicago private-equity community. As founder and president of Prism Capital, Mr. Finkel has overseen fund deployment into a total of 40 portfolio companies through both the Prism Opportunity Fund and the Prism Mezzanine Fund.

Mr. Finkel is a co-founder and former chairman of the Illinois Venture Capital Association which represents Illinois' $100 billion of venture capital and private equity funds, and he received its prestigious Fellows Award. He also received on Prism's behalf the Private Equity Fund Manager of the Year Award for both 2007 and 2008 from Opal Financial. Mr. Finkel was selected to serve on the Illinois State Treasurer's Fund of Fund Review Board and serves on the board of Chicago Junior Achievement and the Governing Board of the Bulletin of the Atomic Scientists.

Prism is an active supporter of small businesses across the country; Mr. Finkel was selected to testify before the House Small Business Committee in support of the SBIC program's reauthorization.

Previously, Mr. Finkel was an investment manager at Wind Point Partners where he invested in both growth and later stage companies. Before entering the world of private equity, he was an investment banker specializing in mergers and acquisitions with PaineWebber. He received an M.B.A. from Harvard Graduate School of Business and a B.A. from Johns Hopkins University. Quoted in *Business Week* and featured on MSNBC's Last Call talking about private equity, Mr. Finkel frequently appears as a speaker at trade conferences and seminars.

David Greising is business columnist and chief business correspondent for the *Chicago Tribune*. In September 2008, he resumed writing a column that first ran in the *Tribune* from 1998 to 2003. As chief business correspondent, Greising is the newspaper's lead writer on globalization and the intersection of politics, business, and economics.

Greising's opinion column features analysis of business and economic news and their impact on readers. Re-launched as the 2008 financial crisis was first exploding, his column has offered incisive and timely analysis of events. As chief business correspondent, Greising has traveled around the world, from the rainforests of South America to the industrial boom towns of China, to report about globalization and its impact on Chicago.

Greising previously worked for *Business Week*, both as its Atlanta bureau chief and in the Chicago bureau. He was a business reporter and columnist for the *Chicago Sun-Times*. He is the author of two business books: *I'd Like the World to Buy a Coke: The Life and Leadership of Robert Goizueta* and *Brokers, Bagmen and Moles: Fraud and Corruption in the Chicago Futures Market*, co-authored by Laurie Morse.

Born in Chicago, Greising is a graduate of DePauw University. He and his wife, Cynthia Hedges Greising, are co-authors of the children's book *Toys Everywhere!*